Fantastic Voyages
of the
Cinematic Imagination

THE SUNY SERIES

HORIZONS OF CINEMA

MURRAY POMERANCE | EDITOR

Also in the series

William Rothman, editor, *Cavell on Film*

J. David Slocum, editor, *Rebel Without a Cause*

Joe McElhaney, *The Death of Classical Cinema*

Kirsten Moana Thompson, *Apocalyptic Dread*

Frances Gateward, editor, *Seoul Searching*

Michael Atkinson, editor, *Exile Cinema*

Bert Cardullo, *Soundings on Cinema*

Paul S. Moore, *Now Playing*

Robin L. Murray and Joseph K. Heumann,
Ecology and Popular Film

William Rothman, editor, *Three Documentary Filmmakers*

Sean Griffin, editor, *Hetero*

Jean-Michel Frodon, editor, *Cinema and the Shoah*

Carolyn Jess-Cooke and Constantine Verevis, editors, *Second Takes*

Fantastic Voyages of the Cinematic Imagination

Georges Méliès's *Trip to the Moon*

Edited by

Matthew Solomon

SUNY PRESS

Cover: G. Méliès, "L'arrivée de l'obus dans la Lune," *Le Nouvel Art cinématographique*, 2d series, no. 5 (January 1930): 82. Billy Rose Theatre Division, The New York Public Library for the Performing Arts, Astor, Lenox and Tilden Foundations.

Published by State University of New York Press, Albany

© 2011 State University of New York

For information, contact State University of New York Press, Albany, NY
www.sunypress.edu

Production by Eileen Meehan
Marketing by Michael Campochiaro

Library of Congress Cataloging-in-Publication Data

Fantastic voyages of the cinematic imagination : Georges Méliès's Trip to the moon / edited by Matthew Solomon.
     p. cm.
  Includes bibliographical references and index.
  ISBN 978-1-4384-3581-7 (hardcover : alk. paper)
  ISBN 978-1-4384-3580-0 (pbk. : alk. paper)
  1. Trip to the moon (Motion picture) 2. Méliès, Georges, 1861–1938—Criticism and interpretation. I. Solomon, Matthew.

  PN1997.T693F36 2011
  791.43'72—dc22   2010025994

10 9 8 7 6 5 4 3 2 1

For Charlie

"A Trip to the Movies: Georges Méliès, Filmmaker and Magician (1861–1938)" by Paolo Cherchi Usai was first published in *Image* 34, nos. 3–4 (1991): 2–11. Reprinted with permission of the George Eastman House.

"Theatricality, Narrativity, and Trickality: Reevaluating the Cinema of Georges Méliès" by André Gaudreault was first published in English in the *Journal of Film and Television* 15, no. 3 (1987): 110–119. Revised version published with permission of Heldref Publications and Taylor & Francis.

"*A Trip to the Moon*: A Composite Film" by Thierry Lefebvre was originally published in French as "*Le Voyage dans la lune*, film composite," in *Méliès, magie et cinéma*, ed. Jacques Malthête and Laurent Mannoni (Paris-Musées, 2002), 171–192. It is published in English translation here with permission of the author.

Contents

Illustrations

Acknowledgments

My greatest thanks go to the contributors who made this volume possible. Each responded with great erudition, insight, and creativity, and I am grateful for all their hard work in this collaborative effort. I am especially grateful to Murray Pomerance, who has shown great enthusiasm for this project from the very beginning when I first discussed it with him in Montreal in November 2006. I offer a special thanks to Paul Hammond, who generously agreed to participate in this volume by translating two essays by Méliès into English. I am extremely grateful to Dean Francisco Soto and the Office of the Humanities and Social Sciences at the College of Staten Island, City University of New York, which provided invaluable support for this project in the initial form of a CSI Summer Research Award that allowed me to examine Méliès material at the Bibliothèque du film in Paris and the Cinémathèque Royale de Belgique in Brussels. I would also like to thank the two anonymous reviewers of the manuscript and to acknowledge the support of James Peltz of SUNY Press.

Serge Bromberg, Jacques Malthête, and David Shepard graciously answered my questions about different versions of *A Trip to the Moon* and Joseph Eckhardt, Frank Kessler, Martin Marks, Luke McKernan, and Mary Elizabeth Ruwell helped me to obtain copies of several hard-to-find documents. Liza Zusman's diligent research in London and New York turned up many useful articles and letters.

Others who helped in various ways were Janet Bergstrom, Nico de Klerk, Paul Falzone, Emma Furderer, Jane Gaines, Doreen Gambichler, Magali Gaudin, Oliver Gaycken, Jaclyn Genega, Charlie Johnston, Giancarlo Lombardi, Jeffrey Man, Laurent Mannoni, Martin Marks, David Mayer, Charles Musser, James Naremore, Adrian Ramos-Rocchio, Régis Robert, Donald Sosin, Paul Spehr, Alexa Davidson Suskin, Christoph Wahl, Watie White, and Eve Wolf. The process of reprinting previously published essays was generously facilitated by Amy

Van Dussen and Janet Infarinato of the George Eastman House, Mary Jaine Winokur of Heldref Publications, Kathy Elrick and Tim Legnani of Taylor and Francis, and Corinne Caradonna of Paris-Musées. Thanks to Paolo Cherchi Usai, André Gaudreault, and Thierry Lefebvre for revisiting their earlier work on Méliès and consenting to have it included in this book. Victoria Duckett and Viva Paci not only wrote chapters but also looked over translations from Italian.

Jennifer Chapman has been a consistent supporter of this book and drew my attention to nuances of the film that otherwise would have escaped me. Throughout the book's gestation, I have been inspired by my son Charlie, whose lively response to *A Trip to the Moon* has been truly infectious. He was always willing to watch the film one more time with me and seems to share my fascination with its many mysteries and surprises. This book is for him.

Matthew Solomon
September 2010

Introduction

MATTHEW SOLOMON

GEORGES MÉLIÈS . . . is the originator of the class of cinematograph films which . . . has given new life to the trade at a time when it was dying out. He conceived the idea of portraying comical, magical and mystical views, and his creations have been imitated without success ever since. . . . The "Trip to the Moon," as well as . . . "The Astronomer's Dream". . . are the personal creations of Mr. Georges Méliès, who himself conceived the ideas, painted the backgrounds, devised the accessories and acted on the stage.

—Complete Catalogue of Genuine and Original "Star" Films, 1905

If it is as a master of trick-films and fantastic spectacles that Méliès is best remembered, by no means all his pictures were of that type.

—Iris Barry, Curator, Museum of Modern Art Film Library, 1939

A Trip to the Moon (1902) is certainly Georges Méliès's best-known film, and of the tens of thousands of individual films made during cinema's first decade, it is perhaps the most recognizable. The image of a cratered moon-face with a spaceship lodged in its eye is one of the most iconic images in all of film history and, more than a century after its initial release, the film's story of a journey to the moon and back continues to amuse many around the world. Long recognized as a pioneering story film with an important impact on American cinema, *A Trip to the Moon* has also been claimed as a foundational entry in the history of several long-standing film genres, including science fiction, fantasy, and even the road movie.[1] The film has been quoted and imitated in audiovisual works ranging from *Around the World in Eighty Days* (1956), to the music video for the Smashing Pumpkins' song "Tonight, Tonight" (1996), and alluded to in literature as different as Louis-Ferdinand Céline's nihilistic interwar novel *Death on the Installment Plan* (1936) and Brian Selznick's illustrated children's book *The Invention of Hugo Cabret* (2007).

From the beginning, *A Trip to the Moon* was a major international success. Between September and December 1902, *A Trip to the Moon* was screened in Paris "entirely in color" at the Théâtre Robert-Houdin after matinee performances on Sundays and Thursdays by the magician Jules-Eugène Legris (who can be seen leading the parade in the film's final two scenes).[2] In addition to showing the film to audiences at his magic theater, Méliès offered both black-and-white and color copies for sale directly through his Star-Film sales office and indirectly through the Warwick Trading Company in London. In addition, unauthorized copies soon became available through several U.S. film producers. According to one account, these copies originated from a print that Méliès—already on the lookout for buyers who intended to dupe his films and resell them— had sold to the Paris photographer Charles Gerschel for exhibition in an Algiers theater on the condition that it be sent directly to Algeria. Gerschel, however, had purchased *A Trip to the Moon* (as well as a number of other Méliès films) for Alfred C. Abadie of the Edison Company. Abadie sent the prints to Edison's laboratories in West Orange, New Jersey, where they were copied and subsequently resold to the Vitagraph Company, which made its own copies.[3] Vitagraph screened the film in theaters through its exhibition service, while other companies sold it as their own for several years; as Charles Musser notes, "Lubin, Selig, and Edison catalogs from 1903–04 listed many dupes . . . and gave particular prominence to Méliès films such as . . . A TRIP TO THE MOON."[4] Consequently, Méliès received but a small fraction of the considerable profits earned by the film through sales of prints and theater admissions.

A Trip to the Moon was a big hit in the United States, where it was first seen less than a month after initially showing in Paris, and could be seen through the remainder of the theatrical season. Reporting the response of enthusiastic New York audiences to the film in October 1902, vaudeville manager Percy Williams simply wrote, "Best moving pictures I ever saw."[5] By year's end, *A Trip to the Moon* had received similarly rave reviews from theaters in other cities across the United States, including Washington, Cleveland, Detroit, New Orleans, and Kansas City.[6] In January 1903, when Thomas Tally reopened his store-front Electric Theater in Los Angeles, he used *A Trip to the Moon* as the featured presentation.[7] In May 1903, after a less-than-inspired batch of new films closed the show at Keith's Theatre in Philadelphia, manager H. A. Daniels commented, "We miss 'The [*sic*] Trip to the Moon.' "[8] When the film screened in Montreal in June 1903, it was presumably already well-known to audiences and was thus described in newspapers as the "famous trip to the moon" and advertised as the "ever-popular 'Trip to the Moon.' "[9]

A Trip to the Moon continued to be a successful subject internationally for several more years. It was distributed in Germany beginning in 1902 under the title *Reise nach dem Mond*.[10] In Italy, it was still being shown as a headline attraction in both permanent theaters and traveling cinemas in 1904, some two years after it had first become available in that country.[11] Well into 1905, *A Trip to the Moon* continued to be screened—and even showcased—in some places. At the Gaîté Montparnasse in April in Paris it was part of a program of several films preceding a live performance.[12] Few early films achieved this sustained popularity and some of the only titles to really rival it over the next few years were subsequent Méliès *féeries* such as *Fairyland, or the Kingdom of the Fairies* (1903) and *An Impossible Voyage* (1904).

After its renown during the early 1900s, *A Trip to the Moon* largely dropped out of sight for the next two decades. In October 1929, however, Jean Mauclaire, the manager of the Studio 28 repertory film theater in Paris, obtained a print from a traveling exhibitor, adding to a cache of Méliès he had discovered in May of that year.[13] Studio 28 was known for screening avant-garde films such as *Un Chien andalou* (1929) and *L'Âge d'or* (1930)—both of which owe something to Méliès's style if not to his sensibility.[14] Mauclaire showed several Méliès films at Studio 28, including *A Trip to the Moon*.[15] According to Méliès, Mauclaire "obtains frequently a great success in showing this film in retrospective performances."[16] Although Mauclaire was reportedly loath to loan the film, he occasionally did.[17] It was almost certainly this print of *A Trip to the Moon* that was part of the program of the Gala Méliès on December 16, 1929, marking the initial culmination of Méliès's rediscovery in France.[18]

During the late 1920s and 1930s, Méliès corresponded with people researching the beginnings of cinema and collecting early films—several were themselves former film pioneers. Jean Acme LeRoy had developed a projection system in 1894, but was unable to profit from it and never received recognition for his invention; he had also been a friend of Georges Méliès's late brother Gaston when the latter lived in New York. LeRoy wanted to assemble a program of early films to show as part of a lecture series on the early history of film, although this plan was cut short when he was partially stricken by paralysis in 1928.[19]

In addition to collecting old films, LeRoy was "preparing a history of the early days in the business and . . . [was] trying to secure reliable data on the early men in the cinema art."[20] LeRoy, along with Merritt Crawford in New York, Maurice Noverre in Brest, and Will Day in London, were film historians *avant la lettre*: each wanted to write a history of cinema that would correct the many omissions and inaccuracies of existing accounts, although their conception of history nevertheless privileged the technological and aesthetic contributions of individual (male) "pioneers."[21] Each wrote to Méliès: he responded expansively to their letters, welcoming the opportunity to document his achievements for posterity. (Méliès's answers to LeRoy's specific queries about *A Trip to the Moon* are included in the Appendix.)

LeRoy had been "in search of 'Trip to the Moon' " since 1927 at least, going so far as to send Méliès a modest sum with which to place "a small want advertisement in the French trade papers."[22] Early in 1930, LeRoy at last obtained a copy of *A Trip to the Moon* from Day.[23] According to Crawford (who claimed to have helped LeRoy negotiate the acquisition of this copy), Day "had a good 'dupe' negative made from his old print . . . [and] LeRoy's print . . . was made from this 'dupe' . . . of 'A TRIP TO THE MOON.' "[24] Day's dupe negative was to be the indirect source of most copies of the film available until recently. While Day declared that the image quality was "as good today as when first shown," his print of *A Trip to the Moon* was incomplete.[25] Indeed, LeRoy's print, which had been made from Day's dupe negative, turns out to have been only 713 feet long, roughly 100 feet shorter than the copies originally sold around the turn of the century.[26]

Both Day and LeRoy realized the print they had was incomplete. LeRoy wrote to Méliès, hoping to obtain the missing footage from him.[27] The only person Méliès could have turned to for LeRoy's request was Mauclaire, who owned the "only print remaining in Paris," although it too was incomplete, "the first picture, and the end, [tableaux] nos. 28–29–30, are missing."[28] Mauclaire's print, like Day's and LeRoy's, lacked the very end, but, unlike theirs, seems to have had the penultimate scene mostly intact. Whether or not Méliès tried to get this additional scene from Mauclaire, it was never restored to LeRoy's print.

During the early 1930s, Méliès occasionally presented his films himself in Paris. On May 20, 1931, he borrowed Mauclaire's print of *A Trip to the Moon* and showed it along with three of his other films to what he described as "a splendid high class public" at the Salle Adyar.[29] Méliès did not own prints of any of his old films, he told Crawford, having "destroyed completely in 1923 . . . all my stock of negative and positive films."[30] If he could somehow obtain enough of his longer films to fill out a program, he might be able to book regular theatrical engagements. During the

Depression, such performances represented one of the only means Méliès had to supplement his meager income from the toy and candy concession he operated in the Montparnasse train station before retiring in 1932. He especially wanted a print of *A Trip to the Moon*, a "production" that, he told LeRoy, "I believe, is unrivalled, though produced by me in 1902, so many years ago. I am sure it will entertain and interest those who see it, as it did when I produced it."[31] It was, he recalled to Day, "my first great success," a film that achieved "such success that, still now, after so many years, the magazines and cinema papers, as well as the ordinary press, remember often this famous 'Voyage dans la lune.' "[32]

LeRoy died in 1932 and the Museum of Modern Art's newly formed Film Library acquired his truncated print of *A Trip to the Moon* when it purchased LeRoy's entire film collection (and what were termed the "non-commercial rights" to the films in it) from his widow in 1935.[33] The following year, the Film Library began circulating copies in 16mm and 35mm and thus it was screened for large numbers of people in the United States and Canada once again. In 1936 the Film Library's first curator, Iris Barry, told a delegation of French film industry officials, "young college and university students in the United States have already been delighted to see, and marveled at, Monsieur Méliès's *A Trip to the Moon*; this film is of such great importance for American cinema."[34] Until 1936 the film had remained largely inaccessible apart from a few isolated screenings such as the ones mentioned previously. Thus the writers of the 1920s and early 1930s who mentioned the film treated it as just one briefly noted example of the fairy tales and magical films Méliès made during his heyday just after the turn-of-the-century.[35]

In 1937 the Museum of Modern Art Film Library made a copy of *A Trip to the Moon* available to the Cinémathèque française through one of its earliest film exchange agreements.[36] On February 10, 1937, Henri Langlois, cofounder of the Cinémathèque, celebrated this agreement with a press screening of *A Trip to the Moon* that included live commentary by Méliès himself.[37] The next month, after Méliès provided commentary for another screening at Langlois's ciné-club, the Cercle du Cinéma, Langlois presented him with a copy of the Cinémathèque's recently acquired print of *A Trip to the Moon*, which he had once believed to be lost.[38] The film had followed a circuitous path of duplication, from London to New York to Paris, through the hands of several collectors and institutions, in order to belatedly return to its creator. By this time, however, Méliès was fully retired and did not have much use for the film. He died less than one year later, on January 21, 1938.

Haidee Wasson argues that the Film Library transformed old films into edifying objects for aesthetic appreciation and informed historical contemplation.[39] The Museum of Modern Art's educational mission created a new mode of film exhibition and reception that fundamentally recontextualized the film viewing experience and specific individual films. The Film Library often circulated *A Trip to the Moon* as part of a program of silent films entitled "Development of Narrative," where it was immediately followed by Edwin S. Porter's *The Great Train Robbery* (1903). As such, it was positioned as a milestone in the history of cinematic storytelling, implying that its "importance for American cinema" (as Barry put it) should be understood largely in narrative terms. The film's place in the Film Library's chronological program of early narrative films was seemingly justified by Porter himself, who acknowledged in a 1940 interview with the *New York Times* that, "From laboratory examination of some of the popular story films of the French pioneer director, Melies [*sic*]—trick pictures like 'A Trip to the Moon'—I came to the conclusion that a picture telling a story might draw the customers back to the theatres, and set to work in this direction."[40] For Porter, there was seemingly no contradiction between a "trick picture" also "telling a story," but more recent debates about the "cinema of attractions" (discussed later) have emphasized the split between these respective impulses in early filmmaking.

Film historians concerned with narrative have mainly stressed the way that *A Trip to the Moon* joins a sequence of spatially and temporally distinct scenes to tell a continuous and coherent story. Despite this emphasis on the use of shot transitions (mainly dissolves) to shift *between* separate spaces, we should not underestimate Méliès's reliance on substitution splices to create instantaneous and often imperceptible transitions or transformations *within* spaces. Méliès spliced together precisely matched shots to create many effects, as Jacques Malthête explains: "In fact, the stop-camera trick was always combined with a splice that was achieved and held together by a practically undetectable gluing generally found in the upper quarter or one-fifth of the frame. All appearances, disappearances, or substitutions were executed during filming, of course, but it was essential that the negative then be edited if the trick was to succeed."[41] By maintaining the framing while altering selected aspects of the mise-en-scène between different takes and then editing these takes together, Méliès transformed the astronomer's telescopes into stools and depicted the shell's collision with the face of the man in the moon (among other effects).

Yet, he also used substitution splices to join performances that were filmed in separate takes into what appears to be a temporally continuous whole. Through careful attention to detail both during filming and editing, Méliès was able to achieve "precise continuity of action over a splice . . . in order to maintain the flow and rhythm of acting which a

Figure 0-1. One of a number of substitution splices in *A Trip to the Moon*.

mere stopping of the camera could not provide."[42] Parts of *A Trip to the Moon* that seem to transpire entirely in long takes are actually made up of several discrete shots of performances by different actors or groups of actors. The most complete version of the film that is currently available shows evidence of more than fifty cuts—many of which often go unnoticed.[43] (See Figure 0-1.) Thus, the substitution splice was not only a means of extending the techniques of stage illusion, but also a way of reconfiguring existing forms of theatrical practice through the new modes of temporality and spatiality made possible by cinematic reproduction.[44] Méliès described the individual sections of his films neither as shots nor scenes, but as "tableaux." Successive tableaux are not necessarily separated from one another in time or space—much less by syntactic markers such as dissolves or cuts.[45]

Méliès's own catalog descriptions of *A Trip to the Moon* list thirty such tableaux. In Star-Film catalogs, *A Trip to the Moon* was given catalog numbers 399 to 411. Méliès assigned individual catalog numbers to each completed twenty-meter length of film in the order it was produced. Thus, *A Trip to the Moon*, which spans thirteen catalog numbers, corresponds to the length of "about" 260 meters given in Méliès's French catalogs.[46] In various other advertisements and catalogs, the film's length is given as 300 meters, 845 feet, and 800 feet.[47] Where mentioned, the "duration of exhibit" or the "duration of the projection" is specified as sixteen or seventeen minutes, roughly corresponding to a projection speed of between thirteen and fifteen frames per second.[48]

While the Museum of Modern Art Film Library's activities helped *A Trip to the Moon* to become part of the canon of world cinema and an indispensable component of countless survey courses, it has come to be known (especially in the United States) in truncated form because these copies were all struck from an incomplete print. This has long been the most readily accessible version of *A Trip to the Moon*. Over the years, it has been seen by hundreds of thousands of people through circulating prints (and other copies derived thereof). It also continues to be widely available in various iterations on the Internet. The Film Library's print ends with the capsule being towed ashore after it returns to earth and splashes down in the ocean. This version is missing two subsequent scenes—five more tableaux. The first of these omitted scenes, the longer of the two by far, includes a parade with a marching band, a military procession, and the lunar capsule, ringed with garlands and emblazoned with the Star-Film trademark rolling past on a float, as well as an awards ceremony in which each of the travelers receives a giant medal, and the Selenite dances for the crowd. In the second of these two scenes, the parade continues in another area where a statue of Barbenfouillis, the expedition's leader, has been erected atop a pedestal bearing the Latin motto, "*labor omnia vincit*" (work conquers all). There, the celebrations continue momentarily.[49] Only in 1997, some ninety-five years after its initial distribution, did a more or less complete version of *A Trip to the Moon* that had been reconstructed by the Cinémathèque Méliès become available once again.[50] In 2000, a colored print was discovered in Spain by Lobster Films.[51]

How much does it matter that so many copies of *A Trip to the Moon* that have been available since the 1930s were and are incomplete? After all, the very notion of a definitive version of any early film is rather anachronistic given that films were sold as "semi-finished products" over which their producers had largely relinquished subsequent control.[52] Indeed, while Méliès could determine how his films were presented at the Théâtre Robert-Houdin, the prints he sold would be supplemented with often idiosyncratic verbal, musical, and sound accompaniment, as well as projected at different speeds, combined with various types of performance, and sometimes even colored and reedited by exhibitors. Méliès implicitly tried to determine the content of the monologues that were spoken alongside his films by publishing detailed descriptions in his catalogs. He also attempted to prevent reediting of his films by using dissolves rather than straight cuts between many scenes.[53] Such efforts to exercise control over how his films were seen and heard hardly entailed a notion of the individual film title as a commodity that existed in a singularly definitive form. Méliès certainly recognized—often with much chagrin, given the widespread piracy of his films—that the sheer fact of mechanical reproduction, along with the possibilities for altering a purchased film, made for many different versions of a single title.

My interest in the scenes missing from many prints of *A Trip to the Moon* has less to do with what Paolo Cherchi Usai has identified as an "obsession for completeness" in contemporary film culture[54]—an obsession that would have been mostly alien to Méliès and his contemporaries—than with the way the omission (or addition) of these final two scenes changes the overall impression of the film. Although it is perfectly legible without the parade, the celebrations, and the commemoration that occurs at the end—one might not even know the Film Library's print was incomplete without reference to the catalog description—the satire of *A Trip to the Moon* is considerably muted without these two final scenes. If, as Elizabeth Ezra writes, "its depiction of the exploration of a faraway place and hostile encounter with alien life forms . . . can easily be read

Figure 0-2. *A Trip to the Moon*—the captured Selenite displayed for the crowd.

as a parable of colonial conflict,"[55] then it is these last few tableaux that secure such a reading.

The ceremony honoring the lunar journey is quite ironic given that the explorers previously squander much of their time on the moon napping and running away—an irony that is underscored by the self-important way the explorers gesture and prance about after they each receive their medals and by the outlandish scale of the medals themselves, which are larger even than their swelled heads. Likewise, the statue erected to honor Barbenfouillis's hard work is rather absurd since a group of

Figure 0-3. Detail of caricature by Méliès [pseud., Geo. Smile], *La Griffe*, January 23, 1890.

workmen are shown constructing the capsule with no help from him or his colleagues. Moreover, they cannot even observe the work without disrupting it, overturning a vat of acid as they tour the workshops. In the end, apart from reaching the moon, their only other accomplishment would seem to be the unprovoked destruction of a number of very fragile moon-dwellers, whom Barbenfouillis mercilessly decimates with sharp blows from his umbrella. The one Selenite who does return to earth is led by a rope around its neck as part of the parade and harshly beaten with a stick until it dances for the crowd.[56] (See Figure 0-2.) This cruel moment, which has gone mostly unremarked to date, reveals the darker side of an ostensible voyage of exploration and unmistakably provides a pointed commentary on the unfortunate consequences of colonialism.

As a satire, *A Trip to the Moon* reprises the sensibility Méliès cultivated drawing political caricatures under the pseudonym "Geo. Smile" for *La Griffe*, the anti-Boulangist weekly published by his cousin Adolphe Méliès from 1889 to 1890. On the cover of the January 23, 1890 issue of

Figure 0-4. *A Trip to the Moon* (detail)—the statue of Barbenfouillis.

La Griffe, for example, Méliès satirized the British Ultimatum (which had forced the Portuguese out of territory in southern Africa) with a caricature of a tall, mustachioed, big-fisted British soldier physically intimidating the much smaller and stouter figure of Portugal. (See Figure 0-3.) In this political cartoon, Méliès highlighted an asymmetry of European military power within colonized Africa, but some twelve years later in *A Trip to the Moon*, he turned from a specific incident between rival colonizing nations to a story that engages with the larger—but no less topical—issue of Western imperial ambition. Méliès mocks the militant nationalism that undergirds such imperial ambitions not only through the massive cannon that is aimed at the moon, but also through groups of chorus girls dressed as marines. Just before the cannon is fired, several marines present the flag with a bugle call while others take their places behind them with rifles by their sides. Later, the marines march in pairs shouldering rifles right behind the capsule in the parade. The film ends with the marines flanking the statue of Barbenfouillis. The statue shows him in a conquering pose, with his foot atop a disgruntled and frowning moon-face with the capsule-bullet still wedged in its eye. One of his hands is held high in a victorious pose and the other is firmly clasping his umbrella (see Figure 0-4), the weapon with which he destroyed the hapless Selenites. Like the British soldier in the caricature, his hands are glaringly oversized, suggesting that Barbenfouillis too is a ham-fisted bully.

The satirical qualities of *A Trip to the Moon* come into even sharper relief by contrasting it with the remake that Segundo de Chomón produced for Pathé-Frères, *Excursion dans la lune* (1908). In *Excursion dans la lune*, Chomón follows *A Trip to the Moon* virtually scene for scene while imitating a number of its most striking tableaux, including the transformation of the astronomer's telescopes into stools, the loading of the capsule into the breech of the cannon, the enlarging moon as the capsule approaches, the lunar snowfall, the umbrella which sprouts into a giant mushroom, the capsule's fall from a precipice, and its plunge through space.[57] *Excursion dans la lune* begins with a group of astronomers in seventeenth-century garb gathered around a fountain in the courtyard of a college, discussing how to get to the moon. The film ends in this same location when the capsule (which has split in two during its return to earth) drops into the fountain. At the very end of the film, "the brave astronomers are decorated with medals and other badges of honor" (as a synopsis published in the trade press describes this scene),[58] but this is a rather fleeting coda that lacks the pomp of the parade, awards ceremony, and dedication of the statue in Méliès's *A Trip to the Moon*.

In a telling revision, the anthropomorphized moon-face in *Excursion dans la lune* nonchalantly swallows the approaching capsule (see Figure

0-5) and belches flames—rather than having it uncomfortably lodged in its eye. In striking contrast to *A Trip to the Moon*, women play dancing moon maidens rather than marines and perform pirouettes rather than wielding rifles. The moon-dwellers, who are described in a trade press synopsis as "peculiar imps" and "multi-colored demons"[59]—their variegated appearance is depicted through stencil-coloring—are not destroyed by blows from the earthlings, but instead they implode and rematerialize at will in puffs of smoke entirely of their own volition. The film concludes not with an ironic celebration of lunar conquest, but with the formation of a couple. One of the astronomers runs off with a dancing moon-maiden and brings her back to earth in the damaged capsule. Instead of being displayed and beaten like the captured moon-dweller in *A Trip to the Moon*, she is welcomed to earth with open arms and quickly betrothed to the astronaut with whom she returns.

The coupling that ends *Excursion dans la lune* looks forward to later modes of narrative closure in film much more than the celebratory parade with which *A Trip to the Moon* concludes, yet Méliès's film has yet to entirely relinquish its important position in the so-called evolution of cinematic storytelling. Teleological models that privilege the development of narrative as the principal axis of film history, however, have mostly been displaced by the recognition that early cinema was often structured by displays of visual spectacle. As Tom Gunning argues

Figure 0-5. *Excursion dans la lune* (1908).

in his influential article on the "cinema of attractions" (developing an argument previously articulated in an essay he coauthored with André Gaudreault): "early cinema was not dominated by the narrative impulse that later asserted its sway over the medium . . . it is a cinema that bases itself on . . . its ability to show something."[60] With this revisionism came a new reading of *A Trip to the Moon* as a prototypical example of a linked series of cinematic attractions much more than an early narrative. Thus, Gunning contends that it is a "plotted trick film" in which the "story simply provides a frame upon which to string a demonstration of the magical possibilities of cinema."[61]

Charles Musser has vigorously disputed this reading, arguing that in *A Trip to the Moon*, "Méliès's cinematic dexterity performs a narrative function," and stressing the "intimate interrelationship between attraction and narrative action" in the film.[62] During the 1980s and 1990s, the respective positions in scholarly debates around the "cinema of attractions" were often mapped onto *A Trip to the Moon*. In the final analysis, Gunning points out, the question of "whether audiences were mainly amazed by the sets, costumes and camera tricks . . . or primarily drawn into its narrative of exploration and discovery can never be absolutely adjudicated."[63] But, Musser's claim—first published in 1994, and nearly just as true when it was republished in 2006—remains: "an extensive analysis of *A Trip to the Moon* still needs to be done."[64] This volume and its contributors respond to Musser's implicit challenge in a variety of ways.

The first two chapters place *A Trip to the Moon* in the context of Méliès's film practice. In chapter 1, "A Trip to the Movies: Georges Méliès, Filmmaker and Magician (1861–1938)," Paolo Cherchi Usai provides a concise introduction to Méliès's filmmaking career, with attention to the technical virtuosity of his productions, his fluid onscreen identity, and his penchant for displaying the female body as a "special effect." Cherchi Usai emphasizes the range of Méliès's oeuvre, which includes not only trick films that derived from his work as a conjuror and designer of stage illusions, but also " 'realist' and political films . . . characterized by a straightforward, polemical attitude." Chapter 2 is a newly revised version of André Gaudreault's crucial revisionist essay, "Theatricality, Narrativity, and Trickality: Reevaluating the Cinema of Georges Méliès," which has been published in French, Italian, and German, but never reprinted in English. Gaudreault argues that Méliès must be understood on his own terms as an early filmmaker rather than as a precursor of— or, alternatively, in opposition to—"the later classical narrative style of filmmaking." Film historian Jean Mitry, for example, associates Méliès's films with "theatricality," claiming that they lack the emphasis on editing found in truly cinematic examples of "narrativity."[65] Gaudreault, however, introduces a third term, "trickality," to describe the strategy that Méliès employed to create illusions that were explicitly acknowledged by actors in the films and presumably appreciated as such by spectators. For Gaudreault, Méliès was neither primarily concerned with storytelling nor—contra Georges Sadoul—confined to a strictly theatrical approach.

In chapter 3, "*A Trip to the Moon*: A Composite Film," Thierry Lefebvre shows that *A Trip to the Moon* was not simply based on the work of Jules Verne (as Méliès himself claimed later in life)—nor is it an amalgamation of Verne and H. G. Wells's novel *The First Men in the Moon*, as Sadoul states[66]—but it is in fact a much more complex and "composite" film that combines elements from many sources. Trips to the moon were taken frequently in the popular culture of the late nineteenth and early twentieth centuries (not only in books, but also in scientific lectures, magic lantern shows, fairground amusements, and theatrical performances). Lefebvre focuses in particular on the film's connections to A Trip to the Moon, a popular attraction at the 1901 Pan-American Exposition in Buffalo, and to the Jacques Offenbach operetta *Le Voyage dans la lune*. Although this operetta was glossed over as an intertext for the film prior to Lefebvre's essay (originally published in French in 2002), it emerges here as a crucial inspiration for Méliès, who appears to have drawn several of the tableaux of *A Trip to the Moon* and selected details of the film's mise-en-scène (including the umbrellas the travelers take to the moon) from it.[67]

In chapter 4, "First-Footing on the Moon: Méliès's Debt to Verne and Wells and His Influence in Great Britain," Ian Christie explores the connections between *A Trip to the Moon* and the works of Verne and Wells. He points out that by the late nineteenth century, "Verne" constituted a veritable multimedia brand that could be consumed not only by reading his stories in newspapers and illustrated books, but also by going to the theater, where both authorized and unauthorized versions of Verne's tales were staged. Much like another "unauthorized" version of Verne, Offenbach's *Le Voyage dans la lune*, Méliès traded on the recognition and appeal of the established "Verne" brand with *A Trip to the Moon*. He may also have been inspired by the recent publication of Wells's *The First Men in the Moon*, although, as Christie notes, Méliès's treatment of the themes of imperialism and colonization in the film is far less ambivalent than either Verne or Wells. In chapter 5, " 'Distance Does Not Exist': Méliès, le Cinéma, and the Moon," Murray Pomerance ruminates on a line of dialogue from Verne's *From the Earth to the Moon* that also resonates with the film: "distance does not exist." Pomerance proposes that *A Trip to the Moon* collapses distance in many ways: through juxtapositions of scenes; through the famous sequence of the moon as one seems to approach its surface; through an emphasis on transformation and (dis)appearance, and ultimately through what he terms the "transitionary image, . . . [which] merges two contradictory, two 'distant' states into a single moving—and thus emotional—experience."

In chapter 6, "Shooting into Outer Space: Reframing Modern Vision," Tom Gunning considers the ways that *A Trip to the Moon* engages with "modern vision"—that is with the extended capacities that technological mediation made available to human sight. With its ability to transcend space, time, and even gravity, cinema epitomizes "modern vision" and early cinema in particular often seems to revel in these possibilities. For Gunning, the linchpin sequence of the approach toward the moon is an archetypal moment of "rocket vision" that exemplifies "modern vision" not only because it seems to adopt the point-of-view of the rocket itself at a crucial moment, but also because it was created—like many others in *A Trip to the Moon*—through a skillful combination of theatrical stagecraft and cinematic technique. This combination owes much to Méliès's work designing illusions for his magic theater, yet it also results in a "hybrid" or "collagelike" sense of space "in which different modes of representation contend." As a whole, the film's spatiality is neither entirely "theatrical" nor fully "cinematic" (in the sense of creating a synthetic space across a series of cuts). Rather, *A Trip to the Moon* is a film in which moving flats painted in trompe l'oeil perspective jostle against superimpositions and substitution splices—a film in which the temporal overlap of the shell landing on the moon twice is entirely consistent with its spatial inconsistencies.

The next two chapters are specific case studies. In chapter 7, "*A Trip to the Moon as Féerie*," Frank Kessler considers *A Trip to the Moon* in generic terms as a *féerie*. Part of what Marian Hannah Winter later broadly categorized as the "theatre of marvels,"[68] the *féerie* was a genre defined by its emphasis on spectacle in the form of sumptuous scenery and costumes, stage effects, and dance performances—all of which typically came together in the apotheosis scenes with which *féeries* conventionally concluded. The *féerie* flourished in nineteenth-century popular theater and was immediately taken up by film producers such as Méliès, Pathé, and others. By positioning *A Trip to the Moon* within a genre history that stretches back to the end of the eighteenth century—rather than as part of the film genres that coalesced later during the twentieth century—Kessler is able to read the film on its own terms as well as to demonstrate, more generally, how early cinema inherited and transformed spectacular theatrical traditions that were inherently skewed toward what Gaudreault and Gunning characterize as "attractions." In chapter 8, "*A Trip to the Moon* as an American Phenomenon," Richard Abel examines the reception of *A Trip to the Moon* in the United States, where many Americans had already taken fictive trips to the moon (or were at least familiar with such imaginary journeys) through novels, theaters, amusement parks, and/or traveling carnival shows. The film was thus received in the United States within a context that activated the public's prior knowledge and experience of these other media. By combing local newspapers from small towns and cities around the country, Abel finds that although *A Trip to the Moon* was widely seen in the US up until the end of 1906, it was almost always identified as an Edison, Biograph, Vitagraph, or Lubin subject. Thus shorn of Méliès's name and its French origins, *A Trip to the Moon* was received in many places—quite surprisingly—as an American production.

In chapter 9, "A Trip to the Fair; or, Moon-Walking in Space," I examine *A Trip to the Moon* as part of the culture of turn-of-the-century World's Fairs, amusement parks, and fairground shows. Fairground exhibitors were one of the primary markets for Méliès's films and, given his close relationship to the realm of fairground exhibition, *A Trip to the Moon* resonates in various ways with the experience of the fairgrounds. In the film, the astronomers do a whole lot of walking and comparatively little actual space travel; as they perambulate through the deep spaces of the film's various scenes, they effectively make stops at a series of "attractions" that are analogous to what one could have seen at a World's Fair. Lefebvre, Gunning, and Abel each note the film's echoes of the A Trip to the Moon ride at the 1901 Buffalo Pan-American Exposition (of which Méliès may or may not have had specific knowledge), but I argue that it also bears the traces of a more generalized fairground conception that can be linked to the 1900 Universal Exposition in Paris (which Méliès certainly knew because he shot a number of nonfiction films there).

In chapter 10, "The Stars Might Be Smiling: A Feminist Forage into a Famous Film," Victoria Duckett uses questions about the place of women in *A Trip to the Moon* as a point-of-departure for a wide-ranging interrogation of its treatment of gender. Women do not travel to the moon in the film, Duckett notes, but they are highly visible agents within the film nevertheless. For Duckett, the lines of women pushing the shell into the breach and waving to the camera, the personified female constellations who look down on the astronomers on the moon, and the women taking part in the revels that follow their return are not just objects of the gaze who (as Laura Mulvey famously describes women in later narrative cinema) "connote *to-be-looked-at-ness*."[69] Instead, she argues that the film's depiction of women creates "a comedic reflection upon . . . gendered difference." By emphasizing Méliès's humor—an aspect of his films that has been underdiscussed[70]—Duckett mounts a compelling feminist analysis that touches on a rich array of intertextual references ranging across the realms of art history, mythology, literature, comic strips, and theater.

In chapter 11, "Impossible Voyages and Extraordinary Adventures in Early Science Fiction Cinema: From Robida to Méliès and Marcel Fabre," Antonio Costa links *A Trip to the Moon* and several of Méliès's other "impossible voyages" to the "science fictions" of French author and illustrator Albert Robida. Costa suggests that Robida's futuristic adventure stories perhaps have more in common with the Mélièsien style than either Verne or Wells, pointing out that Robida's profusely illustrated 1889–1890 novel *Voyages très extraordinaires de Saturnin Farandoul*—like Méliès's *The Conquest of the Pole* (1912)—is more of a parody than an imitation of Verne. He concludes by examining the early Italian film based on this novel, Marcel Fabre's *Le avventure straordinarissime di Saturnino Farandola* (1913).

In chapter 12, "No One-Way Ticket to the Moon," Viva Paci traces the afterlife of Méliès's imagery in *A Trip to the Moon* through the present day, citing examples from Hollywood musicals, experimental film, television, and music videos. Just as *A Trip to the Moon* was a highly intermedial film that borrowed from theater, literature, and the amusement park, so too the film lends itself to such borrowings.[71] Paci argues that the film is a quintessential example of the "cinema of attractions" in which individual "images, elements, and motifs operate and circulate independently, as fully autonomous attractions." She traces this circulation through many unexpected subsequent films that range from Robert Z. Leonard and Busby Berkeley's *Ziegfeld Girl* (1941) and Kenneth Anger's *Rabbit's Moon* (1950) to Al Razutis's *Melies* [*sic*] *Catalogue* (1973) and Baz Luhrmann's *Moulin Rouge!* (2001).

The appendix contains several relevant documents, including a list of the film's thirty tableaux and a detailed synopsis published in English in the September 1902 supplement to the catalog of the Warwick Trading Company. This is followed by Méliès's answers (written in English) to nine questions about the film that were sent to him by LeRoy around 1930. The appendix also contains two important articles Méliès wrote for French cinema periodicals that have been translated by Paul Hammond: "The Marvelous in the Cinema" from 1912 and "The Importance of the Script" from 1932. In the former, Méliès discusses his approach to filmmaking and, in particular, his penchant for "impossible films." The latter contains Méliès's remark that the scenario had limited importance for his own films since the script served merely as a pretext for a series of tricks—a statement that is often quoted vis-à-vis the "cinema of attractions."[72] A full translation of the entire article provides essential background for Méliès's claims and their possible bearing on our under-standing of *A Trip to the Moon*.

To avoid confusion, *A Trip to the Moon* is referred to throughout the book by its English-language title—although it was occasionally called *Trip to the Moon* instead—whereas its French title, *Le Voyage dans la lune*, is reserved for the Offenbach operetta and other productions that went by this name. Likewise, Méliès's other films are referred to here by the English titles under which they circulated, except in cases where this would alter the orthography of an original document or where an exact English release title is unknown.[73] Other film titles are given in the language of the country where they were produced. French works that are frequently cited in this volume—namely, the novels of Verne and Cyrano de Bergerac—are referred to by the titles of their recognized English translations.

Notes

Author's note: Thank you to Charles Silver and Katie Trainor for their help accessing the collections of the Film Department of the Museum of Modern Art, and to the students in my French Directors 1 course at the College of Staten Island during the spring 2009 semester, whose responses to *A Trip to the Moon* spurred many ideas.

1. William Johnson, "Journey into Science Fiction," in *Focus on the Science Fiction Film*, ed. William Johnson (Englewood Cliffs, N.J.: Prentice-Hall, 1972), 3–4; Alec Worley, *Empires of the Imagination: A Critical Survey of Fantasy Cinema from Georges Méliès to The Lord of the Rings* (Jefferson, N.C.: McFarland, 2005), 21–22; Devin Orgeron, *Road Movies: From Muybridge and Méliès to Lynch and Kiarostami* (New York: Palgrave Macmillan, 2008), 32–35. Elizabeth Ezra has claimed that *A Trip to the Moon* "was not only the first science fiction film, but the first cinematic spoof of the genre." *Georges Méliès: The Birth of the* Auteur (Manchester, U.K.: Manchester University Press, 2000), 120.

2. *L'Orchestre*, Sept. 28–Dec. 18, 1902.

3. Letter from Merritt Crawford to George[s] Méliès, Mar. 17, 1931; statement by Arthur White, Nov. 10, 1939, reproduced in *The Merritt Crawford Papers*, ed. Eileen Bowser (Frederick, Md.: University Publications of America, 1986), microfilm, reels 3, 4. See also Charles Musser, *Before the Nickelodeon: Edwin S. Porter and the Edison Manufacturing Company* (Berkeley: University of California Press, 1991), 209.

4. Charles Musser, *A Guide to Motion Picture Catalogs by American Producers and Distributors, 1894–1908: A Microfilm Edition* (Frederick, Md.: University Publications of America, 1985), 11.

5. Percy Williams, "The Orpheum, Week commencing October 27, 1902," unpublished *Managers' Report Books*, vol. 0, p. 33, Keith/Albee Collection, University of Iowa, Iowa City.

6. Richard Abel, *The Red Rooster Scare: Making Cinema American, 1900–1910* (Berkeley: University of California Press, 1999), 7–8.

7. Charles Musser, *The Emergence of Cinema: The American Screen to 1907* (Berkeley: University of California Press, 1990), 299.

8. Quoted in Charles Musser, "Rethinking Early Cinema: Cinema of Attractions and Narrativity," in *The Cinema of Attractions Reloaded*, ed. Wanda Strauven (Amsterdam, Netherlands: Amsterdam University Press, 2006), 394.

9. "Pictures at the Windsor," *Montreal Daily Star*, June 19, 1903, 8; "Meetings and Amusements," *Montreal Daily Star*, June 20, 1903, 12, GRAF-ICS collection, Université de Montréal. References courtesy of Louis Pelletier.

10. Herbert Birett, *Das Filmangebot in Deutschland, 1895–1911* (Munich, Germany: Filmbuchverlag Winterberg, 1991), 541.

11. Mauro Conciatori, " 'Le fantasie luminose' di Georges Méliès nei cin-ematografi italiani," in " *'Verso il centenario': Méliès*," ed. Riccardo Redi (Rome: Di Giacomo, 1987), 52; Aldo Bernardini, *Gli ambulanti: Cinema italiano delle origine* (Gemona, Italy: Cineteca del Friuli, 2001), 92.

12. Jean-Jacques Meusy, *Paris-Palaces, ou les temps des cinémas (1894–1918)*, rev. ed. (Paris: CNRS Éditions, 2002), 121.

13. *L'Ami du peuple du soir*, Dec. 20, 1929, quoted in Georges Sadoul, *Lumière et Méliès*, ed. Bernard Eisenschitz (Paris: Lherminier, 1985), 272.

14. Paul Hammond, *L'Âge d'or* (London: British Film Institute, 1997), 58–60. Méliès himself regarded these "Vanguard films" as "purely disgusting." Letter from Méliès to Crawford, July 3, 1931, *Merritt Crawford Papers*, reel 3.

15. Letter from Méliès to Crawford, Dec. 9, 1930, *Merritt Crawford Papers*, reel 3.

16. Letter from Méliès to Will Day, June 4, 1935, reproduced in *The Will Day Historical Collection of Cinematograph and Moving Picture Equipment*, special issue of *1895* (Oct. 1997): 64.

17. Letter from Méliès to Crawford, Mar. 17, 1931, *Merritt Crawford Papers*, reel 3.

18. On the Gala Méliès, see especially Roland Cosandey, "Georges Méliès as *L'Inescamotable Escamoteur*: A Study in Recognition," in *Lo schermo incantato: Georges Méliès (1861–1938) / A Trip to the Movies: Georges Méliès, Filmmaker and Magician (1861–1938)*, ed. Paolo Cherchi Usai (Rochester: International Museum of Photography at George Eastman House; Pordenone: Edizioni Biblioteca dell'Immagine, Le Giornate del Cinema Muto, 1991), 57–111. See also Maurice Noverre, "Le Gala Méliès," *Nouvel Art cinématographique*, no. 5 (1930): 71–90.

19. Letter from E[ugène] Lauste to Méliès, Feb. 4, 1927; letter from LeRoy to Méliès, February 7, 1927; letter from LeRoy to Méliès, November 14, 1928, files 2/1, 2/2, 2/6, Georges and Gaston Méliès Collection, Special Collections, British Film Institute, London.

20. Letter from LeRoy to Méliès, February 7, 1927, file 2/2, Georges and Gaston Méliès Collection, British Film Institute.

21. Although none ever wrote a book, LeRoy, Crawford, and Noverre published items, respectively, in *Moving Picture World*, *Cinema*, and *Le Nouvel Art cinématographique*. See also Léo Sauvage, *L'Affaire Lumière: Enquête sur les*

origines du cinéma (Paris: Lherminier, 1985), 128–146; Paul Spehr, *The Man Who Made Movies: W. K. L. Dickson* (New Barnet, U.K.: John Libbey, 2008), 636-638; and Cosandey, "Georges Méliès as *L'Inescamotable Escamoteur*," 67–69. Will Day's two-volume manuscript, "25,000 Years to Trap a Shadow," was never published. David Robinson, "L'Ombre qui n'avait jamais été trappée," trans. Laurent Mannoni, *Will Day Historical Collection*, 75–94.

22. Letter from LeRoy to Méliès, May 28, 1927, file 2/4, Georges and Gaston Méliès Collection, British Film Institute; letter from LeRoy to Méliès, Sept. 2, 1929, *Merritt Crawford Papers*, reel 3.

23. Letter from Méliès to LeRoy, Jan. 30, 1930, Georges Méliès subject file, Film Department, Museum of Modern Art, New York.

24. Letter from Crawford to Méliès, June 12, 1931, *Merritt Crawford Papers*, reel 3.

25. Letter from Day to Crawford, June 8, 1931, quoted in letter from Crawford to Méliès, June 12, 1931, *Merritt Crawford Papers*, reel 3.

26 "Films Received from Jean LeRoy," file A–5, Special Collections, Film Department, Museum of Modern Art.

27. Letter from Méliès to Crawford, July 3, 1931, *Merritt Crawford Papers*, reel 3.

28. Letter from Méliès to Day, June 4, 1935, *Will Day Historical Collection*, 64. See also letter from Méliès to Crawford, July 3, 1931, *Merritt Crawford Papers*, reel 3.

29. Letter from Méliès to Crawford, May 21, 1931, *Merritt Crawford Papers*, reel 3.

30. Letter from Méliès to Crawford, Dec. 25, 1930, *Merritt Crawford Papers*, reel 3.

31. Letter from Méliès to LeRoy, Jan. 30, 1930, Georges Méliès subject file, Film Department, Museum of Modern Art.

32. Letter from Méliès to Day, June 4, 1935, *Will Day Historical Collection*, 64. Méliès confirmed that Day's print was incomplete by sending him a list of the film's tableaux transcribed from one of his old catalogs.

33. The sale of the LeRoy collection to the Film Library was brokered by William L. Jamison, who worked for the Film Library during the 1930s and 1940s recovering old films, and E. S. Rinaldi. File A–5, Special Collections, Film Department, Museum of Modern Art.

34. Typescript of speech given June 12, 1936, Box 1, folder 25B, Iris Barry Collection, Film Department, Museum of Modern Art, my translation. This speech was made as part of a film-finding trip Barry made to Europe.

35. See, for example, Terry Ramsaye, *A Million and One Nights: A History of the Motion Picture*, vol. 1 (New York: Simon and Schuster, 1926), 395; and Benjamin B. Hampton, *A History of the Movies* (New York: Covici Friede, 1931), 38.

36. Glenn P. Myrent and Georges P. Langlois, *Henri Langlois: First Citizen of Cinema*, trans. Lisa Nesselson (New York: Twayne, 1995), 39.

37. Laurent Mannoni, *Histoire de la Cinémathèque française* (Paris: Gallimard, 2006), 43.

38. Letter from Méliès to Barry, Mar. 12, 1937, Georges Méliès correspondence, Special Collections, Film Department, Museum of Modern Art.

39. Haidee Wasson, *Museum Movies: The Museum of Modern Art and the Birth of Art Cinema* (Berkeley: University of California Press, 2005).

40. Quoted in Ezra Goodman, "Turn Back the Clock: Reminiscences of Edwin S. Porter, or the History of the Motion Picture," *New York Times*, Jan. 2, 1940, 124.

41. Jacques Malthête, *Méliès, images et illusions* (Paris: Exporégie, 1996), 63, my translation. See also André Gaudreault, "Theatricality, Narrativity, and Trickality: Reevaluating the Cinema of Georges Méliès," trans. Paul Attalah, this volume, 42–43; Tom Gunning, " 'Primitive' Cinema: A Frame-Up? Or the Trick's On Us," in *Early Cinema: Space, Frame, Narrative*, ed. Thomas Elsaesser with Adam Barker (London: British Film Institute, 1990), 97–99; and esp. Gaudreault, "Méliès, the Magician: The Magical Magic of the Magic Image," trans. Timothy Barnard, *Early Popular Visual Culture* 5, no. 2 (2007): 167–174.

42. Gunning, " 'Primitive' Cinema," 98.

43. James Miley, undergraduate paper, College of Staten Island, May 20, 2009.

44. See my *Disappearing Tricks: Silent Film, Houdini, and the New Magic of the Twentieth Century* (Urbana: University of Illinois Press, 2010), 32–37.

45. Compare John Frazer, *Artificially Arranged Scenes: The Films of Georges Méliès* (Boston: G. K. Hall, 1979), 83.

46. *L'Œuvre de Georges Méliès*, ed. Jacques Malthête and Laurent Mannoni (Paris: Éditions de la Martinière, Cinémathèque française, 2008), 335–355. Though Méliès also made a number of films that were not given catalog numbers, this system, which assigned multiple catalog numbers to longer films, has led some to overestimate just how prolific Méliès really was. Star-Film catalog numbers run through 1,556 at least, but this amounts to roughly one-third as many titles. See Jacques Malthête, "Filmographie complète de Georges Méliès," in *Méliès, magie et cinéma*, ed. Malthête and Laurent Mannoni (Paris: Paris-Musées, 2002), 242.

47. *L'Orchestre*, Sept. 28, 1902; *Complete Catalogue of Genuine and Original "Star" Films (Moving Pictures) Manufactured by Geo. Méliès of Paris* (New York: Geo. Méliès, 1903), 25; *Edison Films*, Supplement no. 168 (1903), 5; *Film Catalogue*, Supplement no. 1 (New York: American Mutoscope and Biograph Co., 1903), 28; *Complete Catalogue of Lubin's Films* (1903), 7, reproduced in *Motion Picture Catalogs by American Producers*, reels 1–4. Compare Richard Abel, "*A Trip to the Moon* as an American Phenomenon"; and "A Fantastical . . . *Trip to the Moon*," this volume, 136, 227.

48. Compare *Complete Catalogue of Genuine and Original "Star" Films*, 25; *L'Orchestre*, Sept. 28, 1902.

49. As of 1981, the second of these two scenes was considered "lost" since all available copies of the film did not include it. *Essai de reconstitution du catalogue français de la Star-Film suivi d'une analyse catalographique des films de Georges Méliès recensés en France* (Bois d'Arcy, France: Centre national de la cinématographie, 1981), 111–112. See also Anne Marie Quévrain, "A la redécouverte de Méliès: *Le Voyage dans la lune*," *Cahiers de la Cinémathèque*, no. 35/36 (1982): 160–165.

50. On the Cinémathèque Méliès, which was founded as Les Amis de Georges Méliès by Méliès's granddaughter Madeleine Malthête-Méliès (who worked as Lan-

glois's secretary at the Cinémathèque française from 1943 to 1945), see Madeleine Malthête-Méliès, "La Cinémathèque Méliès: Son histoire et ses activités," *Journal of Film Preservation*, no. 48 (1994): 39–43. See also Frank Kessler and Sabine Lenk, "Ein Leben für Méliès: Ein Interview mit Madeleine Malthête-Méliès, der Enkelin des Zauberers von Montreuil," in *Georges Méliès: Magier der Filmkunst*, ed. Kessler, Lenk, and Martin Loiperdinger, *KINtop* 2 (1993): 93–102.

51. " 'Le Voyage dans la lune' de Méliès en couleurs!" *Le Soir*, Nov. 19, 2002; "Découverte d'un Méliès unique," *Metro*, Nov. 20, 2002: 17, dossiers de presse, Cinémathèque Royale de Belgique, Brussels. Unlike this version, the color films sold by Méliès were hand-colored by women in the employ of Mme. Thuillier of Paris who used magnifying glasses, very fine brushes, and at least four colors of aniline dye (some of which were applied one on top of the other) to painstakingly paint each print frame by frame. Malthête, *Méliès, images et illusions*, 69–72. See also Paul Hammond, *Marvellous Méliès* (London: Gordon Fraser, 1974), 47–48. On colored prints of *A Trip to the Moon*, see also Jacques Malthête, "Les Bandes cinématographiques en couleurs artificielles, un exemple: Les films de Georges Méliès coloriés à la main," *1895*, no. 2 (1987): 7, n. 16; Jacques B. Brunius, "Passé, present, futur du cinéma en couleurs," pt. 1, *Cinéma-tographe*, no. 1 (March 1937): 14.

52. Thomas Elsaesser, unpublished conference paper, cited in Richard Abel, *The Ciné Goes to Town: French Cinema, 1896–1914*, rev. ed. (Berkeley: University of California Press, 1998), 61. See also Elsaesser, "La Notion de genre et le film comme produit 'semi-fini': L'exemple de *Weihnachtsglocken* de Franz Hofer (1914)," *1895*, no. 50 (2006): 67–85.

53. Abel, *The Ciné Goes to Town*, 71.

54. Paolo Cherchi Usai, *Silent Cinema: An Introduction* (London: British Film Institute, 2000), 65.

55. Ezra, *Georges Méliès*, 120. She adds, "When the film was made, France was the second largest colonial power in the world, having emerged from a period of unprecedented imperial expansion at the end of the nineteenth century."

56. Méliès emphasized the way the captured Selenite is forcibly displayed for the amusement of spectators in one of the drawings of tableaux from *A Trip to the Moon* that he made during the 1930s. See *Méliès, magie et cinéma*, 208; compare with photograph on p. 207.

57. My description is based on two prints held by the Film Department of the Museum of Modern Art. A shorter version is reproduced on the DVD *Georges Méliès Encore* (Flicker Alley, 2010).

58. "Latest Films of All Makers," *Views and Film Index*, Feb. 1, 1908, 8. See also Henri Bousquet, *Catalogue Pathé des années 1896 à 1914*, vol. 1 [1907–1908–1909] ([Bures-sur-Yvette, France]: Edition H. Bousquet, 1993), 53.

59. "Latest Films," 8.

60. Tom Gunning, "The Cinema of Attraction[s]: Early Film, Its Spectator and the Avant-Garde," in *The Cinema of Attractions Reloaded*, 381–382. Compare André Gaudreault and Gunning, "Early Cinema as a Challenge to Film History," trans. Joyce Goggin and Wanda Strauven, in *The Cinema of Attractions Reloaded*, 365–380.

61. Gunning, "The Cinema of Attraction[s]," 383.

62. Musser, "Rethinking Early Cinema," 395.

63. Tom Gunning, "Attractions: How They Came into the World," in *The Cinema of Attractions Reloaded*, 38. Gunning continues, "Both undoubtedly played a role and it is the relation between the two aspects that makes up the complex and multi-faceted process of early film spectatorship."

64. Musser, "Rethinking Early Cinema," 395. This article was originally published in *Yale Journal of Criticism* 7, no. 2 (1994): 203–232.

65. Jean Mitry, *Histoire du cinéma: Art et industrie*, vol. 1 [1895–1914] (Paris: Editions Universitaires, 1967), 212–215.

66. Georges Sadoul, *Les Pionniers du cinéma (de Méliès à Pathé), 1897–1909*, vol. 2, *Histoire générale du cinéma* (Paris: Éditions Denoël, 1947), 221–222.

67. Lefebvre thus implicitly problematizes John Frazer's claim that "Offenbach's fantasy operetta . . . was one of the inspirations for Méliès' best-known film, although that relationship is less important than the link between the film and the Jules Verne story." *Artificially Arranged Scenes*, 6. On Verne and Offenbach, see also Laurence Senelick, "Outer Space, Inner Rhythms: The Concurrences of Jules Verne and Jacques Offenbach," *Nineteenth Century Theatre and Film* 30, no. 1 (2003): 1–10. An English version of the French libretto by Eugène Leterrier, Albert Vanloo, and Arnold Mortier was written by Henry S. Leigh: *Le Voyage dans la lune: Grand opera bouffe, in four acts and fifteen tableaux* (London: J. Miles, c.1880).

68. Marian Hannah Winter, *The Theatre of Marvels*, trans. Charles Meldon (New York: Benjamin Blom, 1962).

69. Laura Mulvey, "Visual Pleasure and Narrative Cinema," *Visual and Other Pleasures* (Bloomington: Indiana University Press, 1989), 19.

70. Two notable exceptions are Rae Beth Gordon, *Why the French Love Jerry Lewis: From Cabaret to Early Cinema* (Stanford, Calif.: Stanford University Press, 2001), 163–169, 176–194; and on *A Trip to the Moon* in particular, Gerald Mast, *The Comic Mind: Comedy and the Movies* (Indianapolis: Bobbs-Merrill, 1973), 33–35.

71. On intermediality, see esp. André Gaudreault, *Cinéma et attraction: Pour une nouvelle histoire du cinématographe* (Paris: CNRS Éditions, 2008).

72. Quoted in Gunning, "The Cinema of Attraction[s]," 382; Musser, "Rethinking Early Cinema," 393; André Gaudreault, "From 'Primitive Cinema' to 'Kine-Attractography,' " trans. Timothy Barnard, in *The Cinema of Attractions Reloaded*, 96; and Wanda Strauven, "From 'Primitive Cinema' to 'Marvelous,' " in *The Cinema of Attractions Reloaded*, 112.

73. English-language titles for Méliès's films are taken from the most recent and detailed filmographies in Paolo Cherchi Usai, *Georges Méliès*, rev. ed. (Milan, Italy: Editrice Il Castoro, 2009), 101–150; and *L'Œuvre de Georges Méliès*, 334–356.

1

PAOLO CHERCHI USAI

A Trip to the Movies

Georges Méliès, Filmmaker and Magician (1861–1938)

Portrait of the Artist as a Film Pioneer

IN 1896 MÉLIÈS BUILT A FILM STUDIO MADE of steel and glass in his garden at Montreuil-sous-Bois. Made for his new company, Star-Film, this construction is considered to be the first "classic" film studio of the silent period, a designation manifest in the studio's architectural concept and functional design. Its transparent walls and ceiling caught natural light, and its unusual stage was conceived to allow backdrops to be changed in front of the camera. The design also accommodated Méliès's need to affix the camera firmly to the ground, thus ensuring the stability of the image while filming special effects. For example, the "tracking shots" in some productions are actually optical illusions created by moving or displacing the actors and scenery in front of the stationary lens. By 1905, this studio had established the standard to be followed by its contemporaries.

Worldwide commercial success convinced Méliès to create Star-Film branches outside of France. The most important was the New York branch, established to control and discourage the piracy and plagiarism of his work by other filmmakers.

In 1908 Méliès formed a U.S. production unit directed by his brother, Gaston. His films, mostly low-budget comedies and Westerns, never matched the quality of Georges's work. In 1912 Gaston began production of a series of exotic dramas set on location in the South Seas. This project's disastrous result is believed to have contributed to the financial crisis that ultimately crushed Méliès's career.

Artificially Arranged Scenes

It has been said that Georges Méliès developed all of the basic techniques involved in creating film tricks through his understanding of filmmaking technology and his sensitivity to the possibilities the new medium offered.

Legend claims that the substitution trick was discovered by accident when Méliès was filming *Place de l'Opéra* in 1896. The illusion that an omnibus was magically transformed into a hearse was created when Méliès's camera jammed, resulting in a break in the shooting. By the time that the malfunction was repaired, a hearse had moved into the position where the omnibus had been. Whether or not this story is true, the discovery of the substitution trick led Méliès to realize that film stock could be manipulated during shooting, processing, or printing. Optical illusions could be created such as doubling or multiplying objects and human beings, transforming bodies into microscopic or gigantic entities, dividing the frame into parallel scenes shot separately, dissolving from one scene into another, and superimposing moving images over the main action.

Aside from the novelty of these techniques, the meticulous precision in the tricks' execution is apparent to the contemporary viewer. In the film *The Melomaniac* (1903), Méliès created a sevenfold multiple exposure by rewinding the film inside the camera six times, demonstrating a sense of synchronization and control that is incredible even by today's standards.

The Compulsive Draughtsman

Since his adolescence, Méliès had been possessed by the demon of draftsmanship. Paper materials such as notebooks, letterhead, business cards, used envelopes, and bills were quickly transformed into sketches of the most diverse subjects: magic tricks, caricatures, designs for automated devices, and backdrops. Méliès conceived his tableaux (scenes) from very detailed drawings, a practice that would become standard in the film industry in subsequent decades.

Méliès was a master of scenographic illusion. Vertiginous perspectives, impossible architectural structures, and imaginary descriptions of stars, planets, and underwater environments were all devised by Méliès with a craftsmanship worthy of the European baroque fine arts. It was this ability that made his trompe-l'oeil painted scenes a prevalent feature of his films.

Admittedly, this talent resulted from a variety of technical constraints. The orthochromatic film stock used at that time was sensitive to ultraviolet, violet, and blue light and is only partially sensitive to yellow and green. Red objects appear on the screen as dark spots. To solve this problem he designed scenes and backdrops entirely in shades of grey. Color was then applied manually to each print. Méliès's production stills document the detailed effort that was put into creating extremely elaborate scenes, often shorter than one minute.

Conjuror and Storyteller

One of Méliès's many nicknames was "the magician of Montreuil," referring to his various visual inventions. Although Méliès knew that his fortune derived from his trick films, he always debated the issue with those who saw him as nothing more than an illusionist.

At the beginning of his career he filmed "open air scenes" in which he reconstructed actual events such as the eruption of Mount Pelée and the coronation of King Edward VII. He even staged an underwater scene by placing a fish tank in front of the camera, producing the illusion that the fish were swimming amidst the divers.

Méliès's "realist" and political films were characterized by a straightforward, polemical attitude. Some of these films were not welcomed by the local authorities, as turmoil sometimes ensued at theaters where they were shown.

His repertoire also included historical subjects, adaptations of literary works, and lighthearted variations of operas. Other subjects included publicity, vaudeville, synchronized phonographic sound, and "adult" themes.

The variety of topics in Méliès's production catalog may remind one of an imaginary association of explorers in *An Impossible Voyage* (1904) called the Institute of Incoherent Geography. Méliès's world might well be renamed the "Institute of Incoherent Cinematography," yet the spirit of his cinema is ruled by a strong stylistic and ideological consistency.

The Thousand Faces of Dr. Mabouloff

Georges Méliès played the protagonist in most of his Star-Film productions until 1908. One of the first known examples of his performances is *The*

Vanishing Lady (1896), in which he plays the role of a conjuror. Despite his reputation as a wizard of the screen, Méliès often liked to perform a wide variety of characters such as Don Quixote, Hamlet, Blue Beard, Rip Van Winkle, and the Wandering Jew. His favorite character was the Devil, tempting women and saints, jumping frantically across the stage, provoking the pandemonium that was to become typical of his most popular films.

He often experimented with his optical stunts by trying them himself—walking on walls and ceilings, engaging in conversation with his own image, multiplying his head several times, and even making it explode.

His ever-changing identity was best portrayed in films concerning intergalactic trips and sorcerers' ceremonies, as in each one Méliès created a different name for himself. His favorite was Alcofrisbas; another was Parafaragamus—both were magicians. When he explored the planets, he became Professor Barbenfouillis or the engineer Mabouloff.

Méliès, constantly torn between unabashed playfulness and sheer perfectionism, was obsessed by the idea of multiple identity. He was so aware of his multiplicitous personality that he staged a revealing and somehow disturbing parody of himself in *Going to Bed under Difficulties* (1900), in which he tries to undress and sleep while different clothes in various styles systematically appear, at increasing speed, upon his body.

The Female Body as "Special Effect"

Female personifications of divinities, heroines, suffragettes, witches, fairies, and womanlike illusions caught by the movie camera are so widespread in Georges Méliès's productions that collectively they have become a true subtext of his films. On the surface, the roles women portray reflect the standards of nineteenth-century popular literature, theater, and operetta: they are depicted as mysterious apparitions—unpredictable creatures whose identity cannot be comprehended by the male psyche, as victims driven by fate to their destiny, or even as miraculous saviors.

However, Méliès turned these conventions into narrative archetypes with broader significance. By representing planets and stars as female bodies, he created a metaphor for the glorification of woman as the muse of human inventiveness. While presenting a gentle but straightforward irony targeted at conventions of gender relationships (courtship rituals, clichés of early feminism, portrayals of woman as an object of scientific experiment), Méliès sees in the female body the most perfect manifestation of cinema as an extraordinary mirage.

The Joyful Wisdom

The fifteen years prior to World War I were the last in European history to be dominated by an optimistic view of the future of civilization. Such optimism derived mainly from an aggressive confidence in the possibilities of science and its technological applications: the invention of cinema, the conquest of aerial navigation, the discovery of radioactivity, and the use of the x-ray in medicine.

Méliès lived during the era of the last great geographical expeditions. The success of Jules Verne's novels gave this period a literary legitimacy that rapidly overcame the boundaries of academic circles and penetrated all the social milieux.

From this standpoint, Méliès's film productions represent a true apotheosis in the union of art with science. The famous image from *A Trip to the Moon* (1902), in which a spaceship crashes into the eye of a pastry-faced moon may not only be seen as a symbol of Méliès's aesthetics, but also represents the playful attitude toward science that was typical of the early twentieth century, often manifesting itself in a paradoxically lighthearted, almost provocative, mood. Through this whimsical spirit Méliès expressed his ideal of filmmaking as the fulfillment of a new, superior form of creativity.

Decline and Apotheosis

The career of Méliès as artist and entrepreneur reached a turning point around 1909 when the film industry threatened his scrupulous, craftsmanlike production methods. French film producer Charles Pathé accused Méliès of being a mere artist, and failing to have a sense of business. Méliès replied:

> I am only an artist, so be it. That is something. But it is for just that reason that I cannot agree with you. I say the cinema is an art, for it is the product of all the arts. Now either the cinema will progress and perfect itself to become more and more an art, or if it remains stationary and without possible progress, if the price of the sale is fixed, it will go down in ruin at short notice. . . . For if you businessmen do not have artists to make films for you, I ask, what can you sell?[1]

Pathé refused to distribute his last film, *Le Voyage de la famille Bourrichon* (1912). Oppressed by debts and completely destitute, Méliès interrupted all filmmaking activities in 1913. In an outburst of anger and depression, he set fire to all the Star-Film negatives and sold the remaining positive prints at a loss. Méliès, once among the world's leading film producers, worked with his second wife in a toy and candy kiosk, completely forgotten.

His artistic "resurrection" occurred in 1929, when a group of critics and avant-garde intellectuals discovered that he was still alive and organized a gala in tribute to him. During a formal reception in honor of his appointment to the Légion d'Honneur, Louis Lumière, the inventor of the Cinématographe, saluted Méliès as the "creator of cinematographic spectacle." The "magician of Montreuil" had entered into film history with a standing ovation.

Notes

This chapter was originally written as an introduction to accompany the 1991 Méliès exhibition and film retrospective organized at George Eastman House, International Museum of Photography and Film (Rochester, New York) by the author.

1. Georges Méliès, quoted in John Frazer, *Artificially Arranged Scenes: The Films of Georges Méliès* (Boston: G. K. Hall, 1979), 51.

ANDRÉ GAUDREAULT

Theatricality, Narrativity, and Trickality

Reevaluating the Cinema of Georges Méliès

The fact of the matter, I believe, is that the script *may*, in effect, *have no importance* in certain films.

—Georges Méliès

So much for the scenario which, as I have already said, is the main element, the starting point of the negative.

—Charles Pathé

THE RECENT REEVALUATION OF EARLY cinema (typified by writers such as Noël Burch and the historians who contributed to the 1978 FIAF Brighton project) bases itself on an opposition to a previous teleological concept of film history. The first generation of film historians (such as Lewis Jacobs in the United States and Georges Sadoul in France) saw early filmmakers as marking stages in the development

---

This chapter was translated by Paul Attalah; translation adapted and revised by Tom Gunning and Vivian Sobchack.

of the later classical narrative style of filmmaking. This view led to an evolutionary and progressive model of film history that would move (for example) from Georges Méliès to Edwin Porter to D. W. Griffith, with each seen as demonstrating a further mastery of cinematic technology and form. However, this progressive model has blinded us to the unique characteristics of the work of each of these filmmakers (and others) whose aesthetic projects often differed from one another. Indeed, the central error of those who simply see the early cinema as the primitive precursor of the post-Griffith cinema lies in the fact that they deny this period its own specificity. This error has led to the fact that the filmmakers of this early cinema have been insufficiently studied, and distinctions among them have been too readily ignored.

This teleological view of film history has particularly distorted our understanding of the cinema of Georges Méliès. The goal of my undertaking here is to resituate Méliès's films in their historical context by exploring their most unique characteristics. Such an exploration will allow us to discover in his work certain peculiarities and aspects rarely suspected by those who hold to the traditional teleological view of film history. Thus, the work of *all* the early filmmakers from Porter to Williamson and from Zecca to Hepworth could be subjected to a similar analysis. It is, however, the work of Méliès, the "purest" of the early filmmakers, that provides the best exemplar—simply because Méliès almost always refused every "concession": from Grivolas's money to filming in natural settings.[1] This independence of which he was always so proud (and which led to his ruin), as well as his taste for artificial settings, helped lend his work its singular character.

Jean Mitry notes in his *Histoire du cinéma*, "Most filmmakers, hypnotized by the obvious analogy between filmic spectacle and theatrical representation, preferred to follow Méliès' formula and the path opened up by the Film d'Art: a succession of discontinuous "tableaux," then a succession of scenes wherein every passage from one space or one time to another was specified by an intertitle."[2] Thus Mitry identifies Méliès's aesthetic with the Film d'Art on the basis of their mutual correspondence to theatrical representation. This identification may appear legitimate insofar as much of their production is concerned—notably their use of artificial sets. However, too closely identifying Méliès and the craftsmen of the Film d'Art is dangerous because it too easily associates Méliès's films with one of the main tendencies that supposedly characterizes early cinema: theatricality. Mitry defines the latter as follows: "theatricality, that is to say dramatic construction imitated from the theater and produced according to a staging which is *applied* to the conditions of cinema, a concept which finds its first full achievement in the *L'Assassinat de Duc de Guise*."[3] Many historians identify Méliès's style with what Mitry terms "theatricality."

And although appearances may be on their side (the filmmaker's use of distanced long shots, theatrical sets, entrances and exits on "stage" right and "stage" left, and so forth), this generalization often prevents them from also appreciating the *cinematic* originality of Méliès's films.

Mitry also notes another approach to filmmaking developing in this early period that he opposes to "theatricality" and terms "narrativity." He defines narrativity as "a continuity describing an action freed from the confines of theater—entirely dependent on the dynamic possibilities of editing."[4] Yet, if we understand narrativity as the spatial and temporal articulations made possible through such uniquely cinematic processes as editing, I feel that it is as important an aspect of Méliès's films as of other films of the time.

We are, however, dealing with a form of narrativity quite different from that developed by Griffith and other filmmakers in the second decade of the twentieth century. Méliès demonstrates an alternative attitude toward storytelling, one less focused on the story qua story. He neglects those narratological aspects that mark the early films of Griffith, such as the development of psychological characters, the creation of suspense, and the illusion of realism.

It must be clearly understood that the post-1915 cinema—the narrative representational cinema—is the product of a concept of cinematic narrative that did not exist at the turn of the century. Not that the early filmmakers did not tell stories. Rather, they told stories using a different, more flexible form of narrative. Furthermore, one should note that the desire to tell stories was not the only preoccupation of the early filmmakers. They were, in fact, simultaneously pulled in different directions by numerous interests. They wanted to show objects and people in motion (the time was not far past when you could get people to pay money to see on a screen what they could have seen in real life for free). They wanted to astound and fill people with wonder at the new form of magic made possible by the motion picture camera (many films, obviously including some of Méliès's, existed for that primary purpose). They wanted to show objects and lands that were beyond reach (there were numerous travelogues). And they also wanted to tell stories. However, there was still quite some time before the desire to tell stories first and foremost came to dominate the world of film—and before one form of narrative would be preferred to all others.

If we return to Méliès, it becomes obvious that his main objective was not to create films that told stories. Quite often, as we shall see, the narrative aspect of his films remained totally secondary. As just about everyone agrees, he was bent on creating cinematic spectacle—bringing to the nascent medium elaborate studio sets, makeup, costumes, trick effects, and so forth. But cinematic spectacle is not synonymous with "theatricality." Account must be taken of the distance that separates the world articulated by Méliès's films from both the theatrical world of the Film d'Art and the diegetically sealed world of the narrative film to come.

Consider, for example, the specific spectator/screen relationships that Méliès constructs. These are not the same as those operative in either theatrical or classically narrative cinematic texts. Here, Ingmar Bergman is helpful in reminding us that we can conceive of "illusionism" in relation to audience in several ways:

> When I make a film I am . . . perpetrating a trick. I use a machine built around a human physical imperfection, a machine which allows me to move my audience . . . from a given feeling to its extreme opposite. . . . I am therefore either a trickster or—*if the audience realizes the trick being played*—an illusionist. I mystify and I have at my disposal the most precious and the most amazing of magical machines which has ever in the history of the world fallen into the hands of a mountebank. Therein lies, or ought to lie, for all those who make or sell films, the sources of an irresolvable moral conflict.[5]

At the dawn of cinema, Méliès surely did not suffer Bergman's moral conflict, but his films by their very construction always already point to their illusionary and "screen" existence. Méliès's filmic system (shared by many others of the era) almost always establishes a relationship between spectators and the screen based on the *recognition* of the cinematic illusion. Spectators are never really fooled (nor meant to be)—especially because many of the filmic elements in this system exist precisely to remind viewers that they are watching a film.

For example, in his conjuring films (which may or may not contain the beginnings of a story), Méliès maintains the scenic conventions needed for the smooth unfolding of the magic act: He enters the field of view, directly greets the spectatorial public, points out the best effects, and so forth. In short, he interpellates both the camera and the spectator into the text as he acknowledges their existence through direct address. In his narrative films as well, Méliès or his actors will often address the camera and, thereby, the spectator—demonstrating no particular allegiance to the maintenance of diegetic illusionism, but rather to the *appreciation of illusion* itself. Similarly, Méliès's elaborate sets are so stylized that there could be no doubt as to their patent artificiality. And, finally, the universe that Méliès presents is so utterly "incredible" that there can be no mistaking its obviously constructed and "marvelous" nature. John Frazer has understood this aspect of Méliès well: "When the actors in *A Trip to the Moon* bow and recognize the audience, it is not, as has often been suggested, merely a naive misunderstanding of the distinction between stage and screen. It is an explicit recognition and respect for the audience accustomed to the conventions of the popular stage."[6] These asides to the audience, however, should not be seen simply as the transfer of a stage practice to the cinema in which it has no place because many theatrical plays establish a relationship with their audience that attempts to deny the audience's real presence. Conversely, there is no reason why filmmakers should not act as if the audience were present during the filming, knowing full well they will be present during the showing.

This recognition of the audience's belated (and the camera's immediate) presence presupposes an audience/screen relationship quite different from the one that would come to dominate the Griffith and post-Griffith cinema. In fact, Griffith will turn precisely to the rules of construction of a closed and autonomous universe whose primary condition of existence is the implicit negation of the audience's presence. And in his footsteps, a long line of filmmakers for whom it is of the utmost importance that the spectator be swept away to a diegetically sealed and more or less believable universe will do the same. Noël Burch calls this system of representation based on the constitution of a closed and autonomous universe the "Institutional Mode of Representation."[7] Its characteristic work involves attempts to erase all traces of the process of enunciation that produced the text, in this way inscribing, as Alain Bergala puts it, "a narrative into a chain of images and [producing] the illusion that these images are narrating themselves."[8] This is cinematic illusionism of quite a different kind than that Méliès practiced.

We need now consider the specific nature of Méliès's construction of narrative, the neglected question of his "narrative style." Reading the various commentaries on his work, one gets the impression not only that he was primarily concerned with cinematic spectacle, but also that this spectacle was narratively conceived; Méliès is often called the father of the fiction or narrative film. And yet, Méliès's movement toward narrative was initiated through and developed within the "spectacular" context of his magic act. Beginning with a singular representation of that act in *The Vanishing Lady* (1896), he rapidly moved toward filming acts with an increasing diversity of narrative elements. *Ten Ladies in One Umbrella* (1903) or *The Terrible Turkish Executioner* (1904), for example, are both magical "screen acts" embellished with an elementary narrative development. Moving from *Ten Ladies in One Umbrella* to *The Terrible Turkish Executioner,* however, Méliès introduced a more developed story in terms of action (although not necessarily more elaborate in terms of the cinematic expression of narrativity). *Ten Ladies in One Umbrella* is narratively simple in its fairground framing: "An illusionist standing in front of a fairground stall is playing around at making his hat turn into a balloon. He then turns himself into an Ancient Greek and, with the help of his umbrella, makes ten young maidens appear all dressed in various garb. After they leave, he resumes his normal appearance and changes the balloon which had remained in a corner into a top hat."[9] In comparison, *The Terrible Turkish Executioner* is more complex: "In Constantinople, an executioner is ordered to behead four prisoners. The heads of the condemned men, however, rejoin their bodies and they come back to life. The prisoners take revenge by cutting the executioner in half. He manages to rejoin his two halves and chases after them."[10]

The person of the magician who justifies, supports, and explains the appearances, disappearances, and other physical impossibilities is always present on the stage in *The Vanishing Lady* and on the stage (which is quickly transformed into a Greek backdrop) in *Ten Ladies in One Umbrella*. In *The Terrible Turkish Executioner*, however, the magician is replaced by an executioner in a public square. Moreover, *The Terrible Turkish Executioner* does not show a *magic act* involving successive appearances and disappearances, but a *fantastic action* during which impossible events occur all by themselves without the presence of some mediating deus ex machina that would have caused or "justified" them.

Importantly, however, in this movement toward narrative, Méliès was merely repeating what he had already done on stage and what was becoming increasingly common in the theatrical magic acts of the time: the integration of a series of tricks within a fictional story rather than their discontinuous presentation with a pause between each (for applause) as many magicians and illusionists continue to do even today. According to Paul Hammond, this innovative introduction of narrative is attributable to Maskelyne in the 1880s: "The generation separating the French and English showman had seen Maskelyne develop the use of dramatic narratives to connect and exchange the tricks performed piecemeal by Robert-Houdin."[11]

This narrative element, however, was seen as entirely secondary to the magical effects; thus, Méliès did not consider himself a storyteller. Indeed, here are his own words on the matter (written in 1932): "In these sorts of films, the importance lies in the ingenuity and unexpected nature of the tricks, in the picturesqueness of the sets, in the artistic positioning of the dramatis personae, and also in the invention of the star-turn and the finale. Contrary to the way things are usually done, my procedure for constructing these sorts of works consisted of inventing the details before the whole thing, a *whole* that is nothing other than 'the script.' "[12]

He could hardly state his position more clearly. The scenario, the story line, is merely a means to an end. This view of the function of narrative is exactly the opposite of the narrative system that would become dominant. Méliès usually only tells a story in order to embellish or to tie together the presentation of his latest effects. All his films are "trick-motivated." He tells us, "One can say that the script is, in this case, only the thread intended to link "effects" without much of a relationship to each other, just as the compère of a revue is there to connect together scenes that are extremely incongruous."[13]

I must emphasize here that Méliès holds this view of narrative as functional but secondary not only in those films showing an illusionist doing tricks (*The Vanishing Lady* or *Ten Ladies in One Umbrella*) or in his short one-shot fiction films (*The Terrible Turkish Executioner*), but also in his longer fiction films. Once again Méliès has left us invaluable testimony:

> For twenty years I made fantasy films of all sorts, and my chief preoccupation was, for each film, to find original tricks, a sensational main effect and a grand finale. After which, I used to try and find which era would be most suitable in terms of costuming my characters (often the costumes were required by the tricks, even), and once all this was well established, I got down, last of all, to designing the sets, so as to frame the action in accordance with the chosen period and costumes. As for the script, the "fable," the "tale" in itself, I worked this out at the very end; and I can therefore state that, done thus, the script was without any importance, since my only aim was to use it as an "excuse for mise-en-scène," for tricks or for tableaux with a pleasing effect.[14]

So much for his general approach to narrative. Méliès, however, also gave us accounts of this de-emphasis on narrative and privileging of "tricks" and "picturesque tableaux" in specific films. Thus he said of *Joan of Arc* (1900), "As a lover of the fantastic, I was especially compelled to make this film because of its trick effects, notably the apparitions to Joan of the Archangel Gabriel, of the Saints, and of the flight of her soul to heaven during the stake-burning scene."[15] And of *A Trip to the Moon* (1902), "I then imagined, in using the process of Jules Verne, (gun and shell) to attain the moon, in order to be able to compose a number of original and amusing fairy pictures outside and inside the moon, and to show some monsters, inhabitants of the moon in adding one or two artistical effects (women representing stars, comets, etc) (snow effect, bottom of the sea, etc)."[16] Méliès's use of narrative, then, is totally accessory and the stylistic key to his films is to be found elsewhere. He sees narrativity as pretext rather than text, and it is not determinant in his cinematic imagination and production. No more so than the theatricality that is equally secondary in his work. Indeed, if I may be permitted a neologism, I would like to introduce the notion of "trickality"—a concept that seems to me to best sum up his work.

This emphasis on "trickality," however, does not mean that Méliès's films are exempt from any number of characteristics specific to the systems of cinematic articulation that emphasize theatricality or narrativity. Indeed, film historians have generally underestimated Méliès's unique contribution to the development of narrativity and the processes of editing upon which it is founded. There are two reasons for this underestimation. The first is that, blinded by the analogy between Méliès's films and stage acts, historians have often failed to notice certain particularly developed forms of editing in his films. The second is that, blinded by their teleological understanding of film history, many historians have not seen certain editing operations that are absolutely essential to Méliès's style, but that do *not* resemble the narrative editing that would come to dominate later cinema.

One need only read Georges Sadoul, for example, to realize just how far this blindness can go. Claiming that as a general rule Méliès almost never showed the same object from two points of view (by cutting-in, for example), Sadoul concludes that Méliès's camera never gave a mobile viewpoint on action through changes in the camera's position:

> "*The unity of point of view*" presupposes that the director has set his camera up as the eye of the spectator seated in the middle of a row of theater seats: the "man in the front row." . . . Méliès never imagined that he could leave his seat in the middle of the show to get a better look at the leading lady's smile or to follow her into the dining room when she left the living room.[17]

This characterization of Méliès's work willfully ignores dozens, hundreds, even thousands of meters of his films. In *A Trip to the Moon*, for example, Méliès systematically shifts his point of view and follows his characters as they move from the "Astronomic Club" to the factory, and then to the roof from which the "scientists" can see the foundry. Additionally, in *Fairyland, or the Kingdom of the Fairies* (1903), one very short shot shows us the witch drowning after the previous shot in which Prince Bel Azor has thrown her off a cliff. Indeed, all of Méliès's "feature" films contain similar examples of shifts in point of view in no way justifying Sadoul's claim that, "The passage from one scene to another is not *editing* but a trick, a substitute for quick set changes."[18]

Given this sort of limited description, some of the most important aspects of Méliès's editing technique have been passed over in silence. It is, in fact, particularly odd that historians have never mentioned an example of rapid editing, quite unusual for the period, which can be found in his famous *A Trip to the Moon*. The film contains a succession of four shots in less than twenty seconds! (I have viewed more than 1,500 films from the period between 1895 and 1907 and, as far as I can recall, no other film I have seen contains an example of such rapid editing.) The episode in question deals with the return of the rocket and is constructed in the following narrative sequence of shots:

1. On the moon. The rocket is near an overhang and the astronomers, pursued by the Selenites, rush toward it. Professor Barbenfouillis grabs hold of the rope and makes the rocket tip over into space: 7 seconds. (Figure 2-1)

2. In space. The rocket is in free fall: 2 seconds. (Figure 2-2)

3. Above the ocean. The rocket plunges into the water: 2.5 seconds. (Figure 2-3)

4. At the bottom of the sea. The rocket hits bottom and rises slowly to the surface: 8 seconds. (Figure 2-4)

Obviously, such rapid editing does not happen often in Méliès's films. Nonetheless, all of his feature-length fiction films demonstrate a certain editing flexibility and counter the prevailing opinion according to which Méliès "is quite content, as regards his 'feature' films, to glue end to end his twenty meter negatives as the camera cranks them out."[19]

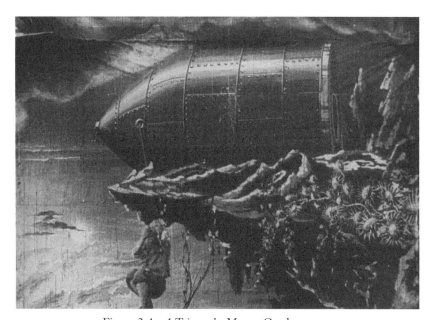

Figure 2-1. *A Trip to the Moon*—On the moon.

Figure 2-2. *A Trip to the Moon*—In space.

Figure 2-3. *A Trip to the Moon*—Above the ocean.

Figure 2-4. *A Trip to the Moon*—At the bottom of the sea.

Filmic expression has at its disposal many types of cuts (cut-ins, cuts on action, eye-line cuts, cuts in relation to the 30–degree rule, and so forth) that help determine various significant visual relations between and among shots (scale, disposition of filmed subjects, angles of vision, and so forth). Certain conventional rules have been formulated and come to stand as Burch's earlier-cited "Institutional Mode of Representation," a mode that has emphasized the practice of matching cuts to make them as "invisible" as possible. This editing rule (and others) began to appear and become institutionalized during the second decade of the twentieth century. Previously, filmmakers had relied on their intuition or had proceeded haphazardly. However, filmmakers were able to make their stories progress primarily through systematic cutting. This need to move the story ahead is most acutely present in Griffith and the filmmakers who came after him. Earlier filmmakers, however, sometimes caused their stories to "stutter" through their editing practice. Indeed, it sometimes happened that from one shot to the next the action would be repeated: There would be a temporal overlap.

Like other early filmmakers, Méliès also used such temporal overlap. Historians frequently mention *A Trip to the Moon* in which the rocket is seen to touch down "twice" on the moon's surface. *An Impossible Voyage*

(1904) is also often cited: The vehicle bursts through the wall of the inn "twice." As might be expected within the context of an evolutionary and teleological view of film history, this "lack" of temporal continuity in the early ("primitive") cinema is often condemned: "Three of four snips of the scissors would have been enough to re-establish the *proper* chronology."[20] But Sadoul once again forgets that the system of early cinema did not "require" the chronological continuity that would later dominate film practice. For Méliès and the other filmmakers of his era, it was more important *to show everything* (the reaction of the people outside the inn before and during the accident of *An Impossible Voyage*, and the activity of the people seated around the table of the inn as well as their reactions to the accident) than to sweep the audience along the continuous path of the uncontrollable vehicle.

Previous historians have noted these types of examples only to point to them as "primitive." Thus, they often conclude that editing was not a crucial part of Méliès's production process or cinematic style. From reading their works, imagining Méliès in a half-darkened room examining his strips of film, carefully finding the exact spot that will have to be cut, taking his scissors, cutting the film and gluing the two ends together, checking the result, and then starting over again if necessary is rather difficult. And yet, that is exactly what Méliès did for almost all of his films. Jacques Malthête, who undertook the enormous task of reconstructing a large part of the films held by the association Les Amis de Georges Méliès, confirms this when he states:

> Indeed, if one were to examine carefully . . . a trick film, one would soon realize that we have for some time been living with false notions and that film historians have missed some important facts. . . . This effect [stop camera] is always associated with a splice. . . . I know of no exception to this rule. Every appearance, disappearance or substitution was of course done in the camera but was always re-cut in the laboratory on the negative, and for a very simple reason: this trick effect . . . will not work if the rhythm is broken. But the inertia of the camera was such that it was impossible to stop on the last frame of the "shot" before the "trick," change the background or the characters, and start up again on the first frame of the "shot" after the "trick" without having a noticeable variation in speed.[21]

Fundamentally, Méliès's films are edited films except that—and the exception is essential—many of his cuts juxtapose two "shots" with the *same* framing: Before and after a stop-camera substitution, the framing remains the same. Certainly this editing technique is quite different from the descriptive or narrative editing of later cinema that primarily relies on the *difference* of framing between cuts. But it remains editing nonetheless, especially when one considers that this type of operation led Méliès to consider and solve the basic problem of match cutting: cutting on movement, matching the positions of filmed subjects, and so forth. In fact, Méliès was one of the first to think of the cinema in terms of cuts! The point here is not to turn Méliès into the father of montage, the precursor of Griffith or Eisenstein. Rather, the point is to recognize that in his work and in many of the other films of the era a type of editing exists that is all too often occulted by the privileged status that film historians regularly grant to the later form of narrative editing.

We are thus led to believe that the question of matching images must have been a major preoccupation for Méliès as well as for the other filmmakers of his time making "trick" films. One only need see a film such as *The Human Fly* (1902) to realize that this was the case. Méliès shows a Russian dancer dancing across walls as though it were the most natural thing in the world. First, we see a man walking across the floor in front of a backdrop. He is about to step onto the wall and

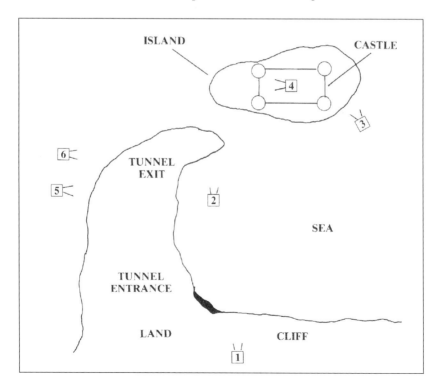

Figure 2-5. *Fairyland*—Diagram of the various camera positions, tableaux 23–29.

at the very instant there occurs a cut that is practically invisible. The filming has been stopped, the backdrop has been laid flat across the studio floor, and the camera has been hoisted up to shoot the scene from a 90-degree angle directly above. Care has been taken to reframe the backdrop exactly as it had been in the previous shot/scene and to maintain the same distance between the camera and the subject. The dancer (played by Méliès) has repositioned himself at the same spot in the scene that is now shot horizontally. The illusion is perfect and is the result of a perfect match cut. Indeed, all stop-camera substitutions require this kind of meticulousness and presuppose an equally precise continuity of action. However, these cuts are used for *magical ends* rather than for the dramatic purposes found later in Griffith's editing. Nonetheless, the fact remains that these match cuts are indeed cuts resulting from a practice of editing that sometimes far outstrips what is normally thought of as editing practice of the time. *The Black Imp* (1905), for example, contains about sixty cuts (stop-action or substitutions) within three and one-half minutes!

Méliès's use of the camera also seems ill-served by traditional historiographic thought about his work. Some experts maintain that the viewpoint of Méliès's camera on the action is stationary. I have already discussed this matter briefly in relation to his shifting perspective in sequences of *A Trip to the Moon* and *Fairyland, or the Kingdom of the Fairies*. However, allow me here to further elaborate a fairly remarkable example of Méliès's creation of the illusion of camera movement between shots within a single space that—had it been shot outdoors by Porter, Zecca, or a member of the "Brighton School"—would certainly have received delirious praise and have caused all teleological historians to speak of yet another cinematic "first." In *Fairyland, or the Kingdom of the Fairies*, the rescue of Princess Azurine is told through a series of shots during which the camera, its position changed for each shot, literally circles the dramatic space. Here is a breakdown of the rescue (see also Figure 2-5):

1. Prince Bel Azor and his companions reach dry land and move into a natural tunnel.

2. The characters emerge at the other end of the tunnel in front of the island where Princess Azurine is held captive. The prince dives into the water. (From shot 1 to shot 2 there is a kind of cut-in.)

3. The prince reaches the island, forces open the castle door, and enters. (The camera has moved in and about 45 degrees right.)

4. Inside the castle, the prince saves the princess. (Locating the exact position of the camera here is impossible.)

5. The prince and princess reach dry land and join up again with the prince's companions. The prince throws the witch off the cliff. (The camera now stands opposite its position in shot 3.)

6. The witch drowns. (The camera is now at the bottom of the cliff although situating the exact shot angle is impossible.)[22]

These various examples of Méliès's editing and his illusion of a shifting point of view on the action demonstrate clearly that we need to reexamine the work of this pioneer filmmaker who pushed the logic of his system of "trickality" right up to the very end of his life—for he took leave of his public under the cover of a *temporal overlap*! His last public appearance was December 16, 1929, at the Salle Pleyel in Paris. This was the Gala Méliès that honored him by showing some of his recently recovered films. At the end of the screening, the audience rose to acclaim Méliès who was nowhere to be found. The lights went down again and another film was projected on the screen. Let us leave the last description of the event to Madeleine Malthête-Méliès:

> Calling upon the method perfected by Méliès twenty-four years earlier . . . which allowed action to move from the screen to the stage . . . the Gala organizers asked him to shoot a very short film; we see him suddenly appear on the screen. . . . Lost in the streets of Paris, he is looking everywhere for the Salle Pleyel . . . on the wall he sees an enormous Gala poster bearing his picture. . . . He dives head first into the poster. Suddenly, the lights go on in the hall. The screen rises and uncovers, in the middle of the stage, a frame to which is nailed the poster we have just seen. Suddenly the paper rips apart and Méliès appears in the flesh.[23]

"Suddenly the paper rips apart," but still a few moments *after* the beginning of the same action had been seen on the screen. An end worthy of one of the most extraordinary of cinematic pioneers using a process that perhaps no one had yet called a mismatch.

Notes

Author's note: This article is an abridged and revised English version of a paper originally given at Cerisy-la-Salle, France, in August 1981, at the symposium

Méliès et la naissance du spectacle cinématographique. (Earlier and quite different versions have been published in French by Klinckcksieck in 1984 and in English by McGill University, Montréal, Working paper Series—Graduate Communication Program, in 1982). The author would like to thank both the Canada Council and the Social Sciences and Humanities Research Council of Canada for grants that enabled this research as well as attendance at the Cerisy Conference.

1. Méliès considered filming in a natural setting a concession to facility. The use of artificial and composed backgrounds was a way for him to distinguish himself from those who, having opted for facility as far as he was concerned, chose to film in natural settings. On this matter, see his 1907 article, "Cinematographic Views," trans. Stuart Liebman, in *French Film Theory and Criticism: A History/Anthology*, ed. Richard Abel, vol. 1 (Princeton, N.J.: Princeton University Press, 1988), 35–47. For the point raised here, see specifically p. 37. This article is appearing in an unabridged and revised translation by Stuart Liebman and Timothy Barnard in my book *Film and Attraction: From Kinematography to Cinema* (Urbana: University of Illinois Press, 2011).

2. Jean Mitry, *Histoire du cinéma: Art et industrie*, vol. 1 (Paris: Editions Universitaires, 1967), 400.

3. Mitry, *Histoire du cinéma*, 370.

4. Mitry, *Histoire du cinéma*, 370.

5. Ingmar Bergman, quoted without any source in the 1980 program of "Cinématographe," the film club of the Collège de Sainte-Foy, Québec City; emphasis added.

6. John Frazer, *Artificially Arranged Scenes: The Films of Georges Méliès* (Boston: G. K. Hall, 1979), 99.

7. Noël Burch, "Porter or Ambivalence," *Screen* 19, no. 4 (1978–79), 98.

8. Alain Bergala, *Initiation à la sémiologie du récit en images* (Paris: Ligue francaise de l'enseignement et de l'éducation permanente, 1977), 38.

9. *Essai de reconstituition du catalogue de la Star-Film suivi d'une analyse catalographique des films de Georges Méliès recensés en France* (Bois d'Arcy, France: Centre national de la cinématographie, 1981), 152.

10. *Essai de reconstituition*, 171.

11. Paul Hammond, *Marvellous Méliès* (London: Gordon Fraser, 1974), 19.

12. Méliès, "The Importance of the Script," trans. Paul Hammond, this volume, 242–243.

13. Méliès, "The Importance of the Script," 243.

14. Méliès, "The Importance of the Script," 243.

15. *Catalogue de l'exposition commémorative du centenaire de Georges Méliès* (Paris: Cinémathéque française, 1961), 28. This is a written statement that dates approximately from 1937.

16. Méliès, "Reply to Questionary [*sic*]," this volume, 233.

17. Georges Sadoul, *Les Pionniers du cinéma (de Méliès du Pathé)*, 1897–1909, vol. 2, *Histoire générale du cinéma*, vol. 2 (Paris: Denoël, 1948), 141; emphasis added.

18. Sadoul, *Les Pionniers du cinéma*, 142; emphasis added.

19. Georges Sadoul, *Georges Méliès* (Paris: Seghers, 1961), 38.

20. Sadoul, *Georges Méliès*, 56; emphasis added.

21. Letter to author, May 1, 1981.

22. I have described the succession of shots as though, across all the shots, we have been dealing with the same background set through which the camera had traveled while changing angles between shots. In fact, Méliès's camera remained in the same place at the back of the studio, and different drawings of the same set were laid out in front of the camera thereby producing the *illusion* of camera movement between shots. It is nonetheless surprising that Méliès should have gone to all the trouble of making five or six backdrops for a scene whose relative unity of space might have allowed him to avoid this découpage. No other filmmaker of the period made such a meticulous découpage, not even in a *natural* setting. Thus, despite the actual fixed position of Méliès's camera, we need to reconceptualize the way we think about his work and to realize that he was deeply concerned with constituting the illusion of camera movement and a variety of ideal viewpoints.

23. Madeleine Malthête-Méliès, *Méliès, l'enchanteur* (Paris: Hachette, 1973), 398–399.

3

THIERRY LEFEBVRE

A Trip to the Moon

A Composite Film

WHEN GEORGES MÉLIÈS MADE *A Trip to the Moon* in May 1902, the exploration of space was no longer a mere utopia. Our own satellite in particular was no longer the "nowhere land" it was once imagined to be by Lucien de Samosate, Francis Godwin, and Cyrano de Bergerac. Over the previous century astronomers had carried out numerous studies of it, using scientific calculations to examine it from every angle, and Auguste Bertsch and Lewis Rutherfurd's astrophotography[1] had popularized its furrowed image among the general public.

And yet, despite its apparent familiarity, the moon remained inaccessible. The kinds of take-offs described by Jules Verne in *From the Earth to the Moon* and by H. G. Wells in *The First Men in the Moon* were absurd: Verne's ballistic model involved a thrust that would have crushed its unfortunate passengers in their seats and reduced them to pulp, whereas Wells's antigravitational model was scarcely different from the dewdrops Cyrano de Bergerac dreamt up several centuries earlier. In 1903, just a few months after *A Trip to the Moon* was released, the Russian Konstantin Eduardovich Tsiolkovsky published *Research into Interplanetary*

This chapter was translated by Timothy Barnard.

Space by Means of Rocket Power, a foundational work in the field that Joseph-Henri Rosny would later call "astronautic theory."

When asked about his motives in making the film, Georges Méliès always remained evasive. "The idea of *Trip to the Moon*," he wrote in 1930, "came to me from the book[s] of Jules Verne, entitled 'From the earth to the moon and round the moon' [*sic*]. In this work the human people could not attain the moon. . . . I then imagined, in using the process of Jules Verne, (gun and shell) to attain the moon, in order to be able to compose a number of original and amusing fairy pictures outside and inside the moon."[2]

Most historians have adopted this minimalist version given by Méliès. Others, beginning with Georges Sadoul, have also remarked on the probable influence of H. G. Wells's *The First Men in the Moon*, which was published in French translation a few months before the film was shot. In general, however, intertextual analysis of *A Trip to the Moon* today has simply vanished, a surprising fact given the film's importance in the history of cinema.

A Trip to the Moon as Attraction

As Jacques Deslandes and Jacques Richard have pointed out, Méliès's film was part of a well-established fairground tradition;[3] they refer to it moreover as a "variation *ad usum populi*" and cite the example of an entertainment of the same name presented by a certain Gorain, a traveling fairground showman at the turn of the century.

Importantly, however, most of these entertainments were seen as forms of popular science and not the sort of fanciful representation that Méliès was interested in. If we are to believe Albert A. Hopkins, Méliès's model was an illustrated lecture entitled "A Trip to the Moon," which was presented for the first time in Berlin in 1887 and later in other countries. This lecture was organized around a series of large painted canvases depicting an eclipse of the sun seen from the earth, lunar mountains seen from a distance of 5,000 miles, Aristarchus Plateau and Promontorium Laplace seen from a distance of 2.5 miles and an eclipse of the sun seen from the moon. Hopkins remarks that, "The surface of the moon is painted on canvas supported on hinged props. . . . A stiff rod joins the hinges and forms the horizon."[4]

As is readily apparent, this kind of entertainment is noticeably different from Méliès's project in that it had no fictional element and did not involve characters acting out roles. In fact it was closer to the cosmography Camille Flammarion and Jean-Henri Fabre used as entertainment than to the unbridled imagination of the magician of Montreuil. Flammarion, moreover, was inspired by the "simulation" staged in Berlin for his Panorama des Mondes (Panorama of Different Worlds), which was intended for the 1900 World's Fair but unfortunately never completed for financial reasons.[5] Fabre, for his part, in the eleventh lesson of his volume *Ciel*, entitled "An Excursion on the Moon," sets out to conquer the moon mentally: "Let's raise ourselves up to the moon. Out of prudence, and for a host of other reasons, we will travel in our minds only."[6] At the end of a "flight" that he employed to illustrate several principles of physics, Fabre landed softly on the moon: "Oof! We're here! Ah, it's nice to fall in our minds only! . . . Where are we? On a rocky slope, similar to some of the bald escarpments found in the Alps. . . . The ground around us rises in steep slopes of bleak bareness and forms a conical pit, a broad hollow, whose bottom is lost in a confusion of mist and heaps of rocks."[7]

Here the journey is only a pretext for a lesson in lunar topography. There is no element of fiction. Therefore, we seemingly must look elsewhere for the model that inspired Méliès.

Georges Sadoul remarked in 1961, "Unlike *The Dreyfus Affair* or *Joan of Arc*, [*A Trip to the Moon*] appears not to have been commissioned by English music halls. And before then French fairground exhibitors did not purchase subjects more than 100 meters in length."[8] Indeed *A Trip to the Moon*'s extravagant budget (10,000 francs, making considerable revenue necessary), its unusual shooting time (three months), and atypical length make quite clear that the U.S. market was this exceptional film's primary target.[9] And so we now turn our attention to the United States.

The Pan-American Exposition in Buffalo

On May 2, 1901, the Pan-American Exposition opened in Buffalo, New York. Patterned after the World's Fair, this prestigious event attracted millions of people and worldwide admiration.

The midway at the heart of the fair comprised numerous attractions, each more spectacular than the last: Eskimo Village, Beautiful Orient, Streets of Mexico, the Aerio-Cycle, and, the most popular of all, A Trip to the Moon. In the language of the day, A Trip to the Moon was a "cyclorama," or a mixture of panoramas and projected views which immersed the viewer in what we today would call a "virtual reality."

After paying an admission fee of fifty cents, viewers entered a large spaceship with thirty seats, the *Luna*, and took their places at the center of a large circular panorama. At the sound of a gong, the ship's wings suddenly began to beat and take-off was simulated. A wind machine went into action. Soon, the painted panoramas were replaced by aerial views of Buffalo and then of the earth, rapidly disappearing into the distance.

After a few tense moments, the ship arrived in the moon's atmosphere and flew overhead for a while before landing in the center of a crater. The passengers were then taken in charge by some sixty dwarves "whose backs had rows of long spikes."[10] These were the Selenites, who cheerfully took the visitors on a tour of caverns, bristling with stalactites, which opened onto an underground castle. There the visitors were introduced to a giant sitting on a throne, the famous Man in the Moon. After a few more adventures, the earthling viewers exited the attraction "through the mouth of a mighty moon-calf"[11] into the light of day.

Designed by Frederic Thompson and Skip Dundy, A Trip to the Moon met with unprecedented success. More than 400,000 people traveled on it to the moon in a six-month period. Among them were Thomas Edison and President William McKinley, the latter the day before he was assassinated at the Buffalo exposition by Leon Czolgosz.[12] On April 26, 1902, just before Méliès began shooting his film, A Trip to the Moon took up residence for the summer at Steeplechase Park, an amusement park where 850,000 new paying viewers rode it to the moon. These figures are out of all proportion with the receipts earned by the entertainments of the same name described by Deslandes and Richard. Finally, the "first electrical and mechanical space extravaganza," as William E. Burroughs described it, moved on May 16, 1903, to the heart of Coney Island, giving birth to its famous Luna Park.

It would be surprising, not to say unbelievable, if Georges Méliès, obsessed as he was with "tricks" and spectacular novelties, was unaware of Thompson and Dundy's attraction and its unprecedented success. In addition, as Charles Musser reports, in May 1901 James White and Edwin Porter shot several short films about the star attractions of the Buffalo exposition, in particular the Aerio-Cycle and A Trip to the Moon.[13] On this occasion Edison published a "Pan-American Supplement," now unfortunately lost, which gave a detailed description of each film. Did Méliès have access to this brochure and the films it describes? Without proof, we are reduced to conjectures.

Several similarities are found between Méliès's film and the Buffalo attraction. In each case, the story unfolds in three distinct parts: the preparations for the journey, the journey itself, and the moon landing are believable enough; the encounter with the Selenites is pure fantasy; and the return to earth mystification pure and simple. The juxtaposition of these three registers was also at the heart of a literary work that we often neglect today to mention when discussing the possible sources of Méliès's film: Edgar Allan Poe's short story "The Unparalleled Adventure of One Hans Pfaall," which dates from 1835.[14]

Another shared feature of these two entertainments was their length, at around twenty minutes. In fact everything points to the idea that Méliès saw his film as a substitute for the famous Buffalo attraction with the idea of providing U.S. amusement parks with a seductive alternative. His instincts, moreover, were remarkable: the film had considerable success in the United States, even if Méliès saw very little of the profits. *A Trip to the Moon* was pirated widely by unscrupulous businessmen and Méliès had to send his brother Gaston in haste to New York in November 1903 to put his affairs in order.[15] On this topic, Fred Balshofer tells a curious anecdote that reveals much about the Méliès clan's wrath: One day, a man appeared at the offices of the American producer Siegmund Lubin and asked to see some of his most recent films. While watching the first images of *A Trip to Mars*, he stood up abruptly and blocked the projector's rays with his raised arm. "Stop the projection!" he cried, visibly furious. The man was none other than Gaston Méliès, and *A Trip to Mars* a barefaced dupe of *A Trip to the Moon*.[16]

Sources of Inspiration

One of the most tenacious pieces of conventional wisdom in film history holds that *A Trip to the Moon* was an "adaptation" of the two Jules Verne novels mentioned earlier, *From the Earth to the Moon* and *Round the Moon*. This "literary adaptation" thesis, clearly championed by Georges Sadoul,[17] is based for the most part on two weak arguments: first, Georges Méliès's own later and highly dubious comments; and second, an *underlying* resemblance between the two novels and Méliès's film. What does it matter if *A Trip to the Moon* does not tell the same story and clearly does not take place in the same context or in the same historical period!

In truth, as I show, *A Trip to the Moon* is a heterogeneous film, taken from a patchwork of sources, which are probably more complex and varied than Méliès made out to be the case.

First of all, as we have seen, the film was undoubtedly motivated by the success in the United States of the amusement park attraction of the same name. In any event, it adopts that attraction's basic elements: a trip to the moon, a moon landing, an encounter with extraterrestrials with a deformity, an underground trek, an interview with the Man in the Moon, and a brutal return to reality back on earth. It is worth mentioning that, of these six points that comprise the adventure proper, only the first and the last appear in Jules Verne's diptych.

The first seven shots in the film, however, do bear some similarity to *From the Earth to the Moon:* the "Astronomic Club" in the film might be based on the Baltimore Gun Club in the novel. The preparations for departure are also described in the Verne novel. The only notable difference, a major one, is the deliberately parodic tone Méliès adopts. Either he is parodying Verne, or he is adapting a preexisting parody.

Sadoul points out the existence of an operetta of the same name while at the same time claiming, paradoxically, that "the film was not an adaptation of a stage show."[18] His reticence in making an explicit connection between this operetta and Méliès's film is due, he claims, to the fact that the operetta had, in his view, been "long forgotten."[19] This is a specious argument in light of Méliès's appetence for this kind of stage entertainment and his self-professed ties to, among other things, the Théâtre du Châtelet![20]

Le Voyage dans la lune was a "fairy-opera" by Jacques Offenbach in four acts and twenty-three tableaux. It was first performed on October 26, 1875, at the Théâtre de la Gaîté and reprised on March 31, 1877, at the Théâtre du Châtelet.[21] Its libretto was written by Albert Vanloo, Eugène Leterrier, and Arnold Mortier.

Vanloo and Leterrier had collaborated on several important operettas, comic operas, and light comedies since the late 1860s.[22] Their venturing into what was not yet called "science fiction" was apparently prompted by Arnold Mortier, whose real name was Arnold Mortje (1843–1925). In 1863 Mortier and E. Lambert de Boisoy had written a piece entitled *La Géant, voyage aérien*. In 1877 he and Philippe Gille adapted Jules Verne's *Le Docteur Ox* (*Dr. Ox*), which Offenbach then set to music.

Le Voyage dans la lune's storyline has no immediate resemblance to Méliès's film. In it, King Vlan, his son Caprice, and their scientific adviser Microscope journey to the moon. There they discover its residents, who resemble humans physically in every respect, but whose behavior, especially their amorous relations, is greatly different. Finally, after several adventures, Prince Caprice finds his soul mate in a charming Selenite princess.

While the two stories are clearly profoundly different, the composition of several scenes reveals certain similarities. Thus the second tableau of the first act places us inside an observatory. Under its dome in the midst of scientific instruments, six astronomers are debating the pros and cons of a trip to the moon. Their names—Cosinus, A-plus-B, Omega, Coefficient, Rectangle, and Phichipsi—are revealing, for they are reminiscent of their counterparts in Méliès's film—Nostradamus, Alcofrisbas, Micromegas, Parafaragaramus, and so forth (Omega thus figures in both works). Throughout this scene, the astronomers "turn their backs on the audience and examine the sky," according to the operetta's libretto.[23] From time to time they sing the following chorus:

> We are astronomers,
> Our eyes fixed on the heavens!
> You're looking at men
> Who live with their noses in the air!

Apart from the element of parody common to both versions, a detail reveals Méliès's specific debt to the earlier work: in Offenbach's opera, as in the 1902 film, the telescopes are able to transform themselves into stools. That such a curious effect recurs is striking, but it is not the only one, as we shall soon see.

The third and fourth tableaux of the fairy opera follow the outline of Jules Verne's story and foretell that of Méliès's film. Initially, we find ourselves in an "immense forge of activity" with bellows, blazing furnaces, and gigantic hammers and anvils. In the background is a red-brick blast furnace.[24] The engineer Microscope reveals to us his plan: "A cannon twenty leagues in length. . . . 300 kilograms of gunpowder will be enough, you understand. . . . We'll place ourselves in front of the moon, we're aiming, we're preparing the final touches. We're leaving, and in a little while . . . we'll be at our destination."[25] Here, scientific arguments are reduced to their simplest expression, like Méliès's film and unlike Verne's novel.

The following tableau is called "The Departure." The change in the set is carried out before the viewer's eyes, a little like the dissolves used systematically in the film. "The back of the forge disappears to reveal a gigantic cannon supposedly twenty leagues long. The breach is passable and is reached by a moving iron staircase. The cannon stretches out above cities and towns across the countryside and is lost to view at the peak of a tall mountain."[26]

This description, which could apply equally well to the seventh tableau of Méliès's film ("The Monster Gun. March Past the Gunners. Fire!!! Saluting the Flag."[27]) is resolutely unlike the original description Jules Verne gives. In *From the Earth to the Moon*, I need not remind the reader, the cannon, "a monster shut up in his stone coffin,"[28] is buried in the ground and thus completely hidden from observers. Vanloo, Leterrier, and Mortier's stage adaptation adopted a perspectival view that Méliès was content to take up "textually": in the film, like in the operetta, the cannon's mouth disappears above a high mountain peak painted in trompe l'oeil.

The film's key scene, the "race through space," is suggested by a dolly forward (in fact it was the moon that moved toward the camera). This internal focalization, which makes the viewer's gaze coincide with that of the rocket ship's "point of view," is also quite explicitly used in the fairy opera at the beginning of the second act. These are its stage directions: "As the curtain rises, soft music. We see the moon wrapped in clouds and occupying the whole stage. Mysterious voices are heard. The moon gradually brightens and *seems to grow nearer*. Confusedly at first, and then more and more distinctly, we see spots, then bizarre clock towers and strange monuments. Finally the circle it forms at the center of the stage *draws aside completely to make way for the next tableau*."[29]

Figure 3-1. Half of a stereoscope card, *Le Voyage dans la lune*—"Le Canon" (Collection Cinémathèque française).

How did the stage hands at the Gaîté and the Châtelet theaters achieve this? Unfortunately, the libretto gives no indication, but the moon's approach appears to have been very clearly suggested. The following tableau depicted the surface of the moon; the spaceship has just crashed into a town inhabited by Selenites: "Music. The house on the left collapses. Day returns and we see the spaceship lying on the ruins of this house. A small window opens and Vlan's head appears."[30]

The sequence of scenes, apart from the "rocket ship in the eye" added by the facetious Méliès, is clearly the same in the operetta and the film: first there is the point of view of the spaceship and the effect of drawing closer to the moon, and second the moon landing seen from the moon's surface. Here, too, the resemblance is disconcerting.

As Sadoul points out, the rest of the opera's libretto differs radically from the film's script. It is no longer the same story. Nevertheless, two transitional tableaux may very well have inspired Méliès.

The operetta's fifteenth tableau ("Fifty Degrees below Zero") indisputably foretells the thirteenth and fourteenth tableaux of the film

("The Snowstorm" and "40 Degrees below Zero!"). So, too, could the stage directions very well apply to the film: "Flammarion-like lunar landscape. Ice and frost. Enormous glaciers. Yawning chasms. Everything is frozen. A pallid sun lights the scene."[31] In the operetta, the snowstorm gives rise to a "great snowflake ballet": "[a]t the back of the stage, female dancers sleeping under the snow slowly awaken and move to the front of the stage."[32] This scene, acted out by the astronauts, can be found in Méliès's film.

The operetta closes on the twenty-third tableau ("The Light of the Earth"), which prefigures the film's tenth tableau ("The Rocket's Vertical Drop into Space"): "The earth had risen, its disc occupying the entire rear of the stage and brightly lighting it, like an aurora borealis."[33] A poster advertising the play shows five people in a lunar landscape watching the earth rise in the background.[34] We should note in passing that there could be no such thing as the "earth rising" on the moon and that in both the fairy opera and the film this scene was pure poetic license.[35]

Finally, if any more proof were needed that the operetta influenced Méliès's masterpiece, we need remark only one of the most obvious things. In the film, the five astronauts journey to the moon encumbered with their umbrellas. These implements, at the very least incongruous for an adventure such as this, are clearly used to describe and stereotype the characters according to a physiognomic principle I have described elsewhere.[36] But what cannot be as easily explained is the object itself: why an umbrella and not a gun, a fire extinguisher, a sewing machine?

Figure 3-2. Stereoscope card, *Le Voyage dans la lune*—"Le Roi Cosmos" (Collection Cinémathèque française).

A sign of the filmmaker's genius, some might say: Méliès was a surrealist before the letter, and the film plunges us into the history of spontaneous art. In fact the real explanation is simpler and, in the end, more rational: the umbrellas in question had already appeared in the operetta by Vanloo and company. In it, King Vlan journeyed to the moon with this accessory. There was a very Cartesian reason for this incongruity: the umbrella functioned as a scepter! The Man in the Moon doubts Vlan's royal blood, "Come now. You're a king? Prove it!" To which Vlan replies, "Right away! Microscope, hand me the umbrella. Here, this is my scepter, mounted on silk. When traveling, it comes in very handy in the rain."[37] No doubt amused by the idea, Méliès no doubt borrowed it, but not without divorcing it from its original context.

H. G. Wells, the Invisible Inspirer

An American fairground attraction and an Offenbach operetta inspired in part by Jules Verne's famous diptych: the circle of sources for *A Trip to the Moon* is gradually widening. Let's now examine Sadoul's hypothesis to the effect that "Méliès, in the film's second part, adapted H. G. Wells as faithfully as he did Jules Verne in the first."[38]

The First Men in the Moon appeared in a French translation by Henry D. Davray in the *Mercure de France* in 1901. It thus seems entirely possible that Méliès read this story and was inspired by it. But was it an "adaptation," as Sadoul suggests? It seems doubtful.

We might note first of all that the lunar surface is considerably different in the two works. Wells pictured luxuriant vegetation, "spiked plants, green cactus masses, fungi, fleshy and lichenous things, strangest radiate and sinuous shapes,"[39] in which strange bovines roamed, whereas Méliès stuck to traditional depictions of the moon with its rocky, austere, and desertlike landscape.

The resemblances between the two works appear only much later and for the most part concern two points: the underground trek and the description of the Selenites. These two features, however, as we have seen, were also at the heart of the attraction at the Pan-American Exposition in Buffalo.

Let us look first at the picture of the Selenite as Wells describes it: short (about five feet in height), he was a "compact, bristling creature, having much of the quality of a complicated insect, with whip-like tentacles and a clanging arm projecting from his shining cylindrical body case. The form of his head was hidden by his enormous many-spiked helmet."[40]

Tentacles, a Wellsian device par excellence also found in *The War of the Worlds*, clearly did not inspire Méliès any more than the "shining cylindrical body case" or the sole "clanging arm." In fact we would look in vain for any similarity at all between the two types of Selenites, apart from the obvious fact that they both depart significantly from established human norms.[41] Their only true points in common are their hostility and their astonishing fragility. Méliès's Selenites, like those in Wells's novel, grab onto the earthlings and keep them at arm's length through the use of cattle prods. They disintegrate under the blows inflicted upon them, as they did in the novel: "My mailed hand seemed to go clean through him. He smashed like—like some softish sort of sweet with liquid in it! He broke right in. He squelched and splashed. It was like hitting a damp toadstool. The flimsy body went spinning a dozen yards, and fell with a flabby impact."[42] In Méliès's film, it is more a matter of exploding than of disintegrating: when struck with force, the Selenites literally go up in smoke. We should note however that Méliès did not wait for Wells's description to put this kind of effect into practice: there is a spectacular example in the film *Fat and Lean Wrestling Match*, which dates from the fall of 1900. There a wrestler, his feet together, jumps onto his opponent's stomach, causing him to explode.[43]

One of the strangest tableaux in Méliès's film shows a cave covered in giant mushrooms. To measure these mushrooms, one of the explorers plants his umbrella in the ground; the umbrella immediately turns into a mushroom and begins to grow before our eyes. This anecdote is suggested metaphorically in Wells's novel: confronted with the luxuriance of the lunar vegetation, the two heroes of the story ponder the reasons for such a phenomenon: "Compared with such a growth the terrestrial puff-ball, which will sometimes swell a foot in diameter in a single night, would be a hopeless laggard. But then the puff-ball grows against a gravitational pull six times that of the moon."[44] Clearly the link is a tenuous one. On the other hand, the accelerated growth of plants is mentioned several times in the Vanloo, Leterrier, and Mortier operetta which, as we have seen, was Méliès's principal source of inspiration. Its stage directions make explicit reference to a mechanical trick that the film would copy. In the sixth tableau of the operetta, the Man in the Moon drops a pinch of tobacco on the ground. To Vlan's great amazement, a plant immediately begins to grow on the spot:

VLAN: "What's that?"

COSMOS: "That's your tobacco, growing. . . . Everything here grows instantly."[45]

During this exchange, the plant continues to grow before our eyes and soon yields flowers and fruit. "Strange," Vlan remarks. "Extraordinary," Microscope adds. There could be no better way to describe the way Méliès makes use of the scene.

Munchausen, by Way of Conclusion

Finally—and here we will conclude our discussion—it would be impossible not to examine the work *The Original Travels of Baron Munchausen*, which Méliès fervently admired and which inspired his curious adaptation of 1911.[46] In chapter 5 of the book, the Baron travels to the moon to recover a silver hatchet he unwisely threw into the air. His description of the adventure follows: "I recollected that Turkey-beans grow very quick, and run up to an astonishing height. I planted one immediately; it grew, and actually fastened itself to one of the moon's horns." The Baron quickly climbed the plant and recovered his hatchet. Unfortunately, in the meantime the plant had dried up, making his return impossible. What did he do?

> I twisted me a rope of that chopped straw, as long and as well as I could make it. This I fastened to one of the moon's horns, and slid down to the end of it. Here I held myself fast with the left hand, and with the hatchet in my right, I cut the long, now useless end of the upper part, which, when tied to the lower end, brought me a good deal lower; this repeated splicing and tying of the rope did not improve its quality, or bring me down to the Sultan's farm. I was four or five miles from the earth at least when it broke; I fell to the ground with such amazing violence that I found myself stunned.[47]

Reading this passage, it is difficult not to think of the twenty-first tableau of *A Trip to the Moon*. There, professor Barbenfouillis, running with the Selenites in pursuit, grabs onto a rope hanging from the tip of the rocket ship, tipping it into space. The following tableau shows him still hanging from his ship, which is plunging on its "vertical drop" toward the earth. Here we are in the presence, as Théophile Gautier wrote in his preface to the French edition of Munchausen's adventures, of an "absurd logic pushed to the extreme and which backs away from nothing."[48]

Begun under the apparent auspices of Jules Verne, *A Trip to the Moon* ends with an indirect tribute to Munchausen, a demonstration of the composite nature of a work that is much more complex than it appears, a complexity I have only begun to explore in this article.

Notes

1. Photographs of planets or stars. The first photographs of the moon date from 1839–1840 (Daguerre and Draper). In 1896 Loewy and Puisieux began publishing their Photographic lunar *atlas*.

2. Georges Méliès, "Reply to Questionary [*sic*]," this volume. 233.

3. Jacques Deslandes and Jacques Richard, *Du cinématographe au cinéma, 1896–1906*, vol. 2, *Histoire comparée du cinéma* (Tournai, Belgium: Casterman, 1968), 441.

4. *Magic: Stage Illusions, Special Effects and Trick Photography*, ed. Albert A. Hopkins (1898; repr., New York: Dover, 1976), 353. The show was presented by the Urania Scientific Theatre.

5. Danielle Chaperon, "Le cinématographe astronomique: Camille Flammarion, un parcours de 1864 à 1898," *1895*, no. 18 (1995), special issue, *Images du réel: La non-fiction en France (1890–1930)*, ed. Thierry Lefebvre, 53–64. Chaperon quotes a few lines from the script, revealing its similarities to the Berlin lecture: "The seaside. Dying waves in the evening, the sun setting behind us. 2 minutes during which night falls. The reddish moon rises. Image of the full moon. Eclipse of the moon. Here, trip to the moon. It grows white, comes nearer and increases in size from 30 cm to 1 meter. We choose a fragment seen in the telescope. Lunar landscape with the earth in the sky. Movement of the earth" (56).

6. Jean-Henri Fabre, *Le Ciel: Leçons élémentaires sur la cosmographie* (1893; repr., Paris: Delagrave, 1922), 133.

7. Fabre, *Le Ciel*, 137, 139.

8. Georges Sadoul, *Lumière et Méliès*, ed. Bernard Eisenschitz (Paris: Lherminier, 1985), 176.

9. This explains, moreover, Méliès's numerous denunciations of the pirating Edison and Lubin practiced. The latter, Méliès claimed, ruined him. From this, we see that the United States was clearly the target market in an attempt to make the film profitable.

10. Jeff Stanton, "Coney Island—Luna Park," http://www.westland.net/coneyisland/articles/lunapark.htm. These Selenite dwarves may have been inspired by a film produced by Siegmund Lubin in 1899, also entitled *A Trip to the Moon*.

11. Stanton, "Coney Island—Luna Park." This was clearly inspired by the H. G. Wells novel *The First Men in the Moon*, published in 1901 by George Newnes in London.

12. William E. Burrows, *This New Ocean: The Story of the First Space Age* (New York: Random House, 1998), chap. 1.

13. Charles Musser, *Before the Nickelodeon: Edwin S. Porter and the Edison Manufacturing Company* (Berkeley: University of California Press, 1991), 175–176.

14. Like Barbenfouillis, who returns to earth hanging from his rocket ship, Hans Pfaall falls to the moon, caught in the netting of his balloon.

15. Jacques Malthête, *Méliès, images et illusions* (Paris: Exporégie, 1996), 158.

16. Fred J. Balshofer and Arthur C. Miller, *One Reel a Week* (Berkeley: University of California Press, 1967), 5–9. This anecdote is repeated and commented

on in Joseph P. Eckhardt, *The King of the Movies: Film Pioneer Siegmund Lubin* (Madison, N.J.: Fairleigh Dickinson University Press, 1997), 46.

17. Sadoul, *Lumière et Méliès*, 174.

18. Sadoul, *Lumière et Méliès*, 174.

19. Sadoul, *Lumière et Méliès*, 174.

20. Translator's note: A Parisian theater and opera house founded in 1808 and still operating today that, in Méliès's day, staged operettas and music-hall programs.

21. The Cinémathèque française has a series of twelve stereoscopic views of unknown origin that were visibly inspired by this operetta in its collection ("Actualités théâtrales" collection, *Voyage dans la lune* series). In these views, the characters are represented by figurines, on their fidelity to the original is doubtful, especially with respect to the sets designed for the Châtelet by Chéret, Fromont, and Cornil. The following are the twelve plates in question: (1) "Caprise" [*sic*]; (2) "La Forge"; (3) "Le Canon"; (4) "Les Sélénites"; (5) "Le Roi Cosmos"; (6) "Le Marché aux femmes"; (7) "Les Charlatans"; (8) "Les Flocons de neige"; (9) "Les Chimères"; (10) "L'Intérieur du volcan"; (11) "Les Hirondelles"; and (12) "Clair de terre." Views nos. 3, 5, and 12 are of particular interest to our discussion here. Nevertheless, that Méliès was directly inspired by them seems unlikely. I believe that he worked from the libretto itself.

22. *Un Mariage aux petites affiches* (1867), *Une Sombre Histoire* (1868), *La Nuit du 15 octobre* (1869), *Un Mari à tiroirs* (1871), *Nabucho* (1871), *La Chouette* (1874), *Giroflé-Girofla* (1874), and so on. They continued to work together until the late 1880s.

23. Albert Vanloo, Eugène Leterrier, and Arnold Mortier, *Le Voyage dans la lune* (Paris: Tresse, 1877), 5.

24. Vanloo, Leterrier, and Mortier, *Le Voyage dans la lune*, 6.

25. Vanloo, Leterrier, and Mortier, *Le Voyage dans la lune*, 7.

26. Vanloo, Leterrier, and Mortier, *Le Voyage dans la lune*, 8.

27. Malthête, *Méliès, images et illusions*, 223.

28. Jules Verne, *From the Earth to the Moon*, trans. Edward Roth (1865; repr., New York: Dover, 1962), chap. 16.

29. Vanloo, Leterrier, and Mortier, *Le Voyage dans la lune*, 9; emphasis added.

30. Vanloo, Leterrier, and Mortier, *Le Voyage dans la lune*, 9.

31. Vanloo, Leterrier, and Mortier, *Le Voyage dans la lune*, 26.

32. Vanloo, Leterrier, and Mortier, *Le Voyage dans la lune*, 26.

33. Vanloo, Leterrier, and Mortier, *Le Voyage dans la lune*, 32.

34. Reproduced in Cécile Py and Christiane Ferenczi, *La Fête foraine d'autrefois* (Lyon, France: La Manufacture, 1987), 49.

35. "The moon sees the sun and other stars apparently turning, rising and setting in a period of fifteen days. But for it the earth remains invariably suspended in the same place in the sky, right in front of the hemisphere we see." Fabre, *Le Ciel*, 158. For a clear explanation of this astronomical phenomenon, see Pierre Rousseau, *Notre Amie la lune* (Paris: Hachette, 1943), 42.

36. Thierry Lefebvre, "Méliès et la physiognomonie: La stigmatisation des personnages fabriqués," in *Georges Méliès, l'illusionniste fin de siècle?* ed. Jacques

Malthête and Michel Marie (Paris: Presses de la Sorbonne nouvelle, 1997), 253–262; see esp. 258.

37. Vanloo, Leterrier, and Mortier, *Le Voyage dans la lune*, 12.

38. Sadoul, *Lumière et Méliès*, 174.

39. H. G. Wells, *The First Men in the Moon*, ed. Leon Stover (1901; repr., Jefferson, N.C.: McFarland, 1998), 110.

40. Wells, *The First Men in the Moon*, 118–119.

41. Except, perhaps, their bristling heads, but we have seen that the Selenites in the Buffalo attraction were also covered with spikes.

42. Wells, *The First Men in the Moon*, 159.

43. *Essai de reconstitution du catalogue français de la Star-Film, suivi d'une analyse catalographique des films de Georges Méliès recensés en France* (Bois d'Arcy, France: Centre national de la cinématographie, 1981), 90. See also the film *The Man with the Rubber Head* (1901).

44. Wells, *The First Men in the Moon*, 102.

45. Vanloo, Leterrier, and Mortier, *Le Voyage dans la lune*, 12.

46. *Les Hallucinations du baron de Münchhausen* (Méliès, 1911). Did Méliès own the French edition of 1862, entitled *Les Aventures du baron de Münchhausen*, as Laurent Mannoni suggests? Gustave Doré's illustrations in that volume are not dissimilar to the anthropomorphism of the moon found in Méliès's film. In each case, our satellite is personified by an isolated, grotesque, and grimacing face.

47. Rudolph Raspe, *The Original Travels of Baron Munchausen* (Chicago: Rand McNally, n.d.), 56–57. Readers should note that the book was reworked many times over the years. Among the writers who "polished" it, we might mention in particular are Rudolph Erich Raspe, credited as the author in the edition of the work quoted here, and Gottfried Bürger.

48. *Aventures du baron de Münchhausen*, trans. and adapted by Théophile Gautier, Jr. (Paris: Hachette, 1997), 49–50.

4

IAN CHRISTIE

First-Footing on the Moon

Méliès's Debt to Verne and Wells, and His Influence in Great Britain

In the end, there's nothing more to say. It's absolutely necessary to create the impossible. Then to photograph it so that it can be seen!!!

—Georges Méliès, "Cinematographic Views"[1]

BETWEEN 1992 AND 2004, DISNEYLAND Paris included an attraction unique to that park, Le Visionarium.[2] Although basically similar to the 360–degree cinemas included in all Disney parks, the Paris version featured Jules Verne, paying tribute to the original source of many of its other attractions, such as Space Mountain and the Nautilus of *Twenty Thousand Leagues under the Sea*.[3] In the scenario for the Visionarium's film presentation, Verne, played by Michel Piccoli, is shown encountering Jeremy Irons as H. G. Wells in a fictitious meeting at the 1900 Universal Exposition, where they are to debate "the probable future." Before this, a robot presenter has taken the two characters and the attraction's spectators on a journey through time, inspired by Wells's *Time Machine*, ostensibly to "convince" Verne that this is feasible.

For the historian of early cinema and its cultural context this counterfactual allegory had considerable charm and poignancy. On the one hand, it proposed a diplomatic acknowledgement of the two fathers of scientific fantasy within a scenario conceived by one of their main twentieth-century beneficiaries and popularizers, the Walt Disney Company. On the other hand, the figure conspicuously missing from this celebration of audiovisual time travel was its progenitor, Georges Méliès, who might have been expected to figure prominently in a French Disneyland, at least until the Visionarium was replaced by Buzz Lightyear's Laser Blast in 2006.[4] Verne remains a fundamental influence on Méliès and, indirectly, Wells. This chapter reexamines the nature and extent of Verne's seminal importance for fantastic fiction as a genre— with Méliès's film marking the moment that it crosses over into moving pictures.

Georges Méliès belonged to the generation that grew up on Verne's *Extraordinary Voyages*.[5] Born in 1861, the third son of a family that was prospering in business, he enjoyed the bourgeois privileges of the era. As Hélène Puiseux observes in her valuable "social reading" of the films, "he attended lycée . . . and like all boys of his age he read Jules Verne openly and Baudelaire secretly."[6] Certainly Verne's *Extraordinary Voyages* would be a lifelong influence, and Baudelaire's translation of Edgar Allan Poe may also have been significant, but the period that young Georges lived through as a youth was also one of political upheaval before the relative calm of the Belle Époque. Louis-Napoleon Bonaparte's coup of 1851 had launched the Second Empire and twenty years of a renewed French pursuit of military glory and imperial conquest. That dream was rudely shattered in 1870 when Prussia defeated France at Sedan and Napoleon's regime was replaced by a republican government, which then bloodily suppressed the Paris Commune in the following year before proclaiming the Third Republic.

These events and conflicts formed the backdrop to Méliès's childhood and youth, and we should not be surprised to find their traces in his films, even if these apparently claim the status of simple entertainment. The fact that these films would include staged representations of contemporary events such as *The Dreyfus Affair* (1899) and *The Coronation of Edward VII* (1902) is evidence enough of the closeness that had developed during the mid-nineteenth century between political reporting and literary fiction. Walter Benjamin's archaeology of French culture during this period includes discussion of the effects of this merging of forms and genres, which began with the introduction of the literary *feuilleton* in French newspapers of the 1830s as a means of maximizing readership.[7] Alongside these, the development of mass-produced illustrated publications, from popular satirical papers such as *Le Charivari* and *La Griffe* (to which Méliès contributed as a cartoonist in 1889–1890) to illustrated popular fiction, also brought about an interpenetration between the verbal and visual, which would be further developed in early film.

Creating the "Verne Effect"

The author who seems to have had the most enduring appeal for Méliès—and whose moon projectile is the basis of *A Trip to the Moon*—was closely implicated in these new forms of "industrialized" literary production. Verne's first novel, *Five Weeks in a Balloon*, only appeared in 1863 after substantial rewriting of the original manuscript demanded by his publisher Pierre-Jules Hetzel. The success of their partnership over the next twenty years owed much to Hetzel's background and determination. Having been forced to leave France by the fall of the Lamartine government in 1852, Hetzel had published another political exile, Victor Hugo, from Brussels. When an amnesty allowed Hetzel to return to Paris, he began to specialize in a new kind of literature for young people that was intended to challenge the prevailing monopoly of religious publishers.[8] Together with another passionate exponent of secular education, Jean Macé, he launched the illustrated bimonthly magazine *Le Magasin d'éducation et de récréation* in 1863, and after the initial success of *Five Weeks* some two-thirds of Verne's *Extraordinary Voyages* would appear as *feuilletons* in this magazine over the next forty-five years.

The *feuilleton* was economically important to authors, but the main vehicle of the Hetzel-Verne collaboration was a series of lavish yet affordable illustrated editions of Verne's novels in a form of hardback binding (*relieure cartonnée*) new to France.[9] Engraved illustrations were central to these, enabling their readers to visualize the spectacular scenes Verne evoked as his travelers journey to the far corners of the world beneath the earth and sea and into space. Hetzel had no doubt as to the importance of the illustrations. He wrote to Verne:

> Issuing instructions to draftsmen for illustrations is necessary to the completion of your manuscripts. You would understand this in relation to theater designs, which are transient, and for a book which is meant to last, it is all the more necessary to understand the need and fulfill it.[10]

Verne would prepare lists of scenes to be illustrated and occasionally request changes, such as when he asked Edouard Riou, illustrator of many of the early *Voyages*, to make the characters in *Twenty Thousand Leagues under the Sea* smaller so that the "corners of the salon could give an idea of the marvels of the *Nautilus*."[11] Hetzel had brought his entrepreneurial skills to the creation of what amounted to a new market: books that balanced education and recreation, intended to be given as presents and to be collected with their vividly colored covers printed on cotton-covered card forming a new décor of bourgeois adolescence.[12] Similar developments were taking place in other countries with publishers staking a claim to this new readership and providing channels through which Verne would become an international "brand," with his texts, often shorn of their encyclopedic detail, forming an important part of juvenile and "prize" series.[13] A global audience had been created for Verne's topographical fantasies.

Meanwhile, the same process of mixing genres that had begun in the press was also under way in the Parisian theater; and once again Verne stood at the midpoint of a development that would also be crucial for Méliès thirty years later. Verne had in fact been attracted to the stage before becoming a novelist and had his first play, *Les Pailles rompues*, a one-act light comedy in the style of Marivaux, presented at the Théâtre Lyrique in 1850 when he was just twenty-two.[14] He had been helped with this early effort by Alexandre Dumas *fils*, the son of the great novelist and a friend. Dumas *père* was himself a successful playwright in the 1830s before becoming an "industrial" producer of historical adventure novels (guided by Hetzel at an earlier stage in his career); and there is clearly a connection between the dynamism of the Parisian stage in the 1830s—dominated by such larger-than-life figures as Frédérick Lemaître, commemorated in Marcel Carné's film *Les Enfants du paradis* (1945)—and the sweep of historical fiction in *The Count of Monte Cristo* and the like.[15] The *feuilleton* had played a major part in boosting Dumas's income to unprecedented levels and broadening his audience, although his Théâtre Historique eventually proved a financial drain and closed in 1850, before reopening, in a sign of the times, as the Théâtre Lyrique.

Theatrical taste was changing and one of the most popular new forms in Paris was musical theater, in which the young Verne also dabbled. The best-known figure in this genre was the German-born composer Jacques Offenbach, who began to create a new kind of comic opera during the 1840s and 1850s. Initially, Offenbach's theater was only licensed to present one-act "opéras comiques" and "opéra-bouffes," but when restrictions were lifted, he seized the opportunity to create longer, more elaborate works, notably *Orphée aux enfers* (1858) and *La Belle Hélène* (1864). Despite their ostensibly classical subjects, these were witty satires, turning mythic characters into highly recognizable contemporary figures in a fluent combination of spoken dialogue and racy musical numbers. *Orphée aux enfers*, for instance, begins with Public Opinion announcing that she is "an improvement" on the Chorus of ancient drama and will keep watch for impropriety—which is clearly threatened from the outset, as Eurydice makes clear her loathing of Orpheus and determination to seek consolation elsewhere. By the 1870s, even this more expansive form was giving way to the more spectacular *"opéra-bouffe-féerie,"* with an emphasis on elaborate scenic effects.[16] *Orpheus*, Offenbach's biggest success to date, was expanded from two to four acts in 1874; and in the following year he composed an *"opéra-féerie" Le Voyage dans la lune*, which although not officially an adaptation prompted Verne to complain of plagiarism from several of his works, including the two "moon" novels.

Meanwhile, Verne himself was enjoying the theatrical success he had yearned for as a young man with two *féerique* adaptations of his most popular works, *Around the World in Eighty Days* (1874) and *Michel Strogoff* (1880). Lavish scenic effects were very much to the fore in these days, with "as handsome as Strogoff" (*beau comme Strogoff*) gaining currency as a conventional compliment.[17] These two spectacles became a Parisian institution, alternating every two years at the Théâtre du Châtelet in an unbroken run of fifty years until 1928. Cowritten by Verne, they involved the contributions of designers, musicians, and performers, making them effectively multimedia works *avant la lettre*, precursors of the filmic spectacle that Mike Todd would create from *Around the World in Eighty Days* to launch his Todd-AO stereoscopic process in 1956. Similarly, in *Le Voyage dans la lune*, shaped as it was according to *féerique* conventions by three librettists, there is little enough *textually* of Verne—no more than the projectile, the Selenite moon-dwellers, and a denouement borrowed from Verne's *Journey to the Center of the Earth*—but there is nonetheless a prevailing "Verne effect."[18] This association and composite provided Méliès with the most immediate inspiration for his 1902 film.

The cultural processes that involved Dumas, Hetzel, Verne, Offenbach, Méliès, and many others have been characterized by the historians of specific media; they have also been seen as components of the Belle Époque constellation. Without trying to increase this complexity, there are perhaps two main conclusion to be drawn that have important implications for the concepts of "authorship," "adaptation," and "influence." First, instead of seeing novels as the central thread of Verne's work it would be more accurate to see these as only one among a multiplicity of new media forms to which he was contributing and by which he was being diffused and stimulated. In the Paris of the Second Empire and early Third Republic, authorship had been industrialized (in Benjamin's phrase) and become, in more modern terms, a matter of branding.[19] Offenbach's *Le Voyage dans la lune* associated two strong brands: the composer and Verne. Méliès's film would imbricate these two with his own rising stock in a process usefully termed "remediation" by Jay David Bolter and Richard Grusin.[20] Second, the role of technology is crucial in this proliferation of forms, from cheap printing to moving pictures—and is Verne's central theme, making him a key figure in fusing the "spirit of the age" with what Benjamin would regard as "the creative forms" of that age's accelerating technological sophistication.[21] In place of "art for art's sake," or the autonomy of the aesthetic, a new fusion of art and technology was under way, encouraged by the proximity of news and fiction in the *feuilleton*, of education and entertainment in the Vernean novel, and of topicality and (neo)classicism in Offenbach. Film would only further this fusion.

Art, Science, and Social Critique:
Verne's Sources and Ambitions for the "Moon" Novels

If Hetzel intervened to shape Verne's first attempt at combining education with entertainment and retained a strong editorial role, this should not obscure Verne's own agenda for a new kind of instructive fiction in the early 1860s. Shortly after *Five Weeks in a Balloon* was greeted by one reviewer as "Edgar Allan Poe with more gaiety and less hallucination," Verne published an essay on Poe in which he regretted that the American writer had not studied the scientific aspects of a journey to the moon more carefully before writing "The Unparalleled Adventure of One Hans Pfaall."[22] Poe's 1835 tale had been translated into French amid the tide of enthusiasm for, generally, his "hallucinatory" qualities, so it is hardly surprising that a deliberately fantastic account of a balloon trip to the moon should have failed to meet Verne's technical standards. For his own novel, Verne consulted his cousin, a mathematics teacher at the Lycée Henri-IV, on the likely acceleration required for a projectile to reach the moon—and the resulting calculations, as has often been noted since the success of the first Apollo mission, turned out to be surprisingly accurate, even if the launch device proposed by Verne would not have delivered such thrust.

Whereas Verne wanted *From the Earth to the Moon* to be scientifically plausible, the novel is no mere didactic account of building a space vehicle. Set in America immediately after the Civil War, it is peopled by larger-than-life characters who belong to the Baltimore Gun Club and frankly miss the opportunities for practical experiment that the war offered. Rather than seek further conflict, their president, Impey Barbicane, conceives the idea of building a massive gun capable of firing a projectile to the moon. Barbicane's plan convinces his fellow club members, but is bitterly opposed by Captain Nicholl, a specialist in armor plating who fought against him during the Civil War and taunts him with a series of public wagers against the project's success. As the project nonetheless proceeds, attracting competition between American states for the honor of hosting its launch site, an international subscription is opened to meet its costs, allowing Verne to offer a *tour d'horizon* of national attitudes toward scientific research. The list of contributors is headed by Russia, testifying to "the scientific taste of the Russians" and their special interest in astronomy; most European countries contribute—apart from England, which treated the appeal with "contemptuous antipathy" and "did not subscribe a single farthing" to the total of $5,446,675 raised.[23]

From the Earth to the Moon reflects Verne's frank enthusiasm for America, a land that he would only visit two years after the novel appeared. The massive gun designed to launch the projectile is finally located in Florida (as was the U.S. space program), and it is named the Columbiad (inspiring the naming of the American shuttle Columbia). The projectile's crew diplomatically consists of Barbicane, his former opponent Nicholl, and an adventurous Frenchman, Michel Ardan, based on Verne's ballooning friend, the photographer Nadar (Felix Tournachon). But the 1865 novel ends with a successful takeoff and a reported observatory sighting of a "new star." The projectile has gone into orbit around the moon, leaving its passengers' fate uncertain. Not until four years later did Verne return to his suspended space mission and continue the story with *Round the Moon*, in which the travelers circle the moon and conclude that it is unpopulated, before managing to break free from their orbit and return to earth, where they safely splash down in the Pacific Ocean off San Francisco, in another anticipation of the spacecraft reentries that became familiar in the 1960s.

Verne's two novels were quickly combined into an omnibus and had become universal juvenile reading by the time H. G. Wells turned to the same theme thirty years later. While Verne had confined himself to what was scientifically conceivable, not allowing his explorers to reach the surface of the moon, Wells's intentions were quite different. His protagonists, the entrepreneurial Bedford and an idealistic inventor Cavor, reach the moon's surface with relative ease, thanks to Cavor's miraculous antigravity substance, "Cavorite," only to discover a remarkable ecology.

Dormant plants spring to life during the brief lunar day, while an entire society lives beneath the moon's surface in a vast network of tunnels and caves. When the two adventurers are separated, Bedford manages to return to earth, where he receives a fragmentary series of messages from Cavor, which explain how Selenite society is organized according to radical eugenic principles.

Eugenics was an issue of deep interest at the time Wells was writing, especially in the "advanced" circles he frequented. The Fabian Society had been formed in 1900, advocating a planned form of socialist society, and for many members such as Wells and George Bernard Shaw this included a commitment to selective breeding to eliminate "failures" and improve the physical and moral quality of the future population.[24] Shaw's play *Man and Superman* (1903) and Wells's own discussion novel *A Modern Utopia* (1905) would advance enforced eugenic programs as vital, and the outline of Selenite society in *The First Men in the Moon* can be seen as a first adumbration of this project in fantastic yet wholly serious form. The Selenites are reported by Cavor to differ greatly "in power and appearance, and yet [are] not different species of creatures, but only different forms of one species"[25] As a result, Cavor explains:

> In the moon . . . every citizen knows his place. He is born to that place, and the elaborate discipline of training and education and surgery he undergoes fits him at last so completely to it that he has neither ideas nor organs for any purpose beyond it. "Why should he?" Phi-oo would ask. If, for example, a Selenite is destined to be a mathematician, his teachers and trainers set out at once to that end.[26]

While there is a famous passage in which Wells allows his hero to reflect on the cost of such specialized breeding, observing a young Selenite being forcibly turned into an "operative," this is in the context of a comparison with contemporary capitalist society:

> That wretched-looking hand-tentacle sticking out of its jar seemed to have a sort of limp appeal for lost possibilities; it haunts me still, although, of course it is really in the end a far more humane proceeding than our earthly method of leaving children to grow into human beings, and then making machines of them.[27]

The climax of the novel takes the form of an extended critique of human civilization on earth, which Cavor explains to the Grand Lunar and his court amid growing incredulity. Wells's model for these chapters is clearly Jonathan Swift's *Gulliver's Travels* (1726), in which Gulliver finds himself embarrassed to justify human behavior to the horselike Houyhnhnms, who classify him as an inferior Yahoo. But there are other elements that feed into this simultaneous portrayal of an alien society and satire on earthly folly. Wells would have been familiar with Bulwer-Lytton's *The Coming Race* (1870), another portrayal of a troglodytic superrace, whereas Cyrano de Bergerac's *Journey to the Moon* (1647) already contained the basic premise of a moon with its own vegetation and creatures who capture the hapless explorer and treat him as inferior.[28]

Wells certainly knew Verne's novels, then entitled in English *A Trip to the Moon*, since he has Bedford mention this to Cavor as they build their space vehicle, adding slyly, "But Cavor was not a reader of fiction."[29] Although he bridled at the comparison early in his career (as did Verne at the end of his life), Wells later summed up the differences between the two:

> [T]here is no literary resemblance whatever between the anticipatory inventions of the great Frenchman and [my] fantasies. His work dealt almost always with actual possibilities of invention and discovery, and he made some remarkable forecasts. . . . But these stories of mine . . . do not pretend to deal with possible things; they are exercises of the imagination in a quite different field.[30]

But despite their obvious differences, there is also an important point of contact in the underlying ideological concerns of the two novels: Both are profoundly ambivalent toward imperialism.[31] Verne has his French astronaut, Michel Ardan, answer Barbicane's question as to why they are heading for the moon:

> "Why?" exclaimed Michel, jumping a yard high, "why? To take possession of the moon in the name of the United States; to add a fortieth State to the Union; to colonize the lunar regions; to cultivate them, to people them, to transport thither all the prodigies of art, of science, and industry; to civilize the Selenites, unless they are more civilized than we are; and to constitute them a republic, if they are not already one!"[32]

Here, it has been suggested, Verne may be parodying the cultural wing of Napoleon's invasion of Egypt in 1798, with its *mission civilisatrice*.[33]

But elsewhere he seems to endorse this aspect of Napoleon's campaign as "a great and beautiful work" and to berate the emperor for giving up Louisiana, "thus relinquishing the last remnant of our colonial empire in America."[34] Wells is equally ambivalent when, in effect, he explores Ardan's second hypothesis. His Selenites *are* more civilized than humans, in terms of having a single global eugenicist state, in line with Fabian principles. The best that Cavor can claim in his interview with the Grand Lunar is that the Anglo-Saxon races have at least got rid of their "autocrats and emperors," replacing them with democracy, although they are still engaged in war and deadly competition for resources.[35] There is no question of earth colonizing the moon, but rather a vague threat of the reverse, which Wells had already explored in his apocalyptic *War of the Worlds* (1898).[36]

　　If both Verne and Wells were ambivalent about the colonial implications of a trip to the moon—implying that there might be nothing to colonize or that the intended colonials may be more advanced than the colonizers—Méliès is more straightforward, making his *Trip* a virtuoso demonstration of modern wizardry and a robust satire on imperial *gloire*. His opening scene, variously described as a paraphrase of Verne's Baltimore Gun Club meeting or as a scientific congress, actually seems closer to the fairy-tale court of Offenbach's operetta, where King Vlan asks his astronomers to devise a way of satisfying his son Caprice's whimsical desire to travel to the moon.[37] His chief scholar Microscope is a plausible prototype for Méliès's Barbenfouillis, and the former's dismissal of the astronomers a parallel to the tumult that greets Barbenfouillis's demonstration. But Méliès's finale confirms his satirical intentions. Unlike any of his sources, he has the space travelers return to a civic reception, parading a captured Selenite on a lead as if in a Roman triumph, and a final image of a statue of Barbenfouillis stamping on a miniature moon. Here, far removed from the fervent partisanship of Verne or the bleak anxiety of Wells, is surely an ironic use of the *féerie* to mock imperial posturing in the tradition of French radicalism. The rocket and the court of the Selenites are indeed a demonstration of power by Méliès/Barbenfouillis—recalling Méliès's hero, the magician Robert-Houdin, being enlisted by the French government to discredit the Algerian marabout magicians in 1856, and doing so by a trick involving electromagnetism.

Hommages à l'anglais

A Trip to the Moon would become Méliès's most famous film and is often, implausibly, described as "the first science-fiction film." Its *féerique* stage settings and dancers point in another direction, toward the long tradition of satirical burlesque, in which the moon and stars are a cipher for pure fantasy—the realm of the Man in the Moon or of Munchhausen's King of the Moon. Arguably Méliès's film had more influence on this tradition in cinema than on science fiction as such. An example of its early influence can be found in the English Robert W. Paul's most famous film, *The '?' Motorist* (1906). Paul knew Méliès from the beginning of his career, having supplied him with projectors in mid-1896, when the Lumières were still refusing to sell their Cinématographe. Méliès had originally discovered the magic theater while living in London in 1884, and he may have discovered that Paul was selling his Theatrograph projectors from magician contacts such as Nevil Maskelyne and David Devant, who were acting as agents for Paul.

Paul, meanwhile, became Britain's leading early producer, and built a studio on the outskirts of London in 1899 which had the same capacity as Méliès's studio to make trick films.[38] Some of Paul's trick films included magician figures, such as *Upside Down: The Human Flies* (1899) and *The Waif and the Wizard* (1901), but the majority did not, although Paul employed an experienced stage magician, Walter Booth, for some years. Of all Paul's trick-based films, *The '?' Motorist* seems at once the most personal and the most mysterious. It is personal insofar as Paul was an enthusiastic pioneer motorist and is known to have chafed at police attitudes toward speeding. *The '?' Motorist* features his own car (possibly with him driving) and shows the car run over a policeman, then up the side of a building and into space, where it passes a smiling moon and runs round the rings of Saturn before returning to earth with a crash, dropping into the middle of a court in session. Making its escape, the car is then transformed into a horse-drawn cart when the police appear again, only to escape by turning back into a car and driving off in triumph. Given the connections between the two filmmakers and their rivalry in the trick film business, it seems unlikely that the car in space and the moon image are not deliberate references to Méliès's well-known *A Trip to the Moon* and *An Impossible Voyage* (1904), whereas the car orbiting Saturn is an original image by Paul. If anything, the tone of the film is even more cavalier than *A Trip to the Moon*, with this devil-may-care motorist diverting into space to show his contempt for the law's efforts to discipline motorists.

Eighty years later another landmark English film paid tribute to Méliès's celebrated *Trip*. In Nick Park's *A Grand Day Out* (1989), the cheese-loving pair Wallace and Gromit decide to pay a visit to the moon as the most famous source of their favorite food. The rocket they build in their basement bears a distinct resemblance to both Méliès's and Verne's squat projectile, and their journey and adventures on the moon—with a robot Selenite who yearns for a skiing holiday on earth—are perhaps the closest approach in modern cinema to the knowing parody of Méliès's original and a tribute to its poetic longevity. While Disney's Space Mountain ride outside Paris still retains traces of its original homage to Verne's imagined America of the Baltimore Gun Club, at the same time aspiring to a more technicist simulacrum of journeying into space, it is in the artisanal cinema of Park's plasticene animation, in Terry Gilliam's and Raúl Ruiz's bricolage, or Guy Maddin's pastiche that we may hope to find a continuation of Méliès's knowing reinvention of popular forms.[39]

Notes

1. Georges Méliès, "Les Vues cinématographiques," in Georges Sadoul, *Lumière et Méliès*, ed. Bernard Eisenschitz (Paris: Lherminier, 1985), 207, my translations throughout.

2. See http://fr.wikipedia.org/wiki/Visionarium#Les_diff.C3.A9rentes_ attractions (accessed May 8, 2008) for details of Le Visionarium and links to transcripts of its contents.

3. The Paris version of the Space Mountain ride originally included the title of Verne's novel, *From the Earth to the Moon*, in its title, with visual references to the Columbiad projectile and the Baltimore Gun Club. It has since been renamed Space Mountain: Mission Two and given a new storyline. See http://en.wikipedia.org/wiki/From_the_Earth_to_the_Moon#Influence_on_popular_culture (accessed May 8, 2008).

4. It is possible that there were negotiations about a Méliès presence in Disneyland, which may well have come to nothing in view of the notorious difficulty of dealing with both the Méliès estate and the Disney Company.

5. Verne's novels were brought out under the collective title *Extraordinary Voyages* (*Voyages extraordinaires*) by his publisher, Pierre-Jules Hetzel.

6. Hélène Puisieux, "Une Voyage a travers l'histoire: Une lecture sociale des films de Méliès," in *Méliès et la naissance du spectacle cinématographique*, ed. Madeleine Malthête-Méliès (Paris: Klincksieck, 1984), 25.

7. Benjamin's exploration formed part of his unfinished "Passage-Work," carried out between 1927 and his death in 1940, and also figures in his essay "The Author as Producer" (1934), in *Understanding Brecht* (London: Verso, 1977), 85–103. For a discussion of Benjamin's analysis, see Susan Buck-Morss, *The Dialectics of Seeing: Walter Benjamin and the Arcades Project* (Cambridge, Mass.: MIT Press, 1989), 136–145.

8. Jean-Paul Dekiss, *Jules Verne: Le Rêve du progrès* (Paris: Gallimard, 1991), 40.

9. Traditionally, in France as elsewhere, books were sold with paper covers, but were bound in calf by those who could afford to do so for their personal

libraries. With increasingly mechanized printing came new, cheaper forms of more durable binding.

10. Hetzel to Verne, 1872, quoted in Olivier Sauzereau, "La Mise en scène d'un texte," in *Le Monde illustré de Jules Verne* (Nantes, France: Actes Sud, 2005), 8.

11. Verne quoted in Sauzereau, "La Mise en scène," 8.

12. Verne's novels appeared at regular intervals in Hetzel's Bibliothèque d'éducation et de récréation, first in small format paperbacks, and later in larger format (28 cm x 19 cm) with elaborate blocked covers aimed at collectors. On this format, see Michel Rœthel, "Les Reliures Hetzel pour l'oeuvre de Jules Verne," in Dekiss, *Jules Verne*, 160–163.

13. In Great Britain, Blackie and Son were leaders in this field, with their "Books for Boys" in the late nineteenth century. Other series were specifically intended as school and Sunday school prizes, such as "Low's Famous Prize and Reward Books," c.1918, from Verne's main English publisher Sampson Low, Marston, and Co., which also included the historical adventure tales of G. A. Henty in its "Illustrated 2/6 series for Boys."

14. See Dekiss, *Jules Verne*, 122.

15. *Les Enfants du paradis* portrays the "Boulevard du crime" of the late 1820s, where different kinds of theater and spectacle jostled for attention, with Pierre Brasseur as the melodramatic Lemaître striving to create a new popular historical theater.

16. On the origins of the *féerie* and its relationship to the English pantomime, see Ian Christie, "*The Magic Sword*: Genealogy of an English Trick Film," *Film History* 16, no. 2 (2004): 163–171.

17. According to the author's grandson, Jean Jules-Verne, in his biography, *Jules Verne* (London: Macdonald and Jane's, 1976), 116. The following information about the fifty-year run of the two plays is from the same source.

18. The French correspondent of the *Times* had no hesitation in comparing Offenbach's work with the stage version of *Around the World*, still running in Paris. See http://en.wikipedia.org/wiki/Le_voyage_dans_la_lune_%28operetta%29 (accessed June 8, 2008).

19. On the industrialization of literature and authorship, see the compilation of Walter Benjamin's texts on Paris and the Second Empire, published as *Charles Baudelaire: A Lyric Poet in the Era of High Capitalism*, trans. Harry Zohn (London: Verso, 1983), esp. 27–33.

20. Jay David Bolter and Richard Grusin, *Remediation: Understanding New Media* (Cambridge, Mass.: MIT Press, 1999).

21. See Buck-Morss, *The Dialectics of Seeing*, 123.

22. Verne's essay appeared in *Le Musée des familles*, another journal of popular education in the same vein as *Le Magasin d'éducation et de récréation*. Dekiss, *Jules Verne*, 48.

23. Quotations from chap. 12 of *De la terre à la lune* (1865). There is no completely satisfactory English translation of this text currently available in book form. The original translation by Lewis Mercier and Eleanor E. King from 1878 is available online at various websites, including http://jv.gilead.org.il/pg/moon/12.html. Another version is *The Annotated Jules Verne, From the Earth to*

the Moon, Direct in Ninety-Seven Hours and Twenty Minutes, ed. and trans. Walter James Miller (New York: Crowell, 1978).

24. On the Fabians and eugenics, see Diane B. Paul, *Controlling Human Heredity: 1865 to the Present* (Atlantic Highlands, N.J.: Humanities Press, 1995), 75–78.

25. H. G. Wells, *The First Men in the Moon* (1901; repr., New York: Random House, 2003), 190.

26. Wells, *The First Men*, 197.

27. Wells, *The First Men*, 201.

28. On sources for Wells's apocalyptic visions and their potential as audiovisual spectacle, see Ian Christie, "Contextualising Paul's Time Machine," *Cinema & Cie*, no. 3 (2003): 49–57.

29. Wells, *The First Men*, 28. Wells may also have borrowed Verne's naming of the potential lunar inhabitants, Selenites, and his discussion of theories about the likelihood of the moon supporting life (see *The First Men in the Moon*, chapter 20).

30. H. G. Wells, preface to *The Scientific Romances of H. G. Wells* (London: Gollancz, 1933), reprinted in *H. G. Wells's Literary Criticism*, ed. Patrick Parrinder and Robert M. Philmus (Sussex, U.K.: Harvester, 1980), 241–243.

31. On the otherwise conservative Verne's ambivalence towards colonialism, see Jean Chesneaux, *Une Lecture politique de Jules Verne* (Paris: Maspero, 1971).

32. Jules Verne, *Round the Moon*, chap. 7, in *Jules Verne: Seven Novels* (New York: Barnes and Noble, 2006), 441.

33. Andrew Martin, *The Mask of the Prophet: The Extraordinary Fictions of Jules Verne* (Oxford, U.K.: Clarendon Press, 1990), 20.

34. Both phrases appear in Verne's *Great Explorers of the Nineteenth Century*, cited in Martin, *The Mask of the Prophet*, 20–21.

35. Wells, *First Men*, 215–217.

36. *The First Men in the Moon* ends with a fragmentary message from Cavor about the Selenites and the discovery of Cavorite, which implies they may already have it. In Wells's earlier *The War of the Worlds* (1898), Martians invade the earth and are only defeated by a bacterial infection to which they succumb.

37. Sadoul, *Lumière et Méliès*, 174; Elizabeth Ezra, *Georges Méliès: The Birth of the Auteur* (Manchester, U.K.: Manchester University Press, 2000), 121. For a synopsis of Offenbach's operetta, see http://en.wikipedia.org/wiki/Le_voyage_dans_la_lune_%28operetta%29 (accessed Sept. 9, 2008).

38. On Paul's trick film work, see Christie, "*The Magic Sword*"; also notes and commentary for *R. W. Paul: The Collected Films, 1895–1908* (DVD, British Film Institute, 2006).

39. There is a deliberate quotation of Méliès's Man-in-the-Moon image in the BBC television series on early cinema *The Last Machine* (1994), in which Terry Gilliam, creator of *The Adventures of Baron Munchausen* (1988), appears narrating as the moon in one episode. Many of Raúl Ruiz's films use a variety of "profilmic" special effects: his *Snakes and Ladders* (1980) uses Méliès-like visual effects to create a dizzying sense of different perspectives on Paris. The Canadian

Guy Maddin uses pastiche of silent-era style in many of his films, including the short *Odilon Redon or the Eye Like a Strange Balloon Mounts Toward Infinity* (1995), based on Redon's painting and Abel Gance's *La Roue* (1923).

Figure 5-1. *A Trip to the Moon*—drawings of earth and moon; moon in distance.

5

MURRAY POMERANCE

"Distance Does Not Exist"

Méliès, le Cinéma, and the Moon

Space

Mais il n'y a rien de commun entre *De la terre à la lune* et mon film
. . . . Il y a la lune, bien sûr, mais Jules Verne ne l'a pas inventée.

—Méliès, as recalled by Lo Duca, 1952

WELL INTO HIS SCATHINGLY satirical science-fiction masterpiece *From the Earth to the Moon* (1865), in which members of the Gun Club of Baltimore have been devotedly conspiring toward the production of a giant cannon that will fire a projectile to the moon, Jules Verne introduces a curious "little round-shouldered" Frenchman:

> He had a strong, leonine head, and he occasionally shook his mane of fiery hair. A short face, broad at the temples, a mustache that bristled like a cat's whiskers, cheeks adorned with little tufts of yellowish hair, and round, distracted, rather nearsighted eyes completed that eminently feline physiognomy. . . . Michel Ardan's personality offered a broad field to observation and analysis. He was

unfailingly inclined to exaggeration and had not yet passed the age
of superlatives. Objects were registered on his retina with inordinate
dimensions, and this led to his associations of gigantic ideas. He
saw everything bigger than natural, except difficulties and men.[1]

In some ways, this Ardan prefigured the existence of Georges Méliès,
who was forty when he made his own *A Trip to the Moon*, a film that
exaggerates everything it touches on and that produces a thoroughly
superlative form of enjoyment, not to say, both anticipating, yet also
standing distinct from, the movies we watch today, as Tom Gunning
suggests.[2]

Ardan makes a presentation to the public, in Tampa (whence the
missile is to set forth), during which he is faced with a crowd of enthusiastic but doubtful admirers: doubtful because his own presence there
is entirely due to the fact that, having claimed that sending an empty
canister to the moon makes no sense, he intends to inhabit the shell
and thus make a voyage himself. Trying to explain that a leap through
space is not so overwhelming a challenge, after all—"The distance from
Neptune to the sun is nothing at all compared to the distances from here
to the stars"—Ardan begins to reason about the size of the solar system:

> Alpha Centauri is 20,000 billion miles away; Sirius 125,000 billion;
> Arcturus 130,000 billion; Polaris 292,000 billion; Capella 425,000
> billion; and other stars are thousands, millions, and billions of billions
> of miles away! How can anyone even consider the wretched little
> distances that separate the planets from the sun? How can anyone
> even maintain that they exist? What an error! What an aberration
> of the senses! . . . To me, the solar system is a solid, homogenous
> body; the planets that compose it touch, press against, and adhere
> to one another, and the space between them is only the space that
> separates the molecules of the most compact metals, such as silver,
> iron, gold, or platinum. I therefore have a right to maintain, and I
> repeat it with a conviction that will be communicated to all of you:
> "Distance" is an empty word, distance does not exist![3]

Ardan's summary comment recalls a Lumière tradition invoked by Gunning, that of "placing the world within one's reach."[4]

In certain interesting ways demonstrated by *A Trip to the Moon*,
cinema is also a domain in which distance does not exist. One might
begin by considering the process and experience of moving through a
film from beginning to end, an experience that later came to be organized as narrative progression but that by the early years of the twentieth

century still retained for audiences' pleasure the characteristics of a chain of tableaux. Each moving image in such a chain is engaging and replete, and the shifts from image to image have the entrancing quality inherent in magical transformations and theatrical scene changes rather than the cause-effect relationship characteristic of narrative movements. Gunning argues that the cinema of attractions "directly solicits spectator attention, inciting visual curiosity, and supplying pleasure through an exciting spectacle."[5] Thus, although one could argue that *A Trip to the Moon* has a distinct fabular quality, that each of its tableaux glows with a fictive light and entrances the viewer with myriad details of action and alignment, still it is not exactly "storytelling," no precise information being displayed to the audience about the change or effect upon any characters as a result of their making a voyage and returning to celebrate it. The characters do not—to paraphrase T. S. Eliot—come back to where they started from and "know the place for the first time." No character's action in this film is followed, developed, expanded upon, or remarked upon as such (such approaches to action are typical of what Gunning and André Gaudreault term the "cinema of narrative integration," after 1907); and therefore for the viewer the experience of watching *A Trip to the Moon* is one of peeping into a strange world in which personalities are interacting and expressing themselves independently of what we would now call "plot." That a group of academics get into a shell and are shot to the moon, that they encounter Selenites there and vanquish them, and that they return alive, do not as consequentialities affect the way we view people moving, gesticulating, pointing, signing, watching, poking, striding, or marching in various of the scenes here: all of this activity has its own intrinsic interest. Gunning notes that for Méliès, narrative plays a role quite distinct from what we find in "traditional narrative film" and he quotes Méliès's own attitude toward the scenario: that he uses it "merely as a pretext for the 'stage effects,' the 'tricks,' or for a nicely arranged tableau."[6]

I do not mean to imply here that as we move through this film, the sequences we discover are reversible logically. The landing on the moon, for instance, takes place after the launch; and to see the scenes in reverse order would confound our understanding of eventfulness and time's compounding. Yet it is also true that as we watch this film, we attach no weight to the logic of the voyage; and watching it backwards is as pleasurable as any other way because each tableau contains all of the elements necessary to attract and hold our interest and no tableau begs a question that *must* be answered in a subsequent one. The action inside each tableau is varied, exquisite, decorative, and surprising—in a superficial way not unlike the charming little movements in certain children's toys, which can engage the attention for hours on end without requiring "narrative" development (Méliès ended his life running a tiny "Confiserie et jouets" shop at the Gare Montparnasse).[7] The film, as Gunning suggests, is a "frame upon which to string a demonstration of the magical possibilities of the cinema."[8]

Yet the action of Méliès's cinematic tableaux is very untoylike, or, more exactly, toylike in a particular way only. Nicolas Dulac and Gaud-reault have made a case that "the temporality of optical toys is closer to that of the machine," basing their argument on a statement of Paul Ricoeur's that "time becomes human to the extent that it is articulated through a narrative mode."[9] The optical temporality of some of these quaint little scenes—the repetitive, cuckoo-clock–like movements of the workmen building the rocket, for example—is not quite human, in that the scenes have an independence from temporal contiguity and narrative pulse; and in that the scenes themselves function like optical toys, with forward and backward motions, openings and closings, probabilities and resolutions working through a kind of metrical calculation as the film unwinds. While we can recognize the human, or quasi-human, nature of the characters, they are all made mechanical by virtue of the storytelling process and the work of Méliès's camera in framing their action. The characters seem to "know only the present tense," as Dulac and Gaudreault put it.[10] And as to Méliès, we may suppose him to have been a kind of toymaster in his filmmaking, to the degree that the pleasure he provides has "as much to do with manipulating the toy as it [does] with the illusion of movement."[11]

I am interested in the ways in which these "magical possibilities of the cinema" may show oneiric characteristics. In *The Interpretation of Dreams* (1900), Freud makes the telling observation of dreams—and similarly representational works of art—that in them logical relationships, such as " 'if,' 'because,' 'as though,' 'although,' 'either–or' and all the other conjunctions, without which we cannot understand a phrase or a sentence," are beyond the pale of what can be managed by the condensa-tion and displacement of dream-work.[12] If we can take it that "the *content* of the dream-thoughts is reproduced by the apparent thinking in our dreams, but not *the relations of the dream-thoughts to one another*,"[13] perhaps the objects in an image work as image-thoughts, and we can understand representation as a mode in which the relation of image-thoughts to one another is similarly difficult or impossible to describe; this would account for a certain vague imposition that we can find in *A Trip to the Moon*—if not also in other silent films—in which various figurations emphatic before us must be connected through the linkages of our own desire as we watch. Thus is the tableau constructed as a dream vision, which is presented to us in a "completed" state,[14] even without the associations between its parts: indeed, especially without those associations.

In the opening scene of *A Trip to the Moon*, Méliès's alter-ego, President Barbenfouillis ("Beard-in-a-Tangle") of the Astronomic Club reveals his plan to send a rocket from the earth to the moon by drawing the projectile on a chalkboard for the various members, costumed as "medieval wizards,"[15] to see. But even at the commencement of this tableau, before he marches into the chamber (in a long dark robe decorated with, among stars and dragons, a smiling personified moon), two forms already appear in preparation on the blackboard on the dais from which Barbenfouillis will speak: a large white circle with parallels of latitude and longitude on it and a considerably smaller circle in the upper right corner of the board. Behind the club members, who are gathered like a choir on risers, a long, six-segmented telescope points through a vaulted arch into the sky where, in an inky patch between masses of cloud, a full moon shines. Later on, a giant gun that will send the rocket shell to the moon will resemble this long telescope in reverse. Now, although no one is looking through the device at the moon, the orb in the sky serves nicely as an equivalence for the smaller white circle on the blackboard—it is, in fact, almost precisely the same size—and thus defines for us the drawing of the moon as opposed to the larger one of the earth. José Ortega y Gasset reminds us that the artist of the Quattrocento "contents himself with representing the distant as smaller than the proximate, but he paints both in the same way. The distinction of planes is, then, merely abstract, and is obtained by pure geometrical perspective. Pictorially, everything in these pictures is in one plane, that is, everything is painted from close-up. The smallest figure, there in the distance, is as complete, spherical and detached as the most important,"[16] and Méliès appears to have used the same sort of (what might be thought unsophisticated) technique for constructing his representation here. The smaller is made to signify the more distant. Yet at the same time it is evident that the smaller is not more distant in fact, but merely, residing on the same surface as the larger, signifying a relation of distance, which relation is itself purely abstract or imaginary, devised from the proximate point of reference. It cannot be said that the moon is far away from this club room in the same way that the club members, ranged on their risers, are far away from the dais. The dais and the club members are arranged in a single space, but the moon outside the window appears to be painted on a scrim, a suggestion of a moon like the suggestion of the moon on the blackboard. As the president explains his plan of a trip to the moon, we see him pointing into the air before his face and twisting about, these actions constituting cinema's only means of expressing the relation between the image-ideas of earth and moon. He points into the air. He points at the large orb on the board. He points at the small one. He gestures to the audience to attend and then with chalk draws above the "earth" a pointed three-segmented device (not unlike the telescopes with which each astronomer has been supplied by a uniformed assistant); then he produces a dotted line ending with an arrow touching the surface of the little "moon." By providing us with the elaborate context of the chamber, the vaulted windows, the sky outside, the clouds, the break in the clouds, the shining moon, the dark blackboard, the orbs drawn on it, the telescopes for seeing (or voyaging through sight), and the club members arrayed like an obedient choir awaiting signals from their conductor, Méliès increases the probability that we will deduce the ideas "from" and "to"; that we will envision a space greater than this in which the moon, here merely signaled, will reside in physical fact; and that the idea of mobilizing an object through that space, or metaphorizing, will occur. The energy and determination evident in the lecturer's rather frenetic gesticulations indicate the centrality, for his audience and for us, of the project to which he alludes.

In each scene of this film there is a dreamlike condensation, whereby the abstract distance we are to imagine existing between the moon and the earth, between the Selenites and the humans, and between the explorers' knowledge and the mysteries beyond their ken, is resolved on a contracted and flat cinematic surface, this resolution constituting the broad effect of Méliès's film "magic." In the succeeding tableau, Barbenfouillis leads his colleagues Nostradamus, Alcofrisbas, Omega, Micromegas, and Parafaragamus to the work site where the enormous shell casing is being prepared, which will carry them to the moon. Workers are feverishly hammering under a skylight that "duplicates the glass-roofed interior of the Montreuil studio" where Méliès in fact produced this film,[17] and the scene is given a delicious clockwork style, in which actions seem mechanically to be repeated ad infinitum with no visible progression. One man lifts and brings down a huge sledge hammer upon an anvil while two others hammer beside him, visitors raise their hands above their heads and lower them or enter the shell and leave it, or turn around and around and around, and two other men, one above and one below, hammer on the shell. We have a distinct sense of movement and energy, but nothing seems to go anywhere; and there seems no distance between the shell as it looks at the beginning of the scene and the shell at the end. One has the sense of an amassing of forces: forces of production, forces of consumption, the urge to polish, and the urge to examine, at one nexus.

Following this we have a long view of a circle of blast furnaces surrounding a huge pit, which will be the mold for the cannon. Each furnace has a tall, vigorously smoking chimney. On cue, all begin to emit molten iron that flows down a series of long troughs into the pit. This scene, a direct inheritance from Verne's very detailed description of the delicate process whereby the cannon barrel is cast, confounds our sense of space, since the pouring liquid that falls into the pit goes offscreen, as does the explosion of steam that emits when the iron is poured. Although the travelers are watching excitedly at right from a rooftop observation post, and again gesticulating wildly, their joy, like ours, seems energized by the flow of molten metal itself, not by a sense that a substance has moved in space from one important location to another. The *mechanism* of the shot gives it impulse: the barreling smoke emerging from the smokestacks; the flowing metal; the exploding steam, the repetitive motions of the figures. Because the pit is dark and round, and the troughs that carry the molten metal slender and lengthy; and because the liquid that flows is hot and white; and because the motion of the liquid into the hole causes the onscreen viewers such a consternation of excitement, it is not hard to imagine the erotogenic possibilities inherent in the tableau, and yet it remains in the abstraction of the viewer's imagination to form the link between the furnaces, the liquid, the dark pit, and the solid gun that we will soon see. This tableau does not frame the connections themselves. Furthermore, even the distance between the furnaces and the pit is obscured for us, first by the rolling liquid, which at its full might as well be stationary as moving, and then by the overwhelming cloud of steam that issues out. Add to this the fact that the tableau works to promise a voyage but not to deliver one, and one can see how Méliès has worked here to avoid traveling while offering his audience a menu of intense excitements all the same.

In the following tableau, we see the travelers mounting to the rooftops and bowing furiously in the direction of the camera (Gunning discusses the "recurring look at the camera by actors" in the cinema of attractions),[18] then climbing into the shell that rests on a track that runs laterally across the screen toward the mouth of the cannon at screen right. A bevy of uniformed girls works to push the shell into the cannon, and then they wave, again at the camera. Here is a variation on the magician's disappearing trick, but performed with less ostentatious technique than one would typically see onstage: the shell, mounted on its track, systematically disappears, that is, proceeds into what we take to be a cannon but cannot see as such. Just as the fluid metal in the preceding scene disappears offscreen, so here the shell itself disappears with the protagonists inside it. We do not have a direct perception of the shell actually going anywhere, that is, to a destination we can see as such. Nor is it necessarily effective for opening a sense of distance to the viewer that destinations be visible, as I shall soon show. We shift to what appears to be a new space, at any rate, positioned behind the gun that points off into the sky and over a range of sharp-peaked mountains. On a signal the fuse is lit, and a puff of smoke indicates that the shell has been fired. This second camera position relative to the gun is in fact achieved only by rotating the viewer through ninety degrees because the end of the barrel, which had previously been at screen right, is now in center-left with the gun pointing away from the camera. In this scene, stunningly, the central dimension commanding our attention runs along the length of the gun barrel away from the camera and into the skies, but it is strikingly evident that along with the sky and the mountains the entirety of the gun has been painted on a flat. The effective depth dimension is therefore only abstractly suggested. That at the end of the shot well-dressed ladies and gentlemen rush in from behind the camera to wave good-bye to the travelers does not accomplish a rendition of optical space that includes the trajectory of the voyage.

The moon is now seen approaching as though from the point of view of the travelers in the shell. A matte shot shows the moon becoming increasingly proximate to the camera's lens (in *The Man with the Rubber Head* [1901], Méliès had mounted himself on a little rail cart to achieve a similar effect).[19] Apparent movement toward the viewer created with moving magic lantern projectors was a typical feature of the late-eighteenth-century Phantasmagoria, especially that of Philidor who, at crucial moments during a projection, "moves his lantern, mounted on wheels or rails, back towards the screen."[20] Stephen Bottomore details an interesting response, an "optical deception worth noticing," in witnesses' reaction to onrushing cars of the Manchester railway in 1830:

> A spectator observing their approach, when at extreme speed, can scarcely divest himself of the idea that they are not enlarging and increasing in size rather than moving. I know not how to explain my meaning better, than by referring to the enlargement of objects in a Phantasmagoria. At first the image is barely discernible, but as it advances from the focal point, it seems to increase beyond all limit. Thus an engine, as it draws near, appears to become rapidly magnified.[21]

Here, suggests Gunning, "the unaccustomed speed of an onrushing locomotive, could be initially processed in terms of the uncanny visual effect of the Phantasmagoria."[22] Suddenly, however, our shell approaches the moon from the side and plunges into the (personified) moon's right eye, which quickly sheds "a custard tear."[23] The "distance" traveled by the shell on its "voyage" in the tableau is only of the slightest degree before it has its effect, the effect taking over the shot. Furthermore, in the early part of the shot, the approach of the moon strikes the viewer as a looming object, freezing the sensibility. Rather than being sensitive to the crossing of distance as the moon "approaches," one fixes on a luminous object getting bigger in one's optical field, threatening by its proximity. Here, of course, we are precisely seeing the destination of the "voyage," but the destination has been severed from the origin. Thus, we have a visual experience corollary to that of the launch, seeing one end of a continuum of motion without reference to the nodes between this spot and the origin. Just as at the launch we did not see the shell actually *going to* any destination, here we cannot see the shell *coming from* one. That the impact of the shell on the moon—that is, the success of earthlings making contact—rather than the voyage itself is central to Méliès, and his audience is made evident even further by the ensuing shot in which we are given a view of a virgin lunar surface, covered with the sorts of stalagmitic projections Méliès might well have read about in H. G. Wells's *The First Men in the Moon* (1901), and suddenly the projectile enters from screen left and lands in front of us. The previous shot, which had purported to show the projectile reaching its destination, is thus immediately erased or negated conceptually, as though the shell both does and does not reach the moon after its travels. Once again, objects exist, space exists, movement exists, and relations between objects can be imagined to exist, but distance itself seems not to.

Succeeding scenes in which the explorers descend beneath the moon's surface to meet the Selenites, are subsequently captured, escape while causing many of the Selenites to explode, and find their way triumphantly back to earth continue to raise the problem of distance in similar ways. It is the spectacle of an elaborate scene, of gesticulating figures, of repeating motions, of the illusion of spewing liquids and vapors—a sort of moving mechanical drawing—that intrigues Méliès. Even the Selenites, who could have signaled a kind of anthropological distance, are constructed dramatically to seem similar to the men who visit them if unable to communicate. They thrash about with wildly moving arms, much as the explorers do, and then suddenly disappear into smoke when prodded with umbrellas. The disappearance is a provocative reaction for the viewer, coming in just at the moment when the Selenites might have been expected to make some response at encountering the earthlings; blowing away like motes of dust, as it were, the Selenites fail to react or

are interrupted in the business of reacting. Wells's voyager had "dreamt
again and again of that bitter, furious creature rising so vigorous and
active out of the unknown sea. It was the most active and malignant
thing of all the living creatures I have yet seen in this world inside the
moon,"[24] yet Méliès's Selenites utterly fail to threaten in this way, to
seem Other, and thus to be separated from those who inspect them by
a measurable distance, as the Selenites created by Ray Harryhausen for
Nathan Juran's film *First Men in the Moon* (1964)—an often amazingly
straightforward representation of Wells's novel—so keenly do.

Time

> Toward the end of the nineteenth century there was a rapid diffusion
> of pocket watches in the general population.
>
> —Mary Ann Doane, *The Emergence of Cinematic Time*

> "I don't want realism, I want magic."
>
> —Blanche DuBois, in *A Streetcar Named Desire*

In her masterful analysis of cinematic time and modernity, Mary Ann
Doane introduces an idea centrally important to the dispassionate analysis
of early film and yet inconceivable or confusing to a watcher of *A Trip to
the Moon*, of cinema as a device for "fixing life and movement, providing
their immutable record."[25] Cinema's investment in an indexical relation
with the world, in which events are taken and held, thus both duplicated
and extended in time, forms a central pillar of her discussion in this
book, and especially colors her treatment of Méliès and the Lumières,
whose films, for Doane, all share an openness and hunger for contingency—the "celebration of the unexpected chance event"—and constitute
"aberrations, moments of resistance, symptoms of the nineteenth-century
epistemological crisis that undermined ideas of law, necessity, and deter-
minism."[26] Perhaps we should work with great care in addressing the
word "contingent" to the films of Méliès, certainly to this film, because
one can see onscreen such powerful evidence of the filmmaker's visual
design, choreography, and commitment to another principle that had
underpinned the world of magic to which he had long been devoted, and
had structurally determined the stage presentations that obsessed him,
namely, transformation. The idea that events might merely transpire, that
the flux of modernity might be imbued in all action, is hard to substantiate in the face of the tracks, the projections, the angles of penetration

and extrusion, the careful diagramming, the vociferous gesturing, the entirely too logical interracial warfare that we see in *A Trip to the Moon*. And transformation is everywhere.

I do not refer simply to the fact that images change, producing what Walter Benjamin called "shocks," which are "potentially traumatic for the spectator."[27] They do change, of course, but more typical of Méliès and structurally more important in *A Trip to the Moon* is the fact that change occurs in a self-referential way onscreen. Outside of this, that frames traverse through the projector one by one (producing the illusion of movement) is hardly more shocking in itself than that people shift and move endlessly through life: they did so before modernity. And art continually moved and changed: the concerti of Beethoven, for example, modulating from key to key or passage to passage—this is premodern and not especially traumatizing (except for those lucky listeners who are stunned by the beauty of these works!) But in a Méliès tableau, two kinds of transformation occur in addition to "normal" movement, and each of these announces itself as such, thereby drawing the viewer's attention not only to the play of light and movement in the fictive screen world, but also to the presence of a filmmaker who is manipulating a medium in order to produce a precise (and far from contingent) psychological and sociological delight.

For Doane, following Georg Simmel, the omnipresence of the watch helped capitalism dissect, manage, and employ both units of time and units of labor; worked to commodify labor; and divided an earlier more diffuse conception of time in such a way that principles of measurement and discipline could be applied to human activity and interaction. Cinema, by its rendition of the contingent, worked to violate the field of piecemeal time that the watch, among other devices, was importing to Western civilization. But if the pocket watch could add the pressure of control and surveillance to the experience of time and space, it could also stun and delight by its purely mechanical continuum, the play of repetitive circular motion that established rhythms, harmonies, and expectations that could be not only fulfilled but also jeopardized or suspended. Doane quotes Stephen Kern to the effect that after the increasingly universalized sharing, measurement, and calculation of time that flowed from the development the railway onward, "The independence of local times began to collapse."[28] But does not this view privilege the "uniqueness and isolation of the local," as Doane puts it? And privilege it on what rationale and at what cost? For Verne's Michel Ardan, after all, this "local" is but a pretext for arguing the unassailable distance between a "here" and a "there" that for him are purely figurative; it is essentially a static theory, based on the presumption of a stationary viewer for whom there are "distances" between one place or experience and another. Once incessant and intense motility is achieved, however, once we begin to see the world as though from a moving position rather than a static one, what does the word "local" or the phrase "independence of local times" actually come to mean? Is not Méliès signaling us to consider the moving point of view as prototypical, given his use of that point-of-view shot, as the moon approaches, in light of the clear fact that it is *not* the rocket's point of view; he is showing us the abstract idea of a moving point of view, in order to suggest, perhaps, that all of the film is to be perceived in this peripatetic way: not necessarily with a world looming toward us, but always with a world through which our anticipation, our orientation, and our interest shift and move. The idea of "the local" is a phantasm itself.

There are basically no timepieces in *A Trip to the Moon*, even though by implication a calculation of sidereal time and of the movements of the celestial orbs must have been undertaken before the gun was shot. We do see one rather riddling clock—hanging inside the open hatch of the projectile first during the loading tableau and then after the explorers have landed. On both occasions, the timepiece reads the same, four o'clock; and because the hour is identical in signature, we can immediately be led to wonder whether a whole day has elapsed between launch and landing, or half a day, or more than one day, or whether time has moved backward, or indeed whether time has frozen altogether. In any event, the clock and its mechanism (its consciousness) appears always to be, and always to have been, *here*. In Verne's book, the members of the Gun Club spend considerable time ascertaining the precise moment at which the projectile must be launched from the earth, and although the use of the pocket watch does not figure heavily in this work either, nevertheless it is intriguingly the case that the entire novel seems something of a clock itself, measuring relentlessly the moments that elapse from the instant at which the project is first conceived; through all of the various preparations and constructions—some of them elaborate—that must take place before there can be a gun; through the mechanical preparation of the gun itself, shipment of the materials, maintenance of social order, and so on, through to the voyagers' final moments of anticipation and readiness, their little celebration deep in the heart of the gun, their actual launch precisely—that is, to the second—on time. Méliès dispenses with this "clockwork" in order to produce a vision that, if it does not exactly appear to integrate and connect the movements of different people in a single plan, still seems to reveal a circling, clocklike, mechanical quality in human action and relationship. Because the film is something like a clock in its circularity, its repetitiveness, its metrical quality, and the precision of its many motions, so is the sole clock within the film less a counter of time than merely a mechanical device—a set of weights and gears and springs that make for up-and-down or back-and-forth movements according to natural law (and simulating what the workmen were shown to do in the construction tableau). A careful study of early clocks, indeed, brings home the idea that they are hardly more than mechanisms for repeating movement; and forcefully and delightfully suggests of the "time" clocks are taken to "count" and "measure" that beyond mechanics, it is an ether impossible to fathom, not a substance with proportion or extensivity at all.[29]

We may think of the precise and mechanical quality of the footsteps of the Selenites, of the mechanical way they are dispensed with, or the mechanical gestures of Barbenfouillis as he gives his lecture, or the mechanical movements of the workmen making the shell. The transformation involved here is a simple one, yet an occasion for real pleasure: every upward movement changes into a downward one (the hammers falling and being lifted, or workmen at screen left pounding an anvil); every downward one changes into an upward one (a hat falling from an academic's head and being retrieved for him); every forward movement into a backward one (a carpenter at screen right planing a board back and forth, removing it from its vise, checking it, inserting it upside down, and planing some more), and so on. The gestures of Barbenfouillis and his clubmates; the gestures of the workers; the flag-waving of the girls surrounding the shell; the movement of the shell into space and then, later, back to earth; the jittery movement of the Selenites taking steps in one direction, then reversing direction again and again. These movements, taken one at a time, are shocking, like "the jolt in the movement of a machine" described by Benjamin, "the workman's gesture that is produced by the automatic operation,"[30] but taken together, rhythmically, they may be experienced fully and directly as flowing transformations.

But a more profound transformation riddles the film and consists in material alternations, replacements, disappearances and appearances, substitutions—the stuff of theatrical magic now applied to the new medium of cinema. The surprise of transformation is rooted in the conceptual "distance" between origins and outcomes, between things and what they turn into; and insofar as we can imagine to ourselves that all objects are precisely and entirely themselves, themselves and not other things, then the "magical" process by which one item is transformed into another really seems to constitute a movement over a distance. But when the transformation is accomplished swiftly and dramatically, that is, with such optical force that attention is drawn to the process of transformation itself rather than to the object being transformed, the two objects,

primary and secondary, appear to be one. There is a metaphorical statement of this formula in Méliès's causing the trip to the moon to take
place so quickly (perhaps in no time at all, according to the clock we
see), so that almost immediately after the launch of the projectile we
see it plunking into the moon's eye: this brings the moon and the earth
together (as they are brought together again when the capsule returns).
Yet we do not need to rely on metaphors. In each sequence of the film
we see dramatic transformations that negate the "distance" or difference
between objects, transformations that collapse space and thrillingly (not
traumatically) undo the local, creating, as did images in the Phantasmagoria of the eighteenth century, an "atmosphere of visual uncertainty . . .
a sense, as one announcement put it, that the specters appeared on the
air itself, immaterially."[31]

I am thinking, for example, of the transitory images that are so
thrilling in this film: in the tableau of the furnaces, the sudden appearance
at left, out of nowhere, of a white flag flapping in the wind, or of the molten liquid; in the tableau of the lecture, the bobbing movements of the
audience, and then the specter of transformation as the voyagers change
out of their club robes into traveling clothes, twisting and gesticulating as
they do so; in the tableaux with the Selenites, the replacement effect as
each creature, struck by an umbrella, morphs into smoke; in the tableau
of the first experience of the moon territory, the replacement effect as
the mushrooms appear to grow, or as star-maidens appear and disappear
in the starry sky; and the contact tableau, in which the moon at first
seems to approach and then suddenly to become humanoid with an eye
that can tear (custard) and a mouth that can move—all this achieved not
only by stop action but also by using an actor with makeup to play the
moon. The Selenite disappearance effect is so powerful and enchanting
for viewers that it withstands considerable repetition, and Méliès must
have expected it would, given his experience with stage disappearance
tricks such as *La Stroubaïka persane* (where a person bound on a platform
suddenly vanished and reappeared in the audience).

The overwhelming effect of these "transitionary images," as we
might call them, beyond the wonder and momentarily thrilling excitement they would have provided for viewers—sufficiently incomplete that
the desire for repetition would have been instantaneously created—was
a sharp sensation of the presence of an unseen, unseeable manipulating
hand, a controlling persona beyond the screen using techniques beyond
our ken for beguiling us. This produces what Gunning calls a "perceptual *vividness*, an increased power over the viewers' senses, one that was
pictorial and visual rather than linguistic"[32]—indeed, a *vividly perceived*
perceptual vividness, a vividness that drew attention to itself, and that
might have been thought sinister, a force that could exert *"undue influence*

on its audience, an attraction compared to bewitchment, hypnosis, casting a spell, or putting the viewer/audience into a trance."[33] The transitionary image, in other words, merges two contradictory, two "distant" states into a single moving—and thus emotional—experience: the Selenite jumping and threatening and the absence of the Selenite; the moon at one position and the moon nearer; the empty furnace apparatus and the furnaces flowing with iron; the moon as a rock and the moon as a face. So it is that in the cinema of Méliès, just as for Michel Ardan, there are moments of extreme enthusiasm and promise in which the impossible can be achieved, and "distance does not exist."

Notes

Author's note: Matthew Solomon has traveled far beyond the distance to which editors are obliged to go in helping me frame this argument, and I am very grateful to him.

1. Jules Verne, *From the Earth to the Moon*, trans. Lowell Bair (1865; repr., New York: Bantam, 1993), 132–133.

2. Tom Gunning, "Lunar Illuminations," in *Film Analysis: A Norton Reader*, ed. Jeffrey Geiger and R. L. Rutsky (New York: Norton, 2005), 65.

3. Verne, *From the Earth*, 140–141.

4. Tom Gunning, "The Cinema of Attractions: Early Film, Its Spectator and the Avant-Garde," in *Early Cinema: Space, Frame, Narrative*, ed. Thomas Elsaesser with Adam Barker (London: British Film Institute, 1990), 56.

5. Gunning, "Cinema of Attractions," 58.

6. Gunning, "Cinema of Attractions," 57. Editor's note: See also Méliès, "The Importance of the Script," this volume, 243.

7. David Robinson, *Georges Méliès: Father of Film Fantasy* (London: Museum of the Moving Image, 1993), 51–53.

8. Gunning, "Cinema of Attractions," 58.

9. Nicolas Dulac and André Gaudreault, "Circularity and Repetition at the Heart of the Attraction: Optical Toys and the Emergence of a New Cultural Series," trans. Timothy Barnard, in *The Cinema of Attractions Reloaded*, ed. Wanda Strauven (Amsterdam, Netherlands: Amsterdam University Press, 2006), 228.

10. Dulac and Gaudreault, "Circularity and Repetition," 228.

11. Dulac and Gaudreault, "Circularity and Repetition," 233.

12. Sigmund Freud, *The Interpretations of Dreams*, trans. A. A. Brill (1900; repr., New York: Random House, 1950), 202.

13. Freud, *Interpretation of Dreams*, 203.

14. Freud, *Interpretation of Dreams*, 203.

15. John Frazer, *Artificially Arranged Scenes: The Films of Georges Méliès* (Boston: G. K. Hall, 1979), 95.

16. José Ortega y Gasset, "On Point of View in the Arts," trans. Paul Snodgress and Joseph Frank, *The Dehumanization of Art and Other Essays on Art, Culture, and Literature* (Princeton, N.J.: Princeton University Press, 1972), 114.

17. Frazer, *Artificially Arranged Scenes*, 95.

18. Gunning, "Cinema of Attractions," 57.

19. Frazer, *Artificially Arranged Scenes*, 96; Paul Hammond, *Marvellous Méliès* (London: Gordon Fraser, 1974), 100.

20. Laurent Mannoni, *The Great Art of Light and Shadow: Archaeology of the Cinema*, trans. Richard Crangle (Exeter, U.K.: University of Exeter Press, 2000), 145.

21. *Blackwood's Magazine*, 1830, quoted in Stephen Bottomore, "The Panicking Audience? Early Cinema and the 'Train Effect,' " *Historical Journal of Film, Radio and Television* 19, no. 2 (1999), 191.

22. Tom Gunning, "Phantasmagoria and the Manufacturing of Illusions and Wonder: Towards a Cultural Optics of the Cinematic Apparatus," in *Le Cinématographe, nouvelle technologie du XXe siècle / The Cinema, A New Technology for the 20th Century*, ed. André Gaudreault, Catherine Russell, and Pierre Véronneau (Lausanne, Switzerland: Editions Payot, 2004), 36.

23. Frazer, *Artificially Arranged Scenes*, 96.

24. H. G. Wells, *The First Men in the Moon* (New York: Modern Library, 2003), 185.

25. Mary Ann Doane, *The Emergence of Cinematic Time: Modernity, Contingency, the Archive* (Cambridge, Mass.: Harvard University Press, 2002), 1.

26. Doane, *Emergence of Cinematic Time*, 138.

27. Doane, *Emergence of Cinematic Time*, 15.

28. Stephen Kern, *The Culture of Time and Space, 1880–1918* (Cambridge, Mass.: Harvard University Press, 1983), 14, quoted in Doane, *Emergence of Cinematic Time*, 5.

29. David Thompson, *Clocks* (London: British Museum Press, 2005).

30. Walter Benjamin, "On Some Motifs in Baudelaire," trans. Harry Zohn, *Illuminations: Essays and Reflections*, ed. Hannah Arendt (New York: Schocken, 1969), 177.

31. Gunning, "Phantasmagoria," 34.

32. Tom Gunning, "Flickers: On Cinema's Power for Evil," in *BAD: Infamy, Darkness, Evil, and Slime on Screen*, ed. Murray Pomerance (Albany: SUNY Press, 2004), 25.

33. Gunning, "Flickers," 25.

6

TOM GUNNING

Shooting into Outer Space

Reframing Modern Vision

IN WIM WENDERS'S DOCUMENTARY tribute to Ozu Yasujiro, *Tokyo-Ga* (1985), the filmmaker searches through modern Tokyo in an attempt to discover some remnant of the film world Ozu had created. At one point on the top of the Tokyo Tower (the world's tallest self-supporting steel tower at 333 meters, 13 meters taller than the Eiffel Tower) he encounters another German tourist filmmaker in search of fresh images, Werner Herzog. Wenders's film recurringly excoriates the modern world of debased images in contrast to the ordered images found in Ozu's films. Television especially, Wenders claims, has inundated the world with false images. High above Tokyo Herzog too mourns the loss of vital images. He is searching, he indicates, for "pure, clear, transparent images," which he feels have vanished from an overdeveloped earth (that crowded Tokyo down into which they peer). He claims he would consider any risk or effort to attain these images: climb huge mountains or travel into outer space on rockets to Mars or Saturn, the National Aeronautics and Space Administration's Skylab or the space shuttle. Wenders, however, indicates his own view that such images must be found on earth, there in the chaos of Tokyo.

This encounter between two Germans high above Tokyo raises for me the issues that the conjunction of modernity, vision, cinema, and global (or indeed extraterrestrial) space bring to us. Lest anyone misunderstand, modern vision is mediated vision, not simply the biological inheritance of the human eye (as fascinating and complex as that may be), but vision that relates to a manmade environment, whether the urbanscape of Tokyo or the vast expanses of the railway systems cutting across natural landscapes. Modern vision thus understood includes the devices that supplement eyesight with the technological effects of enlargement, penetration, or reproduction, from the telescope to the X-ray to the photograph and the cinema. Of course, mechanical devices cannot truly be said to "see," and indeed the difference between these modes of mediated vision and human eyesight is part of what defines modern vision. We are film historians, and like filmmakers Wenders and Herzog, we are speaking about *images*, not simply vision as a biological phenomenon.

Dziga Vertov called his conception of modern vision the camera eye or Kino-Eye, the cinema eye. The camera eye, according to Vertov, constitutes a complex instrument, which included not only all the deviations from the "unarmed human eye" that technology made available, but also a radical rearrangement of space and time, a tool for understanding the modern world. To quote a well-known passage from his manifesto "Kinoks": "Now and forever I free myself from human immobility, I am in constant motion, I draw near, then away from objects, I crawl under, I climb onto them. I move apace with the muzzle of a galloping horse, I plunge full speed into a crowd, I outstrip running soldiers, I fall on my back, I ascend with an airplane, I plunge and soar together with plunging and soaring bodies."[1] Kino-Eye's mastery of space not only included the camera's ability to move, but also the ability of montage to coordinate diverse points upon the globe. As my doctoral student Doron Galili has demonstrated, Vertov believed that the ultimate attainment of this new level of modern vision might come not from film, but from television (which he termed "radio-eye").[2] But does Vertov's utopian conception of a modern mode of vision only lead to Wenders's jeremiad in *Tokyo-Ga* as he watches television in his Tokyo hotel room: "every shitty television set, no matter where, is the center of the world. The Center has become a ludicrous idea, the world as well, the image of the world a ludicrous idea."

Not the least of the complexity of the concept of modern vision lies in its essential ambivalence: its utopian and dystopian aspects; its role in extending the powers of sight into a visionary insight that stitches the globe together; or its role as what Heidegger called the "world picture" in which the world is reduced to an exchangeable and objectifying image, expressive of man's dominance over nature and his fellow man.[3] Modern vision aspires to a victory over space, the technological "far sight" envisioned by both Kino-Eye and television. Herzog's invocation of the view from a rocket ship as both a mode of escape from the chaos of earth and the means of achieving a new sort of vision belongs to a tradition more than a century long. Attaining such vision through a perspective beyond the horizon of the earth appears in both actuality and in fiction and makes clear the way modernity constitutes a technological complex, an environment in which various technologies interact and transform. Paul Virilio in a rather fast and loose manner has shown how cinema grew within a technological environment of modern warfare, including the development of aerial bombardment and surveillance.[4] The use of images as a tool of warfare by other means, certainly forms a part of modern vision, and indeed may underlie Herzog's own aggressive desire to penetrate into dangerous environments such as war zones in search of his pure images. But the pursuit of images from aerial perspectives also derives from the new spaces the modern world makes available, from the sublime desire for mountain top perspectives of romanticism, to the witty illustrations of imaginary balloon voyages by Grandville,[5] to the documentary balloon views of Paris captured by pioneer photographer Nadar,[6] and the photographic panoramas of Eadweard Muybridge.[7] As in the view from the Tokyo Tower, photography and cinema search out an all-encompassing image of space, from Lumière's and Edison's films from the elevator ascending the Eiffel Tower during the 1900 Universal Exposition to the views from satellites presented in Imax.

The symbiosis between the airplane and the cinema forms a rich theme in modern vision, one that some decades ago Angela Dalle Vacche indicated should be explored with the same attention that had been given to the relation between cinema and the railway.[8] I will not undertake this broad and rich task here, but rather a closely related one, already introduced by Herzog on top of the Tokyo Tower: the pursuit of rocket vision. My tutor text is quite frankly a chestnut, probably the best-known early film, Georges Méliès's *A Trip to the Moon* from 1902. As familiar as it is, closely examining this film not only allows us to establish the ambiguous spaces of early film, but also the way this complex and hybrid space found its perfect narrative in the exploration of a space beyond the earth. Through Méliès's film I explore the rocket not only as a mode of transport but also as a vehicle of sight.

A Trip to the Moon may not only be the best-known example of early cinema, but also the best-known silent film. Its widespread availability and rather short running time make it an obvious staple of both introduction to film and film history classes. But more important, the film still provides the entertainment it promised more than a century ago. Its charm remains immediate, its humor and visual attractions still compelling.[9] Even if claiming the film as the first science-fiction film constitutes an anachronistic projection of a later genre, *A Trip to the Moon* does envision a future based on modern technology and forges a link (albeit tongue-in-cheek) with the literature of Verne and Wells. (I must specify that the moon voyage in Verne's novel *From the Earth to the Moon* and Méliès's film remains within the domain of artillery, as the name of the organization that undertakes it in the former, the Baltimore Gun Club, testifies: a shell launched from a giant gun, rather than a self-propelled rocket.) The sources for Méliès's film are diverse and cut across genres. But the lighthearted style of performance (although not entirely foreign to the semi-satirical caricature Verne draws of the rather eccentric Baltimore Gun Club) refers to the burlesque tradition of *féerique* pantomime that Méliès drew on, the magical playlets incorporating transformation and tricks that Méliès offered in his Théâtre Robert-Houdin, patterned on the models of British magical entrepreneur Maskelyne,[10] as well as the comical adaptation of voyages into space in the operetta *Le Voyage dans la lune*,[11] and even on the staging of a trip to the moon as an amusement park attraction in Fred Thompson's Luna Park in Coney Island.[12] *A Trip to the Moon* reflects the intermedial palimpsest that typified early cinema (and I would argue cinema for most of its history) and all these sources contributed to the film's use of space. One could claim that Méliès's film explores the new composite space of cinema as imaginatively as its astronomers did outer space.

The enduring historical significance—and popularity—of *A Trip to the Moon* is undoubtedly overdetermined. Its combination of cinematic tricks and attractions with a simple but very coherent story allows it not only to exemplify both early cinema's dominant as a cinema of attractions but also feed an emerging interest in story films.[13] Its subject matter, exploration of outer space, continued to fascinate audiences for the rest of the century (I remember as a child first seeing an abbreviated version of the film as part of a prologue to Mike Todd's 1956 Verne film adaptation *Around the World in Eighty Days* as an indication of Verne's power of prophecy in the era of the launching of the first satellites). But as with every enduring work of art, *A Trip to the Moon* has been able to be seen in a variety of ways, appear within numerous contexts, and illuminate different aspects of the cinema. In the canonical grand narrative of cinematic development, best formulated by Georges Sadoul and modified (but basically continued) by Jean Mitry, *A Trip to the Moon* represented a primitive step in the evolution of narrative cinema, one dominated by *theatricality*, an approach to cinematic space which maintained a framing of the action within the broad view of the theatrical proscenium arch and simulated what Sadoul called the viewpoint of the *"monsieur de l'orchestre,"* a wide unselective framing with action oriented frontally.[14] In contrast to the emergence of a cinematic style that would break down this theatrical space into separate shots, *A Trip to the Moon* was characterized by a lack of editing, with cuts (or, in many prints of *A Trip to the Moon*, dissolves), which do not construct a dramatic space, but simply move us from location to location, from theatrical tableau to theatrical tableau. For Sadoul and Mitry, who saw the development of editing that would emerge with D. W. Griffith and others as the essential form of cinematic space, *A Trip to the Moon* remained at a primitive stage of this evolution.

This view was disputed by the post-Brighton generation of film historians who revised accounts of early cinema, primarily André Gaudreault, who in polemical exchanges with Mitry especially disputed this description of Méliès and *A Trip to the Moon*.[15] Gaudreault pointed out that in fact the editing in *A Trip to the Moon* is actually more fluid than the traditional description would indicate. Likewise several historians offered a more nuanced account of the theatrical heritage of early cinema (continuing the tradition of A. Nicholas Vardac who described certain forms of nineteenth-century theater as moving toward the more flexible space of cinema, rather than posing its absolute Other).[16] *A Trip to the Moon* derives largely from the spectacular theatrical tradition of the fairy pantomime in which a succession of scene changes provided a major visual attraction of the form. Thus the opening of the film follows the planning, construction, and launching of the moon projectile by moving from elaborate set to elaborate set, following the group of scientists/explorers. Once they land on the moon, we again follow the explorers through even more visually unique sets (the surface of the moon, the lunar caves, the palace of the moon king). Rather than a space constructed through dramatic action, this succession of spectacular displays of set design provides an almost kaleidoscopic series of views.

Gaudreault especially cites one sequence as contradicting the Sadoul/Mitry description of the film's theatricality. The return of the projectile from the moon to the earth moves rapidly through a series of shots, from the spaceship teetering on the edge of the moon, descending through space, penetrating the surface of the ocean, and then floating deep within the sea. As Gaudreault claimed, a sequence of four shots following a single action and lasting only, by his count, twenty seconds, certainly proposes an approach to space that cannot be simply equated with theatricality.[17] Since this revisionist history, a dichotomy between theatricality and cinematic approaches to space no longer holds as the dominant description of space in early cinema. Theater itself has been approached in a more varied manner by historians ranging from David Mayer to Ben Brewster and Lea Jacobs, respecting the range of stage practices and genres.[18] The diverse sources for early cinema discovered in the work of John L. Fell, Charles Musser, Charlie Keil, Frank Kessler, Matthew Solomon, Gaudreault, and others—from comic strips, newspaper and journal illustrations, magic performances and illusions, or magic lantern shows—have complicated our sense of the visual heritage of early cinema.[19]

I want to examine the sequence of landing on the moon. Again a single trajectory of action unites several shots (three or five, depending on how you decide to define and count shots). The first shot shows the huge artillery gun used to launch the projectile toward the moon (in the background, the muzzle of the huge gun pointed toward the heavens and a minuscule distant moon visible through a gap in the clouds are shown in a theatrical flat, painted in exaggerated perspective). The following shot shows a theatrical backdrop of the sky, including an image of the moon that enlarges a bit, as if the camera were drawing closer. A dissolve transforms this painted image of the moon into a grimacing moon-face, a circular cratered form whose center includes a heavily madeup mobile human face—the traditional Man in the Moon. This moon-face enlarges even more, again giving the impression that either the moon or the camera is moving. As the moon-face looms larger, a substitution splice makes a projectile appear on it, as if it had collided with the moon's eye (the projectile appears suddenly, rather than entering the frame, and the moon continues to advance, the face reacting as if it had "something in its eye.")

The next shot shows a set of the lunar surface portrayed in the traditional theatrical recessive flats set in grooves at different depths to portray a deep lunar landscape, marked by craters and stalagmite-like rock formations. The projectile enters from the left, landing on the surface, and the explorers emerge from it, gesticulating broadly their wonder at the scene. The spaceship disappears from view suddenly (whether by a substitution splice or by sinking beneath the stage is a bit unclear). The explorers regroup, as the most distant flat of the lunar landscape sinks slowly out of sight (lowered below the stage surface). Another flat flies into view vertically even further back, showing the "full earth" rising into the sky, and continuing past the top of the frame: a spectacular sight the space travelers fully appreciate. This is followed by a pyrotechnic effect of smoke and flame erupting from one of the craters.

For the remainder of the shot, the black background in the depth of the shot serves as a dark reserve against which a series of spectacular superimpositions appear; the filmic technique of double exposure takes

over from stage machinery. First, a comet travels laterally to the left;
then the stars forming the Big Dipper appear, from which women's faces
emerge, glowering at the explorers who have stretched out to sleep on
the surface below them. Finally three emblematic figures of celestial
entities: Phoebe, the crescent moon; Saturn, both God and Planet; and
two women holding a star, Gemini. The celestial figures cause a snowfall
that awakes the sleeping group, who, shivering, set off in search of shelter
in the crater.

This brief sequence shows how complex and multiple the space
of early cinema can be and demonstrates again that a simple dichotomy
between the theatrical and the cinematic cannot express the dynamic and
varied approaches to space a film like *A Trip to the Moon* offers. This
is a hybrid space, an assemblage of intersecting, and even competing,
spatial practices, reflecting the way early cinema is not only intermedial,
as Gaudreault and others have emphasized, but also multidimensional.
On the one hand, the sequence includes the hallmarks of what would
develop into a cinematic approach, subordinating space to the flow of
action: the shell shooting into space and landing on the moon. Individual
shots merge into a continuous sequence by following the course of this
action.[20] However, the shot of the lunar surface also shows a deliberate—
and delightful—use of the theatrical construction of space through
mobile flats and grooves, flies and traps. More than a century later, this
moonscape set retains its visual power creating an intricately designed
environment, anticipating the surrealist cosmic space of Yves Tanguy,
as well as Mario Bava's marvelous sets for *Planet of the Vampires* (1965).
But Méliès's masterful deployment of theatrical flats frames his use of
filmic superimpositions. The women's heads popping from the stars
employ stage machinery within a filmic technique. Méliès freely (and
effectively) combines filmic techniques as the equivalent of the theatrical
practice of the *vision scene*, using the far background of the stage as an
area in which scenes from radically different or distant spaces could
be revealed (dreams, visions, or as in the versions of *Enoch Arden* or
The Corsican Brothers, simultaneous but distant actions).[21] As opposed to
the naturalistic sets and practices that were taking over serious drama
around this time, Méliès remained faithful to the frankly artificial devices
of popular spectacle. He could also insert cinema into them (as in his
production of films to be projected during *féeries* staged at the Théâtre
du Châtelet).[22] Or he could insert theatrical machines into his films.
Which was host and which was parasite? It is the juxtaposition of these
diverse visual effects that makes the sequences so effective.

Whether or not the collagelike space of such a sequence can be
claimed as an influence on the transformation in space that occurred

in modernist painting in the years that follow (and I think a good case can be made for this influence), Méliès's cinema pushed the visual devices of the nineteenth-century spectacular theater (the operetta, the pantomime, and the magical playlet) into a representation that no longer corresponded simply to the inert space of theatricality or the continuous space composed of different orientations that later cinema achieved through editing. Instead he creates a palimpsest, a playful space of display, with differing modes of representation and even different spatial scales juxtaposed within a single image. The Sadoul/Mitry tradition that casts film history into a linear evolution toward a uniquely cinematic style can only experience this visually impressive display of stage machinery as a residual, outmoded practice. To a nonteleological eye, this sequence reveals the joys of what Bazin called "mixed cinema,"[23] creating a hybrid space whose jagged fit between several modes expresses Méliès's modern pragmatism: a filmmaker in pursuit of visual effects rather than stylistic coherence. In this moon landing Méliès juxtaposes different approaches to space into a sort of collage based in visual display, as different flats move in and out of the frame (laterally left to right, horizontally above and below) and give way to and interact with filmic superimposition.

My work on early cinema refused to characterize the elements of discontinuity in cinematic practice as a primitive awkwardness to be smoothed out as cinema gained greater mastery over its techniques, but instead saw this seeming incoherence as a different mode of address. This can be seen in this film's approach to editing as well, as previous historians have pointed out. Let us return to the cuts that precede the landing. The cut that moves us from the moon-face blinking at the projectile stuck in its eye to the landing on the surface has been analyzed by Gaudreault and Musser as a repeated action edit, or temporal overlap.[24] Such cutting, especially in Edwin S. Porter's *Life of an American Fireman* (1903), became an emblem of the unique editing of early cinema in contrast to the smooth cutting on action that marked classical editing. When an action moves across two locations or orientations (especially moving from interiors to exteriors), early filmmakers frequently stuttered the action, showing its complete trajectory from both orientations, thus causing it to repeat. To put it simply, Méliès shows the spaceship land twice, once in the "long shot" of the moon face and once as the stage machine of the projectile lands on the set of the lunar surface. As some commentators have claimed, a simple snip of the scissor could eliminate such a repetition. Undoubtedly. But *A Trip to the Moon* makes especially clear what else it would eliminate: the spectacular display of two views of the moon landing, not only from different positions, but also in different modes (the comic caricature–like moon-face and the theatrical sensation scene). In Méliès's style spectacle trumps continuity of action, and visual variety triumphs over the diegetic verisimilitude valued by later cinema.

But after revisiting this *locus classicus* of early discontinuity (or nonlinear continuity), I want to rewind a bit further to the moment preceding the projectile pasting the moon in the eye. This series of transforming images (parsing it into shots ultimately obscures its construction) portrays the aerial voyage to the moon through a series of dramatic visual effects. Primary is the effect of motion. Based on Méliès's discussion of other films, we can assume that although the intended effect (and indeed the one achieved) is of a viewpoint traveling toward the moon, Méliès most likely used a static camera and moved the moon toward it. The need for steady registration of the image and the lack of a smooth mode of transport for the camera necessitated this reversal. This solution not only shows Méliès's pragmatic ingenuity in devising optical tricks (his *métier*, as he would claim), but also underscores the point I have often made that the theater of magical illusions constituted a sophisticated laboratory of visual devices designed to cheat and manipulate the senses. As early as the late eighteenth century, the Phantasmagoria had played with the ambiguity of enlargement as a depth cue: a magic lantern slide pulled back from the screen enlarged quickly and could therefore give the impression the image portrayed was rapidly approaching the viewer.[25] This is precisely the perceptual principle Méliès used in representing the approach to the moon; first the graphic image of the moon and then the moon-face increase in size relative to the frame and thus give the impression of a rapid approach toward the viewer. Indeed, the description Méliès issued to accompany the film describes this moment in terms of both approach and enlargement: "The shell coming closer every minute, the moon magnifies rapidly, until finally it attains colossal dimensions."[26] This portrayal of motion through enlargement, or rather of the relativity of motion depending on point of view (the famous perceptual problem of the train leaving the station: which is moving, the train or the platform?) supplies not only a means of conveying the narrative action of the voyage to the moon, but also the unique optical experience of motion, including its embodied ambiguities. Méliès's film does not simply seek a coherent verisimilitude, but rather a series of optical delights and attractions.

Let us look at the spatial, narrative, and perceptual logic of this sequence. Retrospectively it seems to anticipate the spatial flexibility of the cinematic mode. The sequence functions like a point-of-view shot, the view of the explorers as they speed toward the moon. As historians of early cinema have shown, editing or framing that functions like later point-of-view shots appear very early with the variety of films based around views through telescopes, keyholes, or microscopes. The cinematic

logic of alternation between a viewer and what she sees corresponds
to a basic cognitive schema, easily understood and therefore useful in
constructing a visually based narrative syntax. Basically the sequence of
approaching the moon seems to operate this way. However, specifying it
as a point of view becomes difficult because no "watcher" appears in the
sequence (following Edward Branigan's classic description of filmic point
of view no offscreen look is shown).[27] However, as Branigan points out,
we often understand a shot as a point of view without actually seeing a
watcher. Camera movement, as in the unattributed point-of-view shots
that became a part of the visual syntax of the stalker film from the 1970s
on, can cue us that someone is watching the scene even if the actor
remains offscreen. The moving view of the moon seems similar.

I would not deny this reading, even though I find it a bit
anachronistic, assuming the key role of subjective shots so important for
later dramatic cinema. I would prefer to think of this shot as indicating
a nonhuman point of view, the view precisely of the projectile as it arcs
toward the moon. More than simply indicating a view, the shot makes
palpable a trajectory. In effect, this is a peculiarly technological and
modern viewpoint, the viewpoint of the speeding rocket. Although this
interpretation may seems as tendentious (and perhaps as anachronistic)
as describing it as a human subjective shot, I would like to linger on
the fact that so many early point-of-view films are through technological
visual devices (microscopes, telescopes, binoculars, magnifying glasses).[28]
Such devices provide a clear marking for a subjunctive shot, which
partly explains this predilection, but I do not think it explains it away.
Technologically mediated vision fascinated early cinema, portraying a
peculiarly modern perception. The conjunction of vision and devices
wittily doubled the cinema's own medium of viewing and foregrounded
the act of display by framing it.

A Trip to the Moon exemplifies the visual effectiveness of early
cinema's bumpy and playful approach to space. The sequence on the
lunar surface employs jagged juxtapositions, whereas the approach to
the moon plays on the ambiguities of motion and viewpoint. If I have
described this approach to space in formal terms, I also feel it expresses
the film's narrative of achieving a new perspective and envisioning the
new horizons of a world of the future. The spectacle of the earth rising
as seen from the moon epitomizes the witty inversions of a new cosmos in
which visual logic reverses its coordinates. A camera shooting into outer
space means imagining a point of view transcending ordinary human
boundaries, anticipating the later issues of surveillance and the "eye in
the sky" satellites. While the visual surveillance that emerged with World
War I discussed by Virilio remains in the future (the Wright brothers have

not yet taken off), there are direct connections between the aerial balloon photography of Nadar and the sources of *A Trip to the Moon*. In Verne's novels *From the Earth to the Moon* and *Round the Moon* the members of the Baltimore Gun Club who undertake the voyage around the moon are joined shortly before takeoff by a flamboyant adventurer named Michel Ardan. Verne intended, and readers immediately recognized, Ardan as a thinly disguised portrait of the photographer adventurer Nadar.[29] Verne saw launching into outer space as the natural outcome of Nadar's probing visual curiosity, which had led him from photographing the depths of Paris (the catacombs and the sewers) to his aerial views of the city.[30]

I will not launch a second stage of this chapter by discussing the symbiosis between space travel and photography. Raymond Bellour has provided a brilliant reading of the key role photographic and movie images play in Fritz Lang's *The Woman in the Moon* (1929).[31] Outer space was probed by photography before being physically visited by man. Here the voracious nature of modern sight, its expansiveness and acquisitiveness, goes beyond Heidegger's concept of the world picture as the enframing of nature for the use of man, to the digesting of the entire cosmos as image. Méliès's rush toward the moon not only expresses this desire to bring the moon closer in order to capture its image (a theme rehearsed and embodied in an earlier Méliès film from 1898 entitled *The Astronomer's Dream*, expressing the enlargement of the moon seen through a telescope), but also in effect to seize it, to claim it for the explorers. The visual appropriation of this territory in outer space, as various commentators have noted, reflects an era of colonialism in which the exotic becomes a possession. Although the moon explorers do not plant a flag on the lunar surface as the actual U.S. astronauts did decades later, nonetheless in the complete version of the film they bring back to earth a Selenite as captive and trophy, recalling the native peoples of colonialized territories put on display at world expositions at the turn of the century.

The aggressive nature of this territorial gaze hardly rests on this colonial impulse alone, given that the impact of the camera movement becomes visualized as the projectile landing directly in the moon's eye. The synopsis that accompanies the film describes this action as "the shell pierces the eye of the moon."[32] One could describe this violence as the extreme form of modern vision and its literal opening up of a new sort of space. This modern vision is not only mobile, but also aggressive; Walter Benjamin claimed that both Dada and cinema take on a ballistic force that "turned the artwork into a missile,"[33] an image that the Dada film *Entr'acte* (1924) literalized in the penultimate shot of its prologue, showing collaborator Erik Satie and Francis Picabia loading an artillery gun with a shell (their expression as they sniff it identifies its potential effect as olfactory as well as tactile), which then launches out at the audience itself. This movement out from the screen toward the viewer recalls both the looming effect of the Phantasmagoria and the forward rush of the moon as the projectile/viewer approaches. But in Méliès's film the violence of the collision, the shock effect so crucial to Benjamin's concept of modernity, gets transferred from the viewer to the moon itself, which takes it in the eye. Is it accidental that this violence to the moon's eye anticipates perhaps the archetypal image of modernist cinema: the slashed eyeball in Luis Buñuel and Salvador Dali's *Un Chien andalou* (1929), the nauseating yet fascinating image that follows a shot of a cloud crossing a full moon?

I have made numerous claims in this chapter that follow an arc from the nearly undeniable to the more speculative. First, retracing the revisionist history of the early cinema of past decades I claim that *A Trip to the Moon*, like many early films, creates a collagelike space in which different modes of representation contend. I have also claimed that this eclectic style, based in providing the viewer with visual novelty, can be contextualized in relation to modern hyperstimulus of vision and its abstraction of space, a connection that the film itself marks through it portrayal of modern technology. Furthermore, I have claimed that this sort of aggressive visual style, while firmly rooted in the popular arts, could also be experienced as a means of portraying modern perception and provided models for avant-garde modes that appeared somewhat later. My argument does not claim this as the only frame of reference for early cinema, but I do claim it is a rich one. I find these connections exciting. For those who greet them with yawns, I leave them to their own delights.

Film history consists not only in the recovery of the past, but also a trajectory into the future. To my mind these processes are intertwined the way a vision of the past prepares a sense of a future. Whether Méliès's adoption by the avant-garde confused him in his old age (as a similar reception seems to have baffled Henri Rousseau),[34] or whether he recognized in this new generation the high jinx of the Incoherents and the spirit of Montmartre that marked the era of his youth, *A Trip to the Moon* (and its school of Incoherent astronomy)[35] became celebrated by the avant-garde, ranging from the surrealists of the 1920s to American 1960s pop artist Red Grooms.[36] As we know, history is partly based on misappropriations and misreadings, but on those that have the strength to change the way we see things. *A Trip to the Moon* plants the seed of cinema's mission to view the earth from the moon, to imagine a vision outside the common frame of spatial relations, with all its possible dangers and delights. I want to close, then, with a direct quotation of

Méliès's film, perhaps the most beautiful I know, the testament of the greatest documentary filmmaker of the twentieth century, Joris Ivens: the film Ivens made in 1988 with his wife Marceline Loridan, *A Tale of the Wind*.

No other filmmaker pursued cinema's possibility of portraying global space as tirelessly as Ivens did in his sixty-year career. He made films in more than a score of countries, including the Netherlands, the United States, the Soviet Union, Germany, Chile, Australia, North Vietnam, China, Poland, Romania, France, Italy, Spain, and Hungary, covering the transformations of the modern world: its wars, revolutions, and reconstructions.[37] His last film offers both an autobiographical reflection and a portrait of his beloved China. In one sequence Ivens and Loridan recreated a near-fatal heart attack Ivens suffered while filming in China. His hospital room is visited by Monkey, the trickster hero of Chinese opera and of the great epic *Journey to the West*. Finding Ivens inert on his bed, Monkey covers him with a brush painting of a dragon and, with his paintbrush, draws pupils in the dragon's eyes. Magically, a revivifying wind enters the room, blowing open and shattering the glass in the windows, and triggering rapidly cut images of fireworks and a dragon dance in the street below. The shadow of a dragon carrying a man on his tail flies across the hospital wall. Monkey waves out the window to the offscreen celestial traveler. The night sky and moon-face appear in highly scratched footage from Méliès's film. Reediting Méliès's footage, the film cuts to the projectile being loaded in its artillery gun, then landing on the moon. A black-and-white image of a huge mock-up of the moon with the shell piercing its eye appears, its mouth opens, and from it steps Ivens in a long cloak onto a set of the lunar surface; he looks around in wonder, hearing raucous laughter. Ivens encounters the drunken Chinese poet Li Po who drowned when he attempted to embrace the reflection of the moon in water, and a woman seated, like Phoebe in Méliès's film, on the crescent of the moon, but who says she is Chenge, the Chinese "woman in the moon" who fled the earth to escape her husband, but who finds life on the moon boring. Ivens also sees the earth rising above the horizon, and Chenge gives him a telescope to observe more closely.

Ivens uses Méliès's film as a fragment of modern mythology, a viewpoint from which the utopian ideal of a single world can still be envisioned. Probably no filmmaker so devoted himself to the ideal of global revolution and social justice, and few felt as firmly the promises and betrayals of this modern utopia of cinema and politics. His mock-up of the moon combines the moon that suffers the poke in the eye in *A Trip to the Moon* and the voracious swallowing moon that appears in

The Astronomer's Dream. Seeing and swallowing have often fused when one imagines the act of truly absorbed film viewing. The Chinese poet drowns, swallowed by the water as he embraces the reflection of the moon. I have frequently quoted the early film reviewer who described the plunging movement of a phantom ride film as "as an unseen energy swallowing up space," and another review that described an early film taken from a train moving through a tunnel as resembling the penetration of an eye.[38] The cinema from its origins has been fascinated by the image of the eye, seeing it as a portal, not simply to the human soul, but to a new imagined world: the Kino-Eye, uniquely armed to navigate and portray modern space.

Notes

1. Dziga Vertov, "Kinoks: A Revolution," in *Kino-Eye*, trans. Kevin O'Brien, ed. Annette Michelson (Berkeley: University of California Press, 1984), 17.

2. Doron Galili discusses this in his dissertation in progress, "Seeing by Electricity: Vision, Temporality, and Intermediality in Early Television" (University of Chicago).

3. Martin Heidegger, "The Age of the World Picture," *The Question Concerning Technology and Other Essays*, trans. William Lovitt (New York: Harper and Row, 1977), 115–154.

4. Paul Virilio, *War and Cinema: The Logistics of Perception*, trans. Patrick Camiller (New York: Verso, 1989).

5. See, for instance, the illustrations from *Un autre monde* from 1844 of an imaginary balloon trip: J. J. Grandville, *Un autre monde, par Grandville* (1844; facsimile edition, Paris: Libraires associés, 1963), 25–32.

6. Nadar's aerial views from a balloon are discussed in Maria Morris Hambourg, Françoise Heilbrun, and Phillippe Néagu, *Nadar* (New York: Metropolitan Museum of Art, 1995), 27–31, 108–112.

7. Muybridge's panoramas are discussed in Rebecca Solnit, *Motion Studies: Time, Space and Eadweard Muybridge* (London: Bloomsbury, 2003), 153–176.

8. Angela Dalle Vacche made this claim at a symposium devoted to the work of Annette Michelson at New York University in 2003. At the time I strongly disagreed and partly offer here an apologetic rethinking of the issue.

9. On seeing *A Trip to the Moon*, students immediately recognize Méliès as the source for the Smashing Pumpkins' 1996 music video "Tonight, Tonight."

10. Méliès's magical shows and his influences were first detailed by Paul Hammond, *Marvellous Méliès* (London: Gordon Fraser, 1974). Laurent Mannoni, "Méliès, magie et cinéma," in *Méliès, magie et cinéma*, ed. Jacques Malthête and Laurent Mannoni (Paris: Paris-Musées, 2002), 37–51; Christian Fechner, "Le théâtre Robert-Houdin, de Jean Eugène Robert-Houdin à Georges Méliès," in *Méliès, magie et cinéma*, 73–115; and Matthew Solomon, *Disappearing Tricks: Silent Film, Houdini, and the New Magic of the Twentieth Century* (Urbana: University of Illinois Press, 2010), have all greatly supplemented this work.

11. Thierry Lefebvre's wonderful essay "*A Trip to the Moon*: A Composite Film," trans. Timothy Barnard, this volume, 49–63, details the many sources Méliès drew on, including this Offenbach operetta. His concept of the composite film is central to this chapter.

12. The A Trip to the Moon attraction is described in Woody Register, *The Kid of Coney Island: Fred Thompson and the Rise of American Amusements* (New York: Oxford University Press, 2001), 70–99. Lefebvre also discusses this attraction, as does Richard Abel in "*A Trip to the Moon* as an American Phenomenon," this volume, 129–142.

13. Richard Abel, *The Red Rooster Scare: Making Cinema American, 1900–1910* (Berkeley: University of California Press, 1999), 10–19.

14. Georges Sadoul's classic account of Méliès appears in *Les Pionniers du cinéma (de Méliès à Pathé), 1897–1909*, vol. 2, *Histoire générale du cinéma* (Paris: Éditions Denoël, 1947), esp. 141. Jean Mitry discusses Méliès especially in *Histoire du cinéma: Art et industrie*, vol. 1 (Paris: Éditions Universitaires, 1967), 40.

15. André Gaudreault, "Theatricality, Narrativity, and Trickality: Reevaluating the Cinema of Georges Méliès," trans. Paul Attallah, this volume, 31–47.

16. A. Nicholas Vardac, *Stage to Screen: Theatrical Method from Garrick to Griffith* (Cambridge, Mass.: Harvard University Press, 1949).

17. Gaudreault, "Theatricality, Narrativity, and Trickality."

18. David Mayer, *Stagestruck Filmmaker: D. W. Griffith and the American Theatre* (Iowa City: University of Iowa Press, 2009); and Ben Brewster and Lea Jacobs, *Theatre to Cinema: Stage Pictorialism and the Early Feature Film* (New York: Oxford University Press, 1997).

19. Among others, John L. Fell offered pioneering thoughts on these sources in *Film and the Narrative Tradition* (Norman: University of Oklahoma Press, 1974); Charles Musser offered his probing research in his trilogy of early cinema works *Before the Nickelodeon: Edwin S. Porter and the Edison Manufacturing Company* (Berkeley: University of California Press, 1991); *High Class Moving Pictures: Lyman H. Howe and the Forgotten Era of Traveling Exhibition, 1880–1920*, in collaboration with Carol Nelson (Princeton, N.J.: Princeton University Press, 1991); and *The Emergence of Cinema: The American Screen to 1907* (New York: Scribner's, 1990); Charlie Keil, *Early American Cinema in Transition: Story, Style, and Filmmaking, 1907–1913* (Madison: University of Wisconsin, 2001); Frank Kessler, "On Fairies and Technologies," in *Moving Images: From Edison to the Webcam*, ed. John Fullerton and Astrid Söderbergh Widding (Sydney, Australia: John Libbey, 2000), 39–46; Kessler, "In the Realm of the Fairies: Early Cinema between Attraction and Narration," *Iconics* 5 (2000): 7–26; Kessler, "La Féerie—un genre des premiers temps," in *La nascita dei generi cinematografici*, ed. Leonardo Quaresima, Alessandra Raengo, Laura Vichi (Udine, Italy: Forum, 1999), 229–238; Solomon, *Disappearing Tricks*; and André Gaudreault, *Cinéma et attraction: Pour une nouvelle histoire du cinématographe* (Paris: CNRS Éditions, 2008).

20. See for instance the analysis in Pierre Jenn, *Georges Méliès, cinéaste: Le montage cinématographique chez Georges Méliès* (Paris: Albatros, 1984), 50–53.

21. Vardac, *From Stage to Screen*, 17, 34, 70–71, and passim.

22. John Frazer, *Artificially Arranged Scenes: The Films of Georges Méliès* (Boston: G. K. Hall, 1979), 7–8.

23. André Bazin, "In Defense of Mixed Cinema," *What Is Cinema?* trans. and ed. Hugh Gray, vol. 1 (Berkeley: University of California Press, 1967), 53–76.

24. Gaudreault, "Theatricality, Narrativity, and Trickality." Musser speculates on the effect of this temporal overlap cut in Méliès on Porter's *Life of an American Fireman* in *Before the Nickelodeon*, 209. See also Frazer, *Artificially Arranged Scenes*, 96.

25. Tom Gunning, "The Long and Short of It: Centuries of Projecting Shadows from Natural Magic to the Avant-Garde," in *Art of Projection*, ed. Stan Douglas and Christopher Eamon (Ostfildern, Germany: Hatje Cantz Verlag, 2009), 28–29.

26. "A Fantastical . . . *Trip to the Moon*," this volume, 230.

27. Edward Branigan, *Point of View in the Cinema: A Theory of Narration and Subjectivity in Classical Film* (New York: Mouton, 1984), 113–114. Branigan, however, speaks of "delayed POVs," which is not quite the case here.

28. Such early point-of-view films are described and analyzed in *Ce que je vois de mon ciné: La representation du regard dans le cinéma des premiers temps*, ed. André Gaudreault (Paris: Klincksieck, 1988).

29. William Butcher, *Jules Verne: The Definitive Biography* (New York: Thunder's Mouth Press, 2006), 163.

30. Nadar's photographs in the depths of Paris and his aerial views are discussed and reproduced in Hambourg, Heilbrun, and Néagu, *Nadar*, 27–31, 108–112.

31. Raymond Bellour, "Le Machine-Cinéma," in *Les Temps des machines*, ed. Françoise Calvez, *Cinéma et littérature* 8 (Valence: Centre de Recherche et de l'Action Culturelle, 1990), 49–55.

32. "A Fantastical . . . *Trip to the Moon*," this volume, 230.

33. Walter Benjamin, "The Work of Art in the Age of its Technological Reproducibility," 2nd version, trans. Edmund Jephcott and Harry Zohn, *Selected Writings*, ed. Howard Eiland and Michael W. Jennings, vol. 3 (Cambridge, Mass.: Belknap, 2002), 119.

34. Rousseau's reaction to the famous banquet in his honor in 1908 is described in Roger Shattuck, *The Banquet Years: The Origins of the Avant-Garde in France, 1885 to World War I* (New York: Vintage, 1968). A somewhat similar banquet in Méliès's honor was given in 1929.

35. An account of the early Parisian avant-garde movement of the Incoherents contemporary with Méliès can be found in *The Spirit of Montmartre: Cabarets, Humor, and the Avant-Garde, 1875–1905*, ed. Phillip Dennis Cate and Mary Shaw (New Brunswick, N.J.: Jane Voorhees Zimmerli Art Museum, 1996).

36. Pop artist Red Grooms collaborated with filmmaker Rudy Burckhardt on the 1962 film *Shoot the Moon*, which reworks Méliès's film. Viva Paci discusses the many influences that Méliès had on the avant-garde, especially Al Razutis, in "No One-Way Ticket to the Moon," trans. Elizabeth Alsop, this volume, 201–224. I might add that more recently South African animator and artist William Kentridge's *Journey to the Moon* (2003) creates another homage to Méliès's film.

37. Ivens's life is chronicled, somewhat controversially, in Hans Schoots, *Living Dangerously: A Biography of Joris Ivens* (Amsterdam, Netherlands: Amsterdam University Press, 2000).

38. Tom Gunning, " 'Animated Pictures': Tales of Cinema's Forgotten Future, after 100 Years of Films," in *Reinventing Film Studies*, ed. Christine Gledhill and Linda Williams (London: Edward Arnold, 2000), 316–331.

7

Frank Kessler

A Trip to the Moon as *Féerie*

Ashort story by Jules Verne, first published in 1889 and describing a day in the life of an American journalist in the year 2889, opens with the intriguing remark that "in this twenty-ninth century people live right in the middle of a continuous *féerie* without even noticing it."[1] This observation linking technological and scientific progress to the magical world of fairy tales quite probably did not surprise Verne's French readers at the end of the nineteenth century when widely used expressions such as "*la fée électricité*" emphatically conjured up the image of wondrous magic to celebrate the marvels of the modern age. However, the choice of the term "*féerie*," opens up yet another dimension of Verne's metaphor, namely the realm of the spectacular. A popular stage genre throughout the nineteenth century, the *féerie* stood for a form of theatrical entertainment combining visual splendor, fantastic plots, amazing tricks, colorful ballets, and captivating music. All these wonders, on the other hand, were not the result of any kind of magic, but of stagecraft, set design, trick techniques, and a meticulously organized mise-en-scène. Verne's metaphor, thus, complexly intertwines magic and technology, fairy tales and progress, fantasy and science. This, precisely, is the context within which I propose to look at Méliès's 1902 film *A Trip to the Moon*[2]—as a *féerie*; that is, as a film drawing from a long-standing stage tradition that had also found its way into animated pictures where the *féerie* appears indeed from very early on as a generic category.[3]

The *Féerie* on the French Stage

According to a former director of the Théâtre de l'Odéon, Paul Ginisty, one of the earliest historians of the genre and author of a book on the subject published around 1910, the roots of the *féerie* reach back into the sixteenth and seventeenth centuries, when the ballets at the royal court adapted legends and fairy tales, while the so-called *pieces à machines* presented spectacular effects that were created by intricate stage mechanisms.[4] Ginisty identifies three genealogical strands of the *féerie*—ballets, fantastic or magical subject matter, and spectacular effects—which throughout the eighteenth century came together in various forms in fairground theaters as well as in the Comédie-Italienne, the Comédie-Française, and the Opéra-Comique.[5] However, what Ginisty calls the "modern *féerie*" emerged in the last years of the eighteenth century, intimately linked to melodrama, because plays of both genres were written by the same authors, and they were performed in the same theaters.[6] According to him, *Le Pied de mouton*, written by Alphonse-Louis-Dieudonné Martainville and Louis-François Ribié, which premiered at the Gaîté theater on December 6, 1806, is the "model *féerie*," a typical instance of the genre, functioning almost like a blueprint: "In fact, *Le Pied de mouton*, was done over and over again, as it combined all the secrets of the art, the struggle between the spirits, who give a charm to their protégés, the charming lover and his grotesque rival, the exploration of marvelous worlds."[7] The genre then became established as a popular entertainment in the Parisian theater district along the Boulevard du Temple. *Le Pied de mouton* was staged in various adaptations throughout the nineteenth century, and in 1907 Albert Capellani made a film version for Pathé. Indeed, many of the plays quoted by Ginisty are also known as film titles such as *Les Pilules du Diable* (1839), *Les Sept châteaux du Diable* (1844), *La Biche au bois* (1845), and *La Poule aux œufs d'or* (1848), even though stage and screen versions may have differed quite drastically.[8]

Ginisty sees Jacques Offenbach's 1875 *Le Voyage dans la lune* as "the beginning of an evolution," with a different kind of magic, namely modern technology, while *Le Voyage à travers l'impossible* (1882) introduced even something like a "scientific element."[9] As for *Les Quatre cents coups du Diable*, staged in 1904 at the Châtelet, Ginisty remarks that it is one of the plays that "while featuring charms and spirits, [is] not afraid to show modern characters and to mix echoes of contemporary life with the established rites."[10] For the period when he wrote the book, he claims, the *féerie* had more or less ceased to exist. The only hope he expresses lies with poets such as Maurice Maeterlinck and his *The Blue Bird* (1909), whose creativity might lead to yet another evolution of the genre.[11]

In the introduction to his book, however, Ginisty voices a complaint against the overall development that the *féerie* underwent, namely that it abandoned its potential as an art form to become but a "pretext for mechanical artifices," and he looks back on it rather as a touching childhood memory, the magic of which has definitely gone.[12] About one generation earlier the writer Théodore de Banville expressed an equally nostalgic sentiment in one of his stories. In 1866 already he laments the end of the *féerie* as it once used to be, blaming Guilbert de Pixérécourt for having tried to "civilize it, thus planting the first germ of its destruction."[13] He subsequently gives a description of the Théâtre de la Gaîté as it once was that provides an almost contemporary, though slightly poetic, glimpse into the stage practice of the *féerie* in the first half of the nineteenth century:

> In order to imagine it as it was then, one has to dream up some sort of a compromise between the theaters where operas are played and those small shows where we can see the pantomimes. Spectacular sets representing Heaven or Hell, and, for scenes down here on Earth, the most rugged mountainsides with streams, waterfalls, and decrepit pine trees on a cliff; complicated machinery, tricks, illusions, flights through the air, Bengal fire; armies of ballet dancers, supernumeraries, and characters amalgamating all mythology and chivalry, with their lavish and pretentious costumes, produced the overall effect of boulevard theater when that spectacle was still the only nourishment given to the people's artistic appetites.[14]

This account draws a portrait of the *féerie* as a charming, aesthetically not very ambitious form of popular entertainment, trying to impress the audience through spectacular effects and to provide them with all sorts of visual delights. De Banville quite clearly opposes the *féerie* to a more legitimate kind of theater as an art form, hence his observation that de Pixérécourt's attempt to "civilize" it, that is to bring it closer to the established norms of the dramatic stage, contributed to the genre's decline.

De Banville reiterates here a cultural dichotomy, which according to Hassan El Nouty, a literary historian and one of the pioneers of research on nineteenth-century French visual culture, reaches back into the sixteenth century. Until then, theatrical performances had presented a kind of an equilibrium between the "dramatic" and the "spectacular" (or the "literary" and the "visual"), whereas in the sixteenth century aesthetic judgments started to increasingly privilege the former at the expense of the latter.[15] In the seventeenth century, then, "two strands of theater were developing side by side, but separately: 1. One with

limited mise-en-scène and consisting mainly of speech. That is the classical theater. 2. The other, which wanted to be but a feast for the eyes.
These were the so-called *pièces à machines* such as *Naissance de Hercule*
(1649) by Rotrou."[16] In the nineteenth century, the cultural gap between
dramatic art and spectacular delights got even deeper because of the
class bias that added to the elitist condemnation of the latter. El Nouty
quotes Gustave Vapereau proclaiming, "We leave the spectacular plays
to the people and to the children."[17] Among the few defenders of the
féerie El Nouty discusses in particular the ideas of Théophile Gautier,
whose profession that "*le temps des spectacles oculaires est venu*" (the time
of visual spectacle has come) clearly belongs to a dissenting voice.[18] In
contrast, the references to childhood (Ginisty) or childishness (Vapereau)
are but two versions of the rather condescending attitude vis-à-vis the
foregrounding of visual delights on the stage. This also may account for
the conspicuous absence of the *féerie* and other popular stage genres in
the histories of nineteenth-century theater in France.

The *Féerie* from Stage to Screen

Considered as a genre, the *féerie* thus combines several features that
clearly place it within a tradition that favors the visual over the verbal, the
marvelous over the realist, the effect or the trick over drama, amazement
over intellectual engagement. All the elements that characterize this type
of stage show are brought together in a definition Arthur Pougin gives
in his important dictionary of theater terms published in 1885:

> The *féerie* is a spectacular play showing a fantastic or supernatural
> subject where the miraculous element dominates. Thanks to this
> element, which allows the play to neglect the logic of facts as
> well as ideas, the action can evolve freely in a conventional world,
> without having to worry about plausibility. Its sole objective is
> to present the splendor, the illusions and all the power that the
> luxurious staging, the most lavish costumes, the gracefulness of
> the dances, and the charms of music can provide. In other words:
> everything which a most spectacular, most strange, and immensely
> varied scenographic display can come up with to surprise, amaze,
> and enchant the audience.[19]

The *féerie*, in other words, is rather an "attractional" genre (and indeed,
some of the terms characterizing the dichotomy mentioned earlier in the
field of French theater could also describe the opposition between the

cinema of narrative integration and the cinema of attractional display as Tom Gunning and André Gaudreault define it).[20] Even though these plays do present a narrative, what is more important—what constitutes the genre's "dominant," to employ a concept derived from Russian formalists—is the wondrous spectacle, the trick, the illusion, in short: the attraction.

This does not mean that *féeries* did not present narratives, quite the contrary. The plot, however, comes second to the display of spectacular effects and other kinds of attractions.[21] In the entry on trick effects in his dictionary, Pougin explains that this hierarchization occurred at the level of the production process as well: there were in fact people specialized in the invention of elaborate trick effects that they sold to a producer or an author who then built a plot and ultimately an entire *féerie* around them.[22] This, doubtlessly, is the type of practice that Ginisty denounces in his remark quoted earlier, stating that the *féerie* too often had become but a "pretext for mechanical artifices." On the other hand, however, as Pougin notes, tricks were indeed an indispensable ingredient to the *féerie*, as they had the task to make the fantastic appear real to the eyes of the audience.[23] In the terminology Christian Metz proposed with regard to trick effects in cinema, these fall into the category of "invisible *trucage*" (in opposition to visible ones, such as slow motion, blurry images indicating distorted vision of a character, or imperceptible ones, such as the replacement of an actress or actor by a stand-in, a stunt person, and so on):

> Invisible *trucage* is another matter. The spectator could not explain how it was produced nor at exactly what point in the filmic text intervenes. It is invisible because we do not know where it is, we do not see it (whereas we see a blurred focus or a superimposition). But it is perceptible, because we perceive its presence, because we "sense" it, and because that feeling may be indispensable, according to the codes, to an accurate appreciation of the film.[24]

While Metz is analyzing the functioning of tricks in the cinema of narrative integration where, ultimately, tricks and special effects work for the benefit of either the diegetic illusion or the cinematic discourse, his observations also, *mutatis mutandis*, give an accurate account of the way such trick effects function within the context of a cinema, or a theater, of attractions (of attractional display): here, too, the spectator is to appreciate the trick *as* a trick, to understand, with regard to the diegesis, the artificially produced magic as magic the characters experienced, and at the same time to marvel at the prowess of the technicians who succeeded in performing such wonders.[25] Tricks and special effects, in other words, always have a strong "attractional" dimension, but whereas in classical narrative cinema they contribute to the spectators' absorption into the narration, genres oriented toward the spectacular, such as the *féerie*, rather aim at surprising, amazing, and astounding their audiences. Metz in fact cites *The Invisible Man* (1933) as his chief example to illustrate the functioning of "invisible *trucage*," and it suffices to compare this to the way in which similar tricks are used in J. Stuart Blackton's *The Haunted Hotel* (1907) or Segundo de Chomón's *La Maison ensorcelée* (1908) and *Une Excursion incohérente* (1909) to understand the fundamental differences between the two modes of representation.

Given the continuous search for new effects, for new ways to surprise and amaze the audience, animated pictures, too, were included in *féerie* plays. An article in the November 1896 issue of *La Nature* on Georges Demenÿ's Chronophotographe is illustrated by nine frames taken from a film that was "destined to be projected in a *féerie* at the Théâtre du Châtelet."[26] The play in question was *La Biche au bois*; two 58 mm, hand-colored prints of the film actually survive in the collections of the Cinémathèque française and another one at the National Film and Television Archive in Bradford, England.[27] Similarly, in 1905 Georges Méliès created a film for the stage performance of *Les 400 coups du Diable* that he integrated one year later in a film advertised as a "grande féerie en 35 tableaux"[28] with the slightly modified title *Les Quat'cents farces du Diable* (*The Merry Frolics of Satan*).

As a matter of fact, the first films marketed as *féeries* appeared quite early in French sales catalogs. In 1899 already Méliès advertised his film *Cinderella* as a "grand and extraordinary *féerie* in twenty tableaux."[29] And among the categories listed in the Pathé-Frères sales catalogs from 1903 onward one heading grouped *Féeries et contes*, distinguishing thus between *féeries* on the one hand, and filmic adaptations of fairy tales on the other.[30]

The *Féerie* as a Cinematic Genre

Even though generic frontiers are notoriously difficult to establish, a problem that is even more complex in the field of early cinema, several formal elements seem to distinguish the *féerie* from the fairy tale film. Following the stage model, in cinematic *féeries*, ballet scenes suspend the line of action, as in both the 1902 and 1907 versions of Pathé's *Ali Baba et les quarante voleurs*, directed by, respectively, Ferdinand Zecca and Segundo de Chomón. In the scene where Ali Baba's brother Cassim has to hide in the cave because of the unexpected return of the forty thieves, his being discovered and executed is preceded by a dance performed by a group of women who, in the 1902 film, are part of the thieves' entourage, whereas in the 1907 remake they emerge from the depth of the cave. There is no narrative motivation for these ballets, nor are they mentioned in the *Arabian Nights* tale. A second scene, however, is part of the original story: Ali Baba's faithful servant, having discovered that the oil merchant visiting her master is in fact the gang leader in disguise, performs a dance in the course of which she stabs the villain with a dagger. But just like the ballet in the brigands' cave, her dance, too, is staged in such a way that it is oriented toward the camera—and thus the spectator in the theater—and not the diegetic audience to which it is supposedly addressed.

Comparing the 1902 and 1908 versions of Pathé's *La Belle au bois dormant*, the former co-directed by Lucien Nonguet and Ferdinand Zecca, and the latter directed Albert Capellani (or Lucien Nonguet, according to another source), the difference between a *féerie* and a fairy tale film becomes quite obvious. While the 1908 film more or less follows the story line of Charles Perrault's version of the tale with many shots being filmed outdoors, the earlier adaptation adds many episodes to the story. Before he finally discovers the castle of Sleeping Beauty, the prince has to travel to various places, and all of them provide the possibility to present special attractions that go beyond the relatively few trick effects that are needed for a representation of the tale: a ballet in the Kingdom of the Fairies, a spectacular fairy grotto, trick effects in an enchanted cottage, and so on. Furthermore, the later film often uses outdoor scenery, whereas Zecca and Nonguet make abundant use of painted backdrops. And while the 1908 version ends with the wedding at the castle,[31] the 1902 one adopts the conventional closing *tableau* of the stage *féerie*, the so-called apotheosis.[32]

The apotheosis is indeed a special feature, functioning as something like a *mise en abyme* of the splendor and opulence the play seeks to display. Pougin gives the following definition of the term: "This is how the final tableau is called in a *féerie*, in which is offered a most splendid and lavish display of stagecraft. Here the art of the set designer, the costume designer, and the director are exhibited to their fullest degree. . . . [A]ll this makes for a superb spectacle, which will enchant the audience and at the same time affect their senses so that it inevitably will bring success."[33] In *féerie* films the apotheosis is generally announced by an intertitle, and in many cases it is presented in colors. Obviously, *féeries* as such are a genre where the spectacular qualities of colorization are frequently to be found, but the apotheosis is indeed a textual element where this feature is especially important. Thus a Pathé sales catalog of 1902 announces with regard to *La Belle au bois dormant*: "The last *tableau*, or apotheosis, is the only one to be hand-colored."[34]

In addition, the *féerie* as a cinematic genre had a strong presence in the contemporary (French) trade press, the sales catalogs of various companies, and in the way a producer such as Méliès presented himself to his clients, his audience, and his peers. In his famous contribution to the 1907 *Annuaire général et international de la photographie*, Méliès explicitly states that he immediately used his (somewhat legendary) chance discovery of the possibilities of the substitution splice to film his first *féeries*.[35] The term thus circulates in that period in the communication circuits between producers, exhibitors, and spectators, functioning as a generic marker, even though providing a clear-cut definition would probably have been difficult for any of those who used it. However, following Rick Altman's important study on the concept of genre, one could say that, nevertheless, there are recognizable markers at a semantic level (such as, for instance, the diegetic universe, which might be characterized as fantastic or marvelous), at a syntactic level (elements such as the ballets and the apotheosis), and at a pragmatic level (with regard to the way the term functions in contemporary discourses).[36] In that respect, the *féerie* can indeed be considered a genre in early cinema.

A Trip to the Moon as Féerie

So what does it mean to approach Méliès's *A Trip to the Moon* as a *féerie*? In the first instance, this means to not look at the film as a "precursor" of whatever ulterior phenomenon (classical narrative cinema, science fiction, fantastic adventure films, and so forth) but as part of a "cultural series" (as André Gaudreault would call it) that reaches back into the nineteenth century.[37] At the same time, *féerie* films, and *A Trip to the Moon* in particular, while participating in this tradition, or cultural series, also transform it formally as well as thematically. They are, in many respects, a different format, but still visibly rooted in the generic context to which they belong.

In terms of Ginisty's historical overview, *A Trip to the Moon*, just as Offenbach's *Voyage dans la lune*, belongs to the type of *féerie* that combines modern elements with more traditional ones. In this respect, the film presents a rather incoherent diegetic universe, the components of which are juxtaposed without trying to motivate this peculiar kind of blend at the level of a narrative logic. Just as in a stage *féerie* the guiding principle here seems to be the possibility to present a series of spectacular effects.

A 1903 distribution catalog for Star-Film productions in the United States lists the titles of the thirty scenes or "pictures" of which *A Trip to the Moon* is composed.[38] The first one, "The Scientific Congress at the Astronomic Club," already presents the tension between the seemingly modern and the fairy-tale–like fantastic elements that characterize Méliès's film. The scientists participating in the meeting appear in pointed hats and wide robes, looking rather like wizards or ancient astronomers. Young servants enter the meeting hall carrying telescopes, which a little later transform into seats. A comic element is introduced when one of the distinguished members of the Astronomic Club gets into a fight with Professor Barbenfouillis, who proposes the project, and both behave like quarreling schoolboys. When finally the group of men is formed that will take the trip to the moon, they change into relatively modern (but for 1902 still rather old-fashioned looking) travel clothes (Scene 2: Planning the Trip. Appointing the Explorers and Servants. Farewell). The following pictures (Scenes 3 and 4) show the workshop where the projectile is constructed and the foundries where the "monster gun" is cast and thus transfer the action into a modern industrialized environment in an attitude that is both admiring and ironic. The continuous changes in tone and atmosphere clearly indicate right from the start that *A Trip to the Moon* is anything but a faithful adaptation of Jules Verne's novel.

The following scenes (5–7) not only depict the explorers climbing into the rocket and the charging and firing of the huge gun, but also provide the occasion for the corps de ballet, appearing as bluejackets, to display their legs. Again, the generic conventions supersede narrative logic: instead of soldiers (as one would expect from the catalog description, detailing "March Past the Gunners" and "Saluting the Flag" as two events occurring in picture 7), we see a group of ballet dancers. The trip through space and then the famous image of the rocket hitting the moon right in the eye (Scenes 8 and 9; the French expression "*dans l'œil*" is the equivalent of "bull's-eye") is another abrupt change in the mode of representation or, more precisely, in the way the diegesis is constructed. The moon now turns briefly into an anthropomorphic character, disrupting the type of diegetic universe the earlier scenes had established. The landing on the moon and earth rising above its horizon (Scenes 10 and 11); the snowstorm, the descent into the crater, and the discovery of the mushroom grotto (Scenes 13–15); then the encounter and fight with the Selenites, the captivity and their being brought before the king, the escape, the chase, and the departure (Scenes 16–21)—all these episodes are again part of the fantastic diegesis of the *féerie*, whereas Scene 12—"The Dream (the Bolies, the Great Bear, Phoebus, the Twin Stars, Saturn)"—although motivated as a dreamlike apparition, again anthropomorphizes these various celestial bodies. And after the return to earth, the descent to the bottom of the ocean, and the rescue (Scenes 22–25), the remaining tableaux (Scenes 27–30) are dedicated to the celebration of the explorers' exploits and function in a way similar to the customary apotheosis.

A Trip to the Moon is thus indeed a film that, even though it does not take the viewer to the realm of the fairies, is clearly situated within the realm of the *féerie*. The characters (whose names already underscore this genealogy: Barbenfouillis, Alcofrisbas, Nostradamus, Oméga, Micro-mégas, and Parafaragaramus sound rather similar to, for instance, some of the characters' names in Offenbach's *opera-féerie*: Cosmos, Microscope, Cosinus, Grosbedon, and Oméga) and their adventures are subordinate to the wealth of effects and spectacular moments which the film con-tains: substitution splices for transformations and the "exploding" Sel-enites, pyrotechnical tricks for eruptions, steam, smoke, and flames (the foundries, the craters), changes of scale for the trip through space, the simulation of an underwater scene, stage machinery for changing sets and props, group arrangements and parades of the ballet dancers, the stars and planets, comic and fantastic images (the rocket hitting the moon in the eye), fantastic costumes and sceneries, and so on. The characteristic elements of the genre are more or less all present in this film. Looking at *A Trip to the Moon* as a *féerie* thus not only leads to a more accurate understanding of the film in terms of its historical embedding in a cul-tural tradition, but also to more insights into its structural composition and the functioning of its various components with regard to the text as a whole.

More in particular, even though *A Trip to the Moon* clearly presents a narrative with a beginning, a middle, and an end—the adventures of a group of people flying to the moon and back—this narrative sequence does not take place within a coherent diegetic universe, not even if one allows for many fantastic elements in the story. The only logic that is capable of tying everything together is the logic of the genre. The "Right in the Eye!" tableau, for instance, cannot be integrated into the narrative logic, the anthropomorphization of the moon, its all of a sudden having a face and being hit in the eye by the rocket, is incompatible with the tableaux that precede and follow it. However, once this image is seen as an attraction meant to surprise and amuse the spectator within the *féerie* tradition, it is entirely functional in that context. *A Trip to the Moon*, in this respect, plainly illustrates André Gaudreault's contention that Méliès's work belongs to the cultural series of the *féerie* as much as to the emerging new cultural series of what he calls *cinématographie-attraction*.[39]

Between Jules Verne and the *Féerie*

In a 1902 program leaflet of the Cirque féerique Anderson, *A Trip to the Moon* is announced as a "Grande Féerie en 30 tableaux, tirée du roman de Jules Verne."[40] Even though, as Thierry Lefebvre convincingly demonstrates in his above-mentioned analysis, the traces of Verne's work in the film are rather superficial, the explicit reference to it in such a leaflet indicates that contemporary audiences did not perceive the coupling of the fantastic world of the *féerie* with the rationalist nineteenth-century tales of technical progress as a complete mismatch. In fact, Méliès himself continued to exploit the possibilities of this combination in his 1904 *An Impossible Voyage*, which again takes up the title of a Jacques Offenbach work and a reference to Jules Verne. In terms of Hassan El Nouty's study of the French stage in the nineteenth century, the common denominator between them is their orientation toward the spectacular.

Interestingly, a 1907 Pathé production also connects Verne and the *féerie*, even though the film initially seems to focus exclusively on the writer and his books. In *Le Petit Jules Verne*, directed by Gaston Velle and marketed as a *scène à trucs*, a little boy goes to bed and secretly continues reading after his mother has turned out the lights. He falls asleep and starts to dream. A portrait of Jules Verne and his name appear in a vignette above the bed. The dream scene first looks somewhat Méliès-like—the sun, the moon, and a meteor appear. The boy then seems awake and climbs into a balloon that takes him into the air. He looks through a telescope down to earth, and what he sees is represented by nonfiction images in vignettes. Then a storm occurs and he falls into the ocean. He sinks through underwater scenery with corals, shells, and some jellyfish. The corals are transformed into women's heads that subsequently become dancing ballerinas. The jellyfish, too, turn into young women. Then the women disappear, and an octopus attacks the boy. He awakes from the fight, entangled in his bedclothes, which he pulls to pieces with the feathers flying all around.[41]

In this film, the *féerie* elements are part of a fantastic dream triggered by the boy reading a Jules Verne book. Otherwise, however, *Le Petit Jules Verne* presents a relatively tightly organized narrative, combining actuality pictures with artificial sceneries, and in the end rather evokes the abrupt awakenings of Little Nemo from his nightmares. Here the *féerie* and its ballets can be understood almost as a quote or a reference to the genre, and it is quite remarkable that this connection is made in such a context that by no means calls for it. It is almost like a reminiscence of the earlier coalition between Jules Verne's novelistic imagination and the fantasy world of the *féerie*, which is so powerfully present in Méliès's *A Trip to the Moon*.

Notes

Author's note: I would like to thank my research assistant Lotte Harmsen for her help in tracing relevant material for this chapter and Sabine Lenk for comments and suggestions.

1. Jules Verne, *La Journée d'un journaliste américain en 2889* (Paris: Nautilus, 2001), 29. (Unless stated otherwise, all translations from French sources are mine.)

2. For possible literary and other sources for *A Trip to the Moon*, see Thierry Lefebvre, "*A Trip to the Moon*: A Composite Film," trans. Timothy Barnard, this volume, 49–63. I would like, however, to shift the focus from such intertextual relations to a genre perspective.

3. See my "La Féerie—un genre des premiers temps," in *La nascita dei generi cinematografici*, ed. Leonardo Quaresima, Alessandra Raengo, and Laura Vichi (Udine, Italy: Forum, 1999), 229–238.

4. Paul Ginisty, *La Féerie* (Paris: Louis Michaud, n.d. [1910]), 12–24.

5. See Ginisty, *La Féerie*, chaps. 4 and 5. Ginisty of course concentrates on the French situation. In a more international perspective one could also look at, for instance, the Austrian *zauberspiel* and the English tradition of the pantomime, which present both certain similarities with the *féerie*.

6. See Ginisty, *La Féerie*, 66. Ginisty, who slightly earlier had written a book on melodrama, too, claims that in fact the story lines in both genres are quite similar, the main difference being that the role of providence in melodrama is taken over by a fairy in the *féerie*, whereas the villain's part is played by some kind of evil spirit. But obviously, the *féerie* presents everything in a light and comical mood.

7. Ginisty, *La Féerie*, 96.

8. I have discussed such differences with regard to the stage and screen versions of *Ali Baba* in my "In the Realm of the Fairies: Early Cinema between Attraction and Narration," *Iconics* 5 (2000): 7–26; see esp. 11–14.

9. Ginsity, *La Féerie*, 214.

10. Ginisty, *La Féerie*, 216–217.

11. Ginisty, *La Féerie*, chap. 13.

12. Ginisty, *La Féerie*, 9.

13. Théodore de Banville, *Les Parisiennes de Paris* (Paris: Michel Lévy Frères, 1866), 207.

14. De Banville, *Les Parisiennes*, 208–209.

15. Hassan El Nouty, *Théâtre et pré-cinéma: Essai sur la problématique du spectacle au XIXe siècle* (Paris: Eds. A.-G. Nizet, 1978), 16.

16. El Nouty, *Théâtre et pré-cinéma*, 17.

17. El Nouty, *Théâtre et pré-cinéma*, 66–67.

18. El Nouty, *Théâtre et pré-cinéma*, 68.

19. Arthur Pougin, *Dictionnaire historique et pittoresque du théâtre et des arts qui s'y rattachent*, 2 vols. (1885; repr. Plan-de-la-Tour: Eds. d'Aujourd'hui, 1995), 360.

20. See Tom Gunning, "The Cinema of Attractions: Early Film, Its Spectator and the Avant-Garde," in *Early Cinema: Space, Frame, Narrative*, ed. Thomas Elsaesser with Adam Barker (London: British Film Institute, 1990), 56–62; André Gaudreault and Tom Gunning, "Early Cinema as a Challenge to Film History," trans. Joyce Goggin and Wanda Strauven, in *The Cinema of Attractions Reloaded*, ed. Wanda Strauven (Amsterdam, Netherlands: Amsterdam University Press, 2006), 365–380; original French version published in 1989. For my rephrasing of the original couple of concepts see my "The Cinema of Attractions as *Dispositif*" in *The Cinema of Attractions Reloaded*, 57–69.

21. I discuss this point in detail with regard to *féerie* films in my "In the Realm of the Fairies."

22. Pougin, *Dictionnaire historique*, 748. Interestingly, in a retrospective text written in 1932 Méliès describes his own work from the first decade of the century in similar terms. According to him, the story line in those days was but a pretext to link the various tricks. See Georges Méliès, "The Importance of the Script," trans. Paul Hammond, this volume, 241–243. See also André Gaudreault, "Theatricality, Narrativity, and Trickality: Reevaluating the Cinema of Georges Méliès," trans. Paul Attalah, this volume, 31–47, where Gaudreault discusses the role of narrativity in Méliès's films.

23. Pougin, *Dictionnaire historique*. The range of trick effects that could be obtained on the stage is amazing, indeed. Katherine Singer Kovács, "Georges Méliès and the *Féerie*," in *Film before Griffith*, ed. John L. Fell (Berkeley: University of California Press, 1983), 244–257, points to the similarities between nineteenth-century stage effects and the tricks in the films of Méliès. See also the descriptions offered by Ginisty, *La Féerie*, 173–177, and, as an important contemporary source, M. J. Moynet, *L'Envers du théâtre: Machines et décorations* (Paris: Hachette, 1874).

24. Christian Metz, "*Trucage* and the Film," trans. Françoise Meltzer, *Critical Inquiry* 3, no. 4 (1977): 664.

25. On the complex relationship between tricks and the performance of magic by conjurors on the stage around the turn of the century see Matthew Solomon, "Up-to-Date Magic: Theatrical Conjuring and the Trick Film," *Theatre Journal* 58, no. 4 (2006): 595–615.

26. G. Mareschal, "Le Chronophotographe de M. G. Demenÿ," *La Nature*, Nov 21, 1896, 393.

27. See Laurent Mannoni, "Une Féerie de 1896: *La Biche au bois*," *Cinémathèque*, no. 10 (1996): 117–123.

28. The translation of the French term "*tableau*" in contemporary British and American sales catalogs varies. Sometimes they use "picture," sometimes "scene," and sometimes even the French term "tableau." I therefore will use these terms indiscriminately. In French, however, "*scène*" rather referred to a film as a whole (as is the case with Pathé catalog categories such as "*scènes de plein air*" or "*scènes à trucs*"), whereas "*tableau*" denotes a subsection of a staged film.

29. Jacques Malthête, *Méliès, images et illusions* (Paris: Exporégie, 1996), 219.

30. See Henri Bousquet, *Catalogue Pathé des années 1896 à 1914*, vol. 4 [1896–1906] ([Bures-sur-Yvette]: Henri Bousquet, 1996), 1.

31. This is the case at least in the print held by the Netherlands Filmmuseum that was screened at the 2005 edition of the Il Cinema Ritrovato festival in Bologna. According to Henri Bousquet, *Catalogue Pathé des années 1896 à 1914*, vol. 1 [1907–1908–1909] ([Bures-sur-Yvette]: Henri Bousquet, 1993), 67, the Pathé sales catalog mentions an apotheosis, but not the wedding scene, so it could be that here the ending of the tale is coinciding with the apotheosis, whereas in a *féerie* the apotheosis comes after the end of the narrative.

32. See Bousquet, *Catalogue Pathé*, vol. 4, 873, and Bousquet, *Catalogue Pathé*, vol. 1, 67. According to Bousquet both versions were announced as *féeries*, the formal differences between both indicate however that the later film clearly stays closer to the fairy tale.

33. Pougin, *Dictionnaire historique*, 45–46.

34. Henri Bousquet and Riccardo Redi, *Pathé Frères: Les films de la production Pathé*, vol. 1, *Quaderni di cinema*, no. 37 (1988): 79.

35. Georges Méliès, "Cinematographic Views," trans. Stuart Liebman, in *French Film Theory and Criticism: A History/Anthology*, ed. Richard Abel, vol. 1 (Princeton, N.J.: Princeton University Press, 1988), 35–47.

36. See Rick Altman, *Film/Genre* (London: British Film Institute, 1999).

37. See André Gaudreault, "*Les Vues cinématographiques* selon Georges Méliès, ou: comment Mitry et Sadoul avaient peut-être raison d'avoir tort (même si c'est surtout Deslandes qu'il faut relire). . . ," in *Georges Méliès, l'illusionniste fin de siècle*, ed. Jacques Malthête and Michel Marie (Paris: Presses de la Sorbonne Nouvelle, 1997), 111–131. See also Gaudreault's *Cinéma et attraction: Pour une nouvelle histoire du cinématographe* (Paris: CNRS Éditions, 2008).

38. See "A Fantastical . . . *Trip to the Moon*," 227–228, this volume. An identical list of scenes appears in the British distribution catalog of the Charles Urban Trading Co., *Revised List of High-Class Original Copyrighted Bioscope Films*, February 1905, 282. Here the film is announced as "An extraordinary Bioscope Series in 30 pictures." See also the description of the film in Jacques Malthête, *Méliès, images et illusions*, 222–224.

39. Gaudreault, *Cinéma et attraction*, 115–116, 156–158.

40. Reproduced in *Méliès, magie et cinéma*, ed. Jacques Malthête and Laurent Mannoni (Paris: Paris-Musées, 2002), 176. Obviously, the reference to Verne here also serves promotional ends.

41. The film was screened during the 2007 Il Cinema Ritrovato festival in Bologna. See also Bousquet, *Catalogue Pathé*, vol. 1, 44.

8

RICHARD ABEL

A Trip to the Moon as an American Phenomenon

The elaborate story film is a comparatively recent development. One of the earliest that I recall at the present moment was Méliès' "Trip to the Moon," a work that deserves the highest credit when one considers the meager facilities for producing elaborate effects at that time, and the originality called for by such a production.

THIS RARE TRIBUTE TO *A Trip to the Moon* comes near the very end of George Kleine's lengthy 1910 article on nineteenth-century developments in optical projection that eventually led to motion pictures.[1] What Kleine does not mention, however, is that during the time of the film's initial circulation in the United States, there were very few references to the film's maker or to its French origin. In that motion pictures were a relatively new, ephemeral phenomenon in 1902–1903— one of up to a dozen acts on a vaudeville bill, an enticing illustration for a traveling lecturer's program, or an evening entertainment novelty at a summer chautauqua—this absence was not unusual. The attraction for audiences, at least according to advertisements and other publicity, came from the projection apparatus, the exhibition service, or the lecturer/ entertainer.[2] Although a global phenomenon, ever since the Lumière company had demonstrated its apparatus in almost every region of the globe, motion pictures often were inscribed within the broad cultural context of a particular nation, country, or region.[3] This was certainly the case in the United States, where spectacular instances of technological modernity—increasingly framed by imperialistic ambitions following the Spanish-American War (1898–1899)—could be experienced at world's fairs and all kinds of lesser amusement venues. As both a fantasy story and commercial apparition of technological modernity, Méliès's film circulated among a diverse range of popular entertainments called "Trip to the Moon," all of which were either accepted as or transformed into "American" phenomena—as if scrubbed of any "foreign contaminant."[4]

The American Cultural Landscape of "A Trip to the Moon"

Common knowledge has it that Méliès's *A Trip to the Moon* owed much of its narrative to two prior works of fiction, Jules Verne's *From the Earth to the Moon* (1865) and II. G. Wells's *The First Men in the Moon* (1901). Both novels, and particularly Verne's, probably would have been familiar to a range of U.S. readers. *From the Earth to the Moon* was translated into English several times in the 1870s and available, sometimes retitled *A Trip to the Moon*, as one of dozens of free books in magazine or newspaper subscription campaigns such as that of the *Newark Daily Advocate* in 1895.[5] For its part, *The First Men in the Moon* was being favorably reviewed by late 1901, even in newspapers such as the *Atlanta Constitution*.[6] Some Americans could have been familiar as well with Verne's story, however, through an 1875 operetta, also titled *A Trip to the Moon*, with music composed by Jacques Offenbach, or through Adolphe d'Ennery's melodrama adaptation.[7] The operetta, for instance, was popular enough at the Tivoli in Oakland that, in June 1896, the show was held over for an extra week.[8] From Wisconsin to Texas, other folks would have been familiar with the American Travesty Company's tour of John Gilbert's "Off the Earth" or "A Trip to the Moon," billed as a "fantastic operatic travesty" starring Eddie Foy.[9] This "lunar travesty" even poked fun at the growing trend of mass consumption: "The sublunary transactions of the play occur in a department store where everything is on sale from stamps to steamboats, and where cries of 'X Cash' mingle with the girole [?] of the saleswoman and the unconventional specialties of the customers."[10] The dream of traveling to the moon was so widespread by the turn of the last century that a teacher in Upper Montclair, New Jersey, asked her students "to write an original story of a trip to the moon," and the one written by eleven-year-old Marion Eloise Serffer was printed in newspapers as far away as Massachusetts.[11]

The most important precedent for Méliès's film, and what greatly heightened its initial appeal, however, came in a major attraction at the 1901 Pan-American Exposition in Buffalo. An intriguing segue to that attraction came in one of the many newspaper articles on the slightly prior 1900 Paris Exposition. Billed as "the scientific wonder of wonders," this was "the great Lunar telescope" that promised to "be less trouble than Jules Verne's imaginary trip to the moon to bring Luna down to earth."[12] For the Pan-American Exposition's midway, Frederic Thompson and Elmer "Skip" Dundy created a wonderment that would outdo the Lunar telescope and offer a "realization" of Verne's and Wells's imaginary voyages. Their attraction, a dramatic cyclorama ride dubbed A Trip to the Moon, proved to be a spectacular "eye-catcher" and superb "coiner." To lure visitors to Buffalo, the exposition organizers also heavily promoted A Trip to the Moon in small and midsize city newspapers across the country. As early as the summer of 1900, several papers in Pennsylvania, for instance, printed much the same story of the cyclorama—"one of the midway illusions that will excite wonder and interest"—accompanied by a line drawing of the building's entrance and, in one case, a model of the spaceship.[13] Other papers from Fort Wayne to Des Moines published

Figure 8-1. A Trip to the Moon, Pan-American Exposition, 1900.

a full-page story, "The Wonders of the Pan-American Exposition," in which one of the two attractions featured in both line drawings and text was A Trip to the Moon, described as "one of the most novel . . . of new wonders" stretching over the midway's half-mile length.[14] According to this story, visitors would board the spaceship Luna, fly above the earth's surface, voyage through the starry heavens, land on the lunar surface, take a guided tour of the Man in the Moon's palaces (where, it was assumed, "ladies [would be] especially interested in the show windows of the moon shop"), and return to earth safe and satisfied. Unlike the "savage" realm of the Selenites in Méliès's film, the cyclorama's moon world incorporated the consuming desires of the earlier travesty show.

When the Pan-American Exposition finally opened in June 1901, newspaper stories often paid more attention to the midway amusements than to the more educational exhibits in the Albright Gallery of Art, the Temple of Music, or the New York state building.[15] They also consistently mentioned and often praised A Trip to the Moon as one of the most popular attractions. Fortuitously located near the entrance, it was "about the first trip you take when you reach the Midway," wrote one visitor from Oshkosh, Wisconsin, and "everybody does [it]," added another from Hayward, California.[16] Among them was Nebraska Senator and former presidential candidate William Jennings Bryan, who, while extolling the beauty and noble purpose of the exposition, with his family took in the midway shows, notably A Trip to the Moon.[17] Although "many in the audience [found] the effects so realistic," according to Robert Rydell, that they "suffered from motion sickness," the editor of the *Connellsville Courier* (Pennsylvania) was struck with awe in a lengthy description of his own tour of this "wonderful illusion," and the *Syracuse Post-Standard* reprinted a *New York Herald* story that singled out A Trip to the Moon (its ingenuity worthy of Verne and Wells) as one of the midway's "most startling illusions—wonderful combinations of electricity and mechanism—signal triumphs of the switchboard age."[18] As late as October, the *New Castle News* (Pennsylvania) featured a special story about "the sights awaiting tourists who take 'A Trip to the Moon,' on Frederic Thompson's airship 'Luna,' " accompanied by a line drawing of "a street in Moon City, with the palace of the Man in the Moon in the background."[19] Well before the Exposition closed in November 1901, Thompson and Dundy already were licensing "a theatrical company" to tour a smaller version of the cyclorama to local fairs and carnivals, but they themselves had even bigger plans.[20]

Those plans had a partner in George Tilyou, who built Steeplechase Park on Coney Island in 1897. When Tilyou visited the Pan-American Exposition, looking for new attractions, he "was captivated," John Kasson

Figure 8-2. A Trip to the Moon (inside attraction), 1901.

writes, by A Trip to the Moon.[21] An offer of hefty profits quickly convinced
Thompson and Dundy to move the cyclorama to Steeplechase Park for
the 1902 season, and the relocation at first proved costly when a March
snowstorm destroyed the newly erected building.[22] Despite this calamity
and an unusually wet summer, according to Edo McCullough, the park,
"thanks to A Trip to the Moon, did handsomely."[23] So handsomely
that, coincident with the release of the Méliès film, Thompson and
Dundy could purchase the old Sea Lion Park nearby, tear it down, and
construct an even more elaborate "mysterious palace of play" called

Luna Park to rival Steeplechase.[24] A Trip to the Moon was intended as a stellar attraction in this new "White City" park, and, before being electrocuted for killing a trainer (filmed to promote direct current by Edison in 1903), an elephant named Topsy was given the task of pushing the main building three-quarters of a mile to the new site.[25] Thompson and Dundy enlarged the original cyclorama as a crucial part of their plan to further rejuvenate Coney Island, and the press elevated Luna into a kind of permanent New York World's Fair.[26] A Trip to the Moon fit perfectly into what Kasson described as the new park's "illusions of extravagance and ostentatious display . . . its orgy of ebullient forms, bright colors, and sumptuous ornament."[27] Thompson himself provided the rationale: "Everything must be different from ordinary experience. What is presented to [visitors] must have life, action, motion, sensation, surprise, shock, swiftness or else comedy."[28] So successful was the "old" attraction over the course of the next three years that he had to revoke his initial decision to remove it in late 1905, partly because it was simply too painful to abandon the "child" that had "started him on his career."[29]

At the same time that A Trip to the Moon was drawing so many crowds at Steeplechase Park, not one but several smaller versions of the attraction were touring local fairs and carnivals. Those tours were particularly popular in the Midwest throughout the summer.[30] One of the earliest appearances, for instance, came one week early in June 1902, at the Elks' Carnival in Dayton, Ohio, where a newspaper description made it closely resemble the original at the Pan-American Exposition.[31] Other venues included the Merchants' Grand Street Carnival in Benton Harbor, Michigan; the Elks' Carnival in Lima, Ohio; the Knights of Pythias Grand Carnival Jubilee in Mansfield, Ohio; and the Fall Festival in Fort Wayne, Indiana.[32] That fall, A Trip to the Moon could be found further south among the attractions at the Interstate Fair in Atlanta, where another newspaper story reminded fair visitors of its "phenomenal run at the Pan-American exposition and at Coney Island," and at the Seawall Carnival in Galveston, Texas.[33] Once Thompson and Dundy's enlarged cyclorama was established at Luna, the smaller attraction continued to tour, but to fewer venues. It reappeared in Des Moines, Iowa, for instance, at the Iowa State Fair in August 1903, but a severe storm destroyed the tent in which the ride was housed, allowing a reporter to imagine that "it had departed in earnest for some of the celestial planets, and would not come down in time to enable the proprietor to operate on the public."[34] A year later, however, it settled down intact for a week at the Merchants' Free Street Fair in Iowa City.[35] In one form or another, the story of A Trip to the Moon remained so popular that now amateur groups even took up producing stage versions, probably drawn from the Gilbert travesty. For three nights in January 1905, for instance, the Amusement Club in Athens, Ohio, staged their version of "Trip to the Moon"; two months later the Fine Arts Fakirs Association opened an exhibit hall at the John Crouse College of Fine Arts in Syracuse, one of whose rooms was devoted to "A Trip to the Moon"; and for two nights in October that year the YMCA in Piqua, Ohio, mounted a "gorgeous spectacular production" under that name in May's Opera House.[36] In the summer of 1906, even the 4-Paw-Sells Circus came up with a "most daring and dreadful feat" called Salvo's Trip to the Moon, in which riders plunged down a "precipitous roadway," past a "delicately poised and frail shaped imitation of the moon," and then miraculously through an unnerving "meteoric wheel."[37]

A Trip to the Moon, the Motion Picture

Given a cultural landscape in which most Americans, even in small towns, would have read about, seen, or even experienced one or more amusements that represented some kind of imaginary journey to the moon that—with the exception of Jules Verne (who was popular globally)—was assumed to be "American," motion picture audiences probably could not have been better prepared for the arrival of Méliès's spectacle film. And the French magician turned filmmaker most likely would have had some inkling of such propitious conditions before producing his *A Trip to the Moon* in the summer of 1902. Moreover, something over which Méliès had no control made those conditions even more conducive to his film's reception.

Three years earlier, trade press ads for both American Vitagraph and Lubin had included among their motion picture "headline attractions" for summer parks a film entitled either "The Man in the Moon or the Astrologer's Dream" or "The Astrologer's Dream and Trip to the Moon."[38] Uncredited, not unexpectedly (Lubin's film also was a dupe), this title most likely was Méliès's *The Astronomer's Dream or the Man in the Moon* (1898), in which the moon suddenly looms as a monstrous head filling an astronomer's study window, swallows him, and spits out the indigestible bits, from which he magically is reconstituted by a benevolent moon goddess. When this film appeared in vaudeville houses, chautauquas, and fairs, however, its title always turned into *Trip to the Moon.* In October 1899, the San Antonio Fair had this *Trip to the Moon* paired with a version of *The Passion Play,* "on exhibition at the great entrance of the Main building"; a month later the same pair appeared in the city's St. Joseph's Hall.[39] In April 1900, the Music Hall in Lowell, Massachusetts, one week had as its "closing attraction . . . a series of moving pictures of scenes of the Sixth Massachusetts regiment's experiences during the late war, and 'A Trip to the Moon.' "[40] In July 1900, on a Waterloo, Iowa, chautauqua program, the same film was shown with a more recent fairy play also produced by the unidentified Méliès, *Cinderella* (1899).[41] Over the course of the next two years, especially after Edison finally offered its own dupe of Méliès's film for sale,[42] this *Trip to the Moon* remained a staple of exhibition services supplying vaudeville houses. In October 1901, a three-day program at Myers Grand in Janesville, Wisconsin, included "the biograph moving pictures telling the story of 'The Trip to the Moon.' "[43] A month later, Brown's Opera House in Waterloo featured a special three-night program featuring the Kinodrome service, one of whose films was *A Trip to the Moon*.[44] Finally, in July 1902, the amusement park in Lincoln, Nebraska, advertised a weeklong evening program of "wonderful pictures" with *A Trip to the Moon* joining *The Great Passion Play*, *Cinderella*, and, for "the first time," the volcanic eruption, *Mt. Pelee in Action*.[45]

When Méliès's *A Trip to the Moon* (260 meters in length) eventually was imported into the United States, in October 1902, both Edison and American Biograph advertised that they had copies for sale. However, the prints had slightly different titles and varied slightly in length: Edison's was *A Voyage to the Moon* (850 feet), and Biograph's was *A Trip to the Moon* (800 feet).[46] Only Biograph identified theirs (again Edison's print was a dupe) as "Méliès's Magnificent Spectacle" and offered an "illustrated bulletin, with full details," presumably as a lecture (in English) to accompany the film.[47] Beginning in November, *A Trip to the Moon* (as it usually was titled) began to feature on vaudeville programs across the country—from the Keith circuit in the Northeast and Midwest and Orpheum circuit (headquartered in Chicago) in the Midwest and West to Grover's Garden in Lynn, Massachusetts, the Casto Theatre in Lowell, Massachusetts or Huber's 14th Street Museum in New York City.[48] By March 1903, the film even was being shown free for shoppers (presumably women and their children) in department store recital halls such as that at Simpson Crawford, "New York's Finest Retail Store."[49] When, in early April 1903, Keith's Union Square Theatre (New York City) switched its exhibition service from American Biograph to American Vitagraph, one of its first programs included *A Trip to the Moon*—"the best moving picture film which I have ever seen," reported manager S. K. Hodgdon. "It held the audience to the finish and was received with a hearty round of applause."[50] Yet during these first six months of *A Trip to the Moon*'s circulation, T. L. Tally, who repeatedly presented the film at his Electric Theater in Los Angeles, was the only exhibitor to name Méliès (from Paris) as its maker.[51]

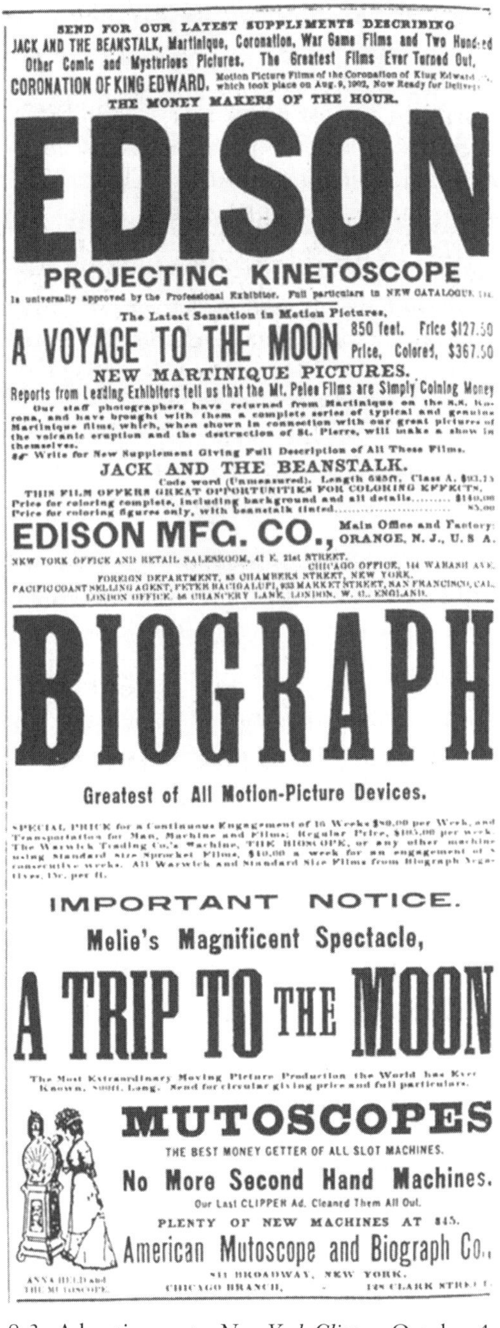

SEND FOR OUR LATEST SUPPLIMENTS DESCRIBING
JACK AND THE BEANSTALK, Martinique, Coronation, War Game Films and Two Hundred
Other Comic and Mysterious Pictures. The Greatest Films Ever Turned Out.
CORONATION OF KING EDWARD. Motion Picture Films of the Coronation of King Edward, which took place on Aug. 9, 1902, Now Ready for Delivery.
THE MONEY MAKERS OF THE HOUR.

EDISON

PROJECTING KINETOSCOPE
Is universally approved by the Professional Exhibitor. Full particulars in NEW CATALOGUE [illegible]

The Latest Sensation in Motion Pictures,
A VOYAGE TO THE MOON 850 feet. Price $127.50 Price, Colored, $367.50

NEW MARTINIQUE PICTURES.
Reports from Leading Exhibiters tell us that the Mt. Pelee Films are Simply Coining Money
Our staff photographers have returned from Martinique on the S.S. Korona, and have brought with them a complete series of typical and genuine Martinique films, which, when shown in connection with our great pictures of the volcanic eruption and the destruction of St. Pierre, will make a show in themselves.
Write for New Supplement Giving Full Description of All These Films.

JACK AND THE BEANSTALK.
Code word (Unmeasured). Length 625ft. Class A, $93.75
THIS FILM OFFERS GREAT OPPORTUNITIES FOR COLORING EFFECTS.
Price for coloring complete, including background and all details.......... $140.00
Price for coloring figures only, with beanstalk tinted.......... $5.00

EDISON MFG. CO., Main Office and Factory: ORANGE, N. J., U. S. A.
NEW YORK OFFICE AND RETAIL SALESROOM, 41 E. 21st STREET.
CHICAGO OFFICE, 144 WABASH AVE.
FOREIGN DEPARTMENT, 83 CHAMBERS STREET, NEW YORK.
PACIFIC COAST SELLING AGENT, PETER BACIGALUPI, 933 MARKET STREET, SAN FRANCISCO, CAL.
LONDON OFFICE, 56 CHANCERY LANE, LONDON, W. C., ENGLAND.

BIOGRAPH

Greatest of All Motion-Picture Devices.

SPECIAL PRICE for a Continuous Engagement of 16 Weeks $80.00 per Week, and Transportation for Man, Machine and Films; Regular Price, $105.00 per week. The Warwick Trading Co.'s Machine, THE BIOSCOPE, or any other machine using Standard Size Sprocket Films, $10.00 a week for an engagement of [illegible] consecutive weeks. All Warwick and Standard Size Films from Biograph Negatives, 15c. per ft.

IMPORTANT NOTICE.
Melie's Magnificent Spectacle,
A TRIP TO THE MOON
The Most Extraordinary Moving Picture Production the World has Ever Known. 500ft. Long. Send for circular giving price and full particulars.

MUTOSCOPES
THE BEST MONEY GETTER OF ALL SLOT MACHINES.
No More Second Hand Machines.
Our Last CLIPPER Ad. Cleaned Them All Out.
PLENTY OF NEW MACHINES AT $45.
American Mutoscope and Biograph Co.,
841 BROADWAY, NEW YORK.
CHICAGO BRANCH, - 128 CLARK STREET.
ANNA HELD and THE MUTOSCOPE.

Figure 8-3. Advertisements, *New York Clipper*, October 4, 1902.

Throughout the remaining months of 1903, as family vaudeville houses, town halls, chautauquas, and fairs or carnivals took up the film's exhibition, *A Trip to the Moon* became increasingly associated with Edison. Occasionally newspaper ads or notices would mention that it was a "Vitagraph picture," such as in Houston and Reno, Nevada.[52] Later in the year, it also was in the repertory of International Bioscope, a touring exhibition service that supplied towns such as Traverse City, Michigan.[53] Perhaps only once, at the Eagles' Street Carnival in Lincoln, was it ever linked to a French source: "a stupendous production direct from its European triumph . . . a most marvelous portrayal of the story of the same name by the famous French novelist, Jules Verne."[54] For the most part, however, *A Trip to Moon* was promoted, as it was in March at the Whitney Family Theater in Fitchburg, Massachusetts, as a "wonderful Edison moving picture."[55] That summer the "Edison Moving Picture Company" appeared for the fourth time to provide entertainment at the Waterloo chautauqua in Iowa, and " 'Trip to the Moon' was the most interesting picture" shown to packed audiences.[56] That fall, at Washington Hall in Trenton, New Jersey, "Prof. Neuman, the Great" was accompanied by the "Edison Kinetoscope" and "Trip to the Moon," the first of just three films.[57] Along with others, most especially Edison's *The Great Train Robbery* (1903), *A Trip to the Moon* continued to circulate for the next three years—from family vaudeville houses in Waterloo, Reno, and Ogden, Utah, or town halls in Frederick, Maryland, and Cedar Rapids, Iowa, to early nickelodeons in Altoona and Titusville, Pennsylvania.[58] Yet only Edison's name consistently stuck to the film, whether at the 1904 summer Mardi Gras Carnival in Butte, Montana, or at an evening entertainment of the First Baptist Church in Atlanta in January 1906.[59] Not only was *A Trip to the Moon* almost wholly assimilated into the American cultural landscape, as if the memory of its French launch had been lost after its return to earth on another continent, Méliès's "spectacular production" also had been rebranded to further burnish the Edison name—and his, as well as a newly imperial America's, highly competitive mastery of technological innovation.

Fading "Originals" in the American Cultural Landscape

By at least the spring of 1903, Méliès was well aware of the discrepancy between the wide distribution of his films (often in duped prints) and the less-than-stellar profits from their sales in the United States. In May, he finally sought to right this imbalance by sending his brother Gaston to open a sales office and printing laboratory in New York City to curtail the circulation of "bad and fraudulent copies" of "genuine and original" films stamped with his Star-Film brand.[60] Unlike Pathé-Frères' much more substantial investment in a similar strategy the following year, Méliès's effort was only partially successful.[61] The New York office undoubtedly sold more "original" film prints, perhaps even of *A Trip to the Moon* (whose title the initial ads highlighted), but in circulation they often could not escape being seen as one more in a series of "American" phenomena, and even exploited to shore up a local public institution. In Coshocton, Ohio, for instance, the receipts from an exhibition of *A Trip to the Moon* apparently contributed to the purchase of new books for the town library.[62] Hardly ever did the French filmmaker's name, unlike Edison's, remain attached to any of his films: in late December 1903 a rare ad for the Grand Opera House in Butte noted that *Fairyland or The Queen among the Fairies*, the lengthy fairy play that followed *A Trip to the Moon*, was "copyrighted by Georges Méliès of Paris."[63] Despite the continuing popularity of *A Trip to the Moon* and other Méliès films in the United States, neither his name nor that of Star-Film did more than flicker briefly in the American cultural landscape. At least another six years would pass before George Kleine would make an effort, however much an afterthought, to resurrect Méliès and reassert the significance of *A Trip to the Moon* for the early development of American cinema.

Notes

1. George Kleine, "Progress of Optical Projection in the Last Fifty Years," *Film Index*, May 28, 1910, 27.

2. See, for instance, Richard Abel, *The Red Rooster Scare: Making Cinema American, 1900–1910* (Berkeley: University of California Press, 1999), 2–6.

3. For a lively debate about how early motion pictures might be figured differently and productively by concepts such as the "national," "global," and "transnational," see *Early Cinema and the "National"* ed. Richard Abel, Giorgio Bertellini, and Rob King (New Barnet, U.K.: Libbey, 2008).

4. This chapter could not have been written without the research made possible by newspaperarchive.com, an increasingly productive source (whatever its limitations) for accessing thousands of newspapers in small towns and midsize cities in the United States. I thank Michael Aronson for first alerting me to this research source.

5. "Advocate's Great Book Offer," *Newark (N.J.) Daily Advocate*, Jan. 15, 1895, 2.

6. Lucian L. Knight, "The Literary World," *Atlanta Constitution*, Nov. 10, 1901, 39.

7. John Frazer, *Artificially Arranged Scenes: The Films of Georges Méliès* (Boston: Hall, 1979), 6–7.

8. "The Tivoli," *Oakland (Calif.) Tribune*, June 20, 1896, 12; and June 27, 1896, 12.

9. "Amusements," *Galveston (Texas) Daily News*, Jan. 28, 1897, 38

10. "A Trip to the Moon," *Waukesha (Wisc.) Freeman*, Oct. 29, 1896, 3.

11. Marion Eloise Serffer, "A Trip to the Moon," *Fitchburg (Mass.) Daily Sentinel*, June 15, 1898, 8.

12. "Biggest Telescope Ever Made," *Nebraska State Journal*, Mar. 5, 1899, 16.

13. "A Trip to the Moon," *Warren (Pa.) Evening Democrat*, July 25, 1900, 2; *Tyrone (Pa.) Daily Herald*, Aug. 2, 1900, 3; *Bedford (Pa.) Gazette*, Aug. 10, 1900, 2.

14. "Wonders of the Pan-American Exposition," *Fort Wayne (Ind.) Journal-Gazette*, July 22, 1900, 13; *Des Moines (Iowa) Daily News*, Aug. 1, 1900, 5.

15. See, for instance, the early full-page story, "Pan-American's Midway," *Des Moines (Iowa) Daily News*, Mar. 23, 1901, 10.

16. "At the Buffalo Exposition," *Daily Northwestern (Evanston, Ill.)*, July 13, 1901, 4; "A Rainbow City," *Hayward (Calif.) Daily Review*, July 26, 1901, 2.

17. "Bryan at the Exposition," *Sunday State Journal (Oshkosh, Wisc.)*, June 23, 1901, 1.

18. Robert Rydell, *All the World's a Fair: Visions of Empire at American International Expositions, 1876–1916* (Chicago: University of Chicago Press, 1984), 151; "The Pan-American Midway: Things the Editor Saw There," *Connellsville (Pa.) Courier*, July 26, 1901, 7; "Mysteries of the Midway at the Pan-American," *Syracuse (N.Y.) Post-Standard*, July 21, 1901, 19. See also "Doing the Pan-American," *Iowa State Reporter*, Sept. 24, 1901, 6.

19. "A Trip to the Moon," *New Castle (Pa.) News*, Oct. 9, 1901, 16.

20. "Five Thousand People Go to Buffalo This Morning," *Syracuse (N.Y.) Post-Standard*, Aug. 22, 1901, 6; "San Antonio Fair," *Galveston (Texas) Daily News*, Oct. 8, 1901, 7; "Riotous Scenes in Closing of Exposition at Buffalo," *Decatur (Ill.) Daily Review*, Nov. 4, 1901, 1.

21. John Kasson, *Amusing the Millions: Coney Island at the Turn of the Century* (New York: Hill and Wang, 1978), 61.

22. "Snow Storms and Floods in the United States," *(Winnipeg) Manitoba Morning Free Press*, Mar. 7, 1902, 8.

23. Edo McCoullough, *Good Old Coney Island: A Sentimental Journey into the Past* (New York: Scribner's, 1957), 303.

24. Kasson, *Amusing the Millions*, 63.

25. "Elephant as a House Mover," *Syracuse (N.Y.) Post-Standard*, Nov. 3, 1902, 2; "Coney's New Midway," *Atlanta Constitution*, Nov. 30, 1902, n. p.

26. "Coney Island Rejuvenated," *New York Times*, Apr. 12, 1903, 28.

27. Kasson, *Amusing the Millions*, 63, 65.

28. Kasson, *Amusing the Millions*, 66.

29. "April's First Sunday Calls Out All New York," *New York Times*, Apr. 2, 1906, 9.

30. Somewhat incongruously, "The Great Midway Attraction" allegedly was featured at the Opera House in Titusville, Pennsylvania, in late April 1902—see the Titusville Opera House ad, *Titusville (Pa.) Herald*, Apr. 25, 1902, 3.

31. "Dayton Elks' Carnival," *Hamilton (Ohio) Evening Democrat*, May 30, 1902, 2.

32. "The Fair Next Week," *Daily Palladium (Benton, Mich.)*, July 5, 1902, 4; Elks' Carnival ad, *Lima (Ohio) Times-Democrat*, July 5, 1902, 2; Knights of Pythias Grand Carnival Jubilee ad, *Mansfield (Ohio) News*, July 29, 1902, 6; Fall Festival ad, *Fort Wayne (Ind.) Sentinel*, Aug. 20, 1902, 23.

33. "Fair in Full Blast Draws Spectators," *Atlanta Constitution*, Oct. 11, 1902, 3; "Seawall Carnival," *Galveston (Texas) Daily News*, Nov. 23, 1902, 8.

34. "Tent Blown Down," *Iowa State Reporter*, Aug. 28, 1903, 2.

35. Merchants' Free State Fair ad, *Iowa City Daily Press*, July 18, 1904, 8.

36. "Trip to the Moon," *Athens (Ohio) Messenger*, Jan. 19, 1905, 5; "Surprises for Town and Gown at Fine Arts College Monday," *Syracuse (N.Y.) Post-Standard*, Mar. 24, 1905, 3; "Trip to the Moon," *Piqua (Ohio) Daily Call*, Oct. 9, 1905, 5.

37 "Salvo's Trip to the Moon," *Piqua (Ohio) Daily Call*, May 7, 1906, 2.

38. Vitagraph ad, *New York Clipper*, May 13, 1899, 217; Lubin ad, *New York Clipper*, June 10, 1899, 300.

39. "Sunday at the Fair," *San Antonio (Texas) Daily Light*, Oct. 30, 1899, 5; "The Passion Play," *San Antonio (Texas) Daily Light*, Nov. 10, 1899, 8.

40. "Clever Show," *Lowell (Mass.) Sun*, Apr. 26, 1900, 2.

41. "Building the South," *Waterloo (Iowa) Daily Courier*, July 11, 1900, 5.

42. Edison ad, *New York Clipper*, Dec. 1, 1900, 896.

43. "Amusement Notes," *Janesville (Wisc.) Daily Gazette*, Oct. 8, 1901, 3.

44. Brown's Opera House ad, *Waterloo (Iowa) Daily Reporter*, Nov. 1, 1901, 4.

45. Lincoln Park ad, *Lincoln (Neb.) Evening News*, July 5, 1902, 5.

46. Edison and Biograph ads, *New York Clipper*, Oct. 4, 1902, 712. Lubin offered its own dupe of *A Trip to Moon*, a puzzling 1,200 feet in length—see the Lubin ad, *New York Clipper*, Oct. 11, 1902, 733.

47. Biograph ad, *New York Clipper*, Oct. 18, 1902, 760.

48. "Casto Theatre," *Lowell (Mass.) Sun*, Dec. 22, 1902, 6; the Huber's 14th Street Museum ad, *New York Times*, Jan. 25, 1903, 14. For details about the film's circulation on the Keith and Orpheum circuits and in other vaudeville venues, from New Haven, Connecticut, and Washington, D.C., to Cincinnati, Indianapolis, Detroit, and New Orleans, see Abel, *The Red Rooster Scare*, 7.

49. Simpson Crawford Co. ad, *New York Times*, Mar. 10, 1903, 3.

50. "New York City," *New York Clipper*, Apr. 11, 1903, 168. See also the American Vitagraph ad, *New York Clipper*, Mar. 21, 1903, 108.

51. "Amusements," *Los Angeles Times*, Jan. 18, 1903, 1.1; Feb. 28, 1903, 1.

52. "Amusements," *Galveston (Texas) Daily News*, Apr. 5, 1903, 8; "A Trip to the Moon," *Reno (Nev.) Evening Gazette*, Dec. 3, 1903, 5.

53. "News of the Theatres," *Traverse City (Mich.) Daily Eagle*, Dec. 3, 1903, 3.

54. "Bally Ho!" *Lincoln (Neb.) Evening News*, May 18, 1903, 7.

55. Whitney Family Theater ad, *Fitchburg (Mass.) Daily Sentinel*, Mar. 12, 1903, n. p.

56. "Chautauqua Attractions," *Waterloo (Iowa) Daily Reporter*, June 30, 1903, 4.

57. "Amusements," *Trenton (N.J.) Times*, Oct. 7, 1903, 9.

58. Pastime ad, *Ogden (Utah) Standard*, May 10, 1904, 5; "A New Program," *Cedar Rapids (Iowa) Daily Republican*, Aug. 19, 1904, 5; Electric Theatre ad, *Waterloo (Iowa) Daily Reporter*, Jan. 23, 1905, 6; Grand Theater ad, *Reno (Nev.)*

Evening Gazette, July 29, 1905, 6; "Moving Pictures," *Frederick (Md.) Daily News*, Jan. 13, 1906, 5; "The Pictorium Program," *Altoona (Pa.) Mirror*, June 25, 1906, 1; "A Trip to the Moon," *Titusville (Pa.) Herald*, Dec. 18, 1906, 2.

59. "Other Features," *Anaconda (Mont.) Standard*, Aug. 31, 1904, 5; "Entertainment at First Baptist Church," *Atlanta Constitution*, Jan. 22, 1905, 2.

60. Geo. Méliès ad, *New York Clipper*, May 9, 1903, 276; Star-Film ad, *New York Clipper*, June 6, 1903, 368.

61. For a lengthy analysis of Pathé-Frères's extremely successful investment in selling its films in the United States, see Abel, *The Red Rooster Scare*, 20–37, 48–73.

62. "New Books for Library," *Coshocton (Ohio) Democratic Standard*, Apr. 22, 1904, 2.

63. "Butte News," *Anaconda (Mont.) Standard*, Dec. 21, 1903, 11. In a similarly rare case, Méliès's next big fairy play, *An Impossible Voyage* (1904) was at least once identified as "the latest Parisian film." See the Grand Theater ad, *The (Portland) Oregonian*, Dec. 25, 1904, 19. T. L. Tally also identified *Fairyland* as a "Parisian" production when he screened it at his Lyric Theatre in Los Angeles: "Clever Moving Pictures," *Los Angeles Times*, Oct. 11, 1903, 6.2, reprinted in Abel, *The Red Rooster Scare*, 13.

9

Matthew Solomon

A Trip to the Fair; or, Moon-Walking in Space

A *Trip to the Moon had its* first successes on the fairgrounds. Méliès recalled that when potential buyers balked at the long length of the film and its correspondingly high price, he screened it in a fairground booth at the Foire du Trône as part of a show put on by one of his clients, who were "nearly all fairground showmen." Méliès reported that the film was an immediate hit with fairgoers, a "truly popular audience," who enthusiastically laughed at some tableaux and vigorously applauded others. According to Méliès, the film was an overnight sensation as news of the crowd's response spread rapidly through the "world of the fairgrounds." Soon "every fairground showman in France had heard about the triumphant success of *A Trip to the Moon*."[1] While one must be cautious about the accuracy of this account, which is reenacted in Georges Franju's film *Le Grand Méliès* (1953), Méliès's emphasis on fairground audiences as both litmus test for *A Trip to the Moon* and a catalyst for its popularity is telling. Fairground shows were an important exhibition context for the film, but just as important are the ways *A Trip to the Moon* engages with the wider realm of fairground amusement.

A Trip to the Moon is a fairground film that provides the travelers in the film—and, by extension, its audiences—with many of the sights and thrills of a turn-of-the-century amusement park or World's Fair.

One reason its fantasy of lunar travel may have been so compelling is that the voyage to the moon is presented in the form of a trip to the fair. For a film ostensibly about space travel, it is remarkable just how much *A Trip to the Moon* is propelled not so much by the movement of the capsule through space, but by the comparatively pedestrian act of walking. Dissolves between many scenes are bridged by the movement of the group of travelers as they walk or run from one space to a more or less adjacent one. Sometimes screen direction is consistent, but often it is not, giving the impression not of a travel in a straight line, but of walking and running back and forth—and ultimately in circles (the film ends with a group of revelers dancing in a ring around a statue of Barbenfouillis). While *A Trip to the Moon* is said to have influenced Edwin S. Porter, we might conclude that it anticipates Porter's *Rube and Mandy at Coney Island* (1903) perhaps more than it prefigures either *The Great Train Robbery* (1903) or *Life of an American Fireman* (1903).[2]

Throughout much of the film, Méliès, as Professor Barbenfouillis, plays a role analogous to that of guide—rather than magician—leading the group on a perambulatory path from one site to the next. Just as guides transitioned among World's Fair sites with the phrase, "Next we will take a passing glance,"[3] many of the film's tableaux offer the group "passing glances" at a variety of fairground sights.[4] Like visitors to a fair or exposition, the travelers in *A Trip to the Moon* make metaphorical stops at a series of attractions. The film begins with a Scientific Congress of astronomers analogous to the many specialized congresses convened as part of World's Fairs.[5] The next two scenes show locations reminiscent of the 1900 Universal Exposition in Paris.[6] The workshop in which the shell is constructed resembles the Palace of Machines and the casting of the cannon recalls the massive pavilion of the French foundry Schneider and Co., where visitors to the Exposition could see the process of casting large-scale artillery and an enormous cannon. World's Fairs were supposed to be peaceful international gatherings (despite the conspicuous presence of French army and navy exhibits at the Universal Exposition), but as one skeptical contemporaneous commentator noted, "Schneider's great gun seems to threaten the Exhibition. . . . [T]he Paris Exhibition has taught us that the triumph of the modern world is purely mechanical. We can threaten our enemies more efficiently, we can kill space and time with greater ease."[7] Through its spatial and temporal ellipses, *A Trip to the Moon* effectively "kills" space and time, but the film's giant cannon and lines of soldiers and sailors remind us of the military buildup that was the flip side of the World's Fairs' emphasis on twentieth-century technological prowess.

Other subsequent tableaux in the film bear a distinct resemblance to fairground attractions. These include a sort of thrill ride as the capsule plummets earthward with two figures barely clinging to it—a fall that ends with a kind of shoot-the-chutes when the capsule plunges into the sea.[8] The shot in which the capsule sinks to the bottom of the sea and bobs to the surface—one of Méliès's signature "underwater views"[9]—simulates what might have been seen at an aquarium such as the one at the Universal Exposition. There is a boat ride, followed later by a parade and the public display of the Selenite. Led by a rope at the end of the procession, the tribally-costumed Selenite dances for the crowd, an episode that suggests a parody of ethnological and colonial exhibits like those at the Universal Exposition, where (as one contemporaneous commentator ironically put it), "strange men . . . are gathered from distant provinces to make a liberal and instructive entertainment."[10] The film concludes with a celebratory marching band parade that files past a statue commemorating the recently completed voyage.

Like a fairgoer's transit between and within various places within the fairgrounds, the travelers' movements in *A Trip to the Moon* take place across and through a series of distinctively spatial "attractions."[11] Although the temporality and visuality of the "cinema of attractions" have each received much attention, the spatiality of cinematic attractions has largely been overlooked. This spatial dimension reconciles what

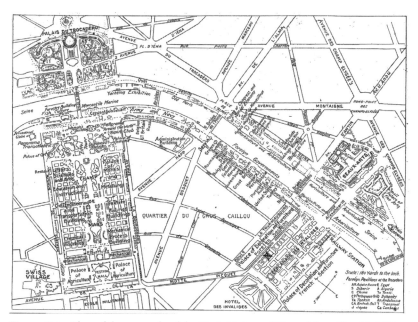

Figure 9-1. Plan of the grounds of the Paris Universal Exposition, *New York Times*, April 8, 1900.

is sometimes conceived as a dichotomy between attractions and narrative because these tableaux are at once attraction sites and story scenes. More to the point, the spatial dimension of the film's attractions (and the movement of individuals relative to them) creates perhaps the most significant analogy between the film and the amusement park: "At Coney Island and other amusement parks . . . audience and activity frequently merged. . . . Customers participated intimately in the spectacle around them. . . . [through] settings and attractions that immediately affected behavior."[12] With *A Trip to the Moon*, Méliès implicates cinema in the "new mass culture" of the amusement park by staging the voyage (along with the preparations that precede it and the celebrations that follow) as a series of participatory attractions. Thus, the iconic anthropomorphized moon of *A Trip to the Moon* is not so very different from the grimacing "funny face" that looked down on visitors to Coney Island's Steeplechase Park.

Méliès, *le barnum*

Although he directed one of the world's most famous magic theaters, Méliès's ties to fairground and traveling exhibition also made him something of a *barnum*. The term "*barnum*" was derived from the name of the American showman P. T. Barnum and had entered the French lexicon (in both initial capped and lowercased forms) during the mid-nineteenth century to refer to impresarios of theatrical and fairground spectacle.[13] As it was used at the beginning of the twentieth century in the French magic circles Méliès moved within, the word "*barnum*" had connotations of humbug and cheap amusement.[14] Some of the earliest advertisements for moving pictures in the fairground trade journal *L'Industriel forain* targeted "exhibitors, *barnums*, and fairground prestidigitators."[15]

Among what Richard Abel terms the "Big Four" firms of the turn-of-the-century French cinema (Lumière, Méliès, Pathé, and Gaumont),[16] Pathé and Méliès were most closely tied to fairground exhibition. After hearing an Edison phonograph at the fair in Vincennes in 1894, Charles Pathé had purchased his own phonograph and exhibited it in a series of fairs in the provinces beyond Paris. He went into business supplying other fairground exhibitors with phonographs and cylinders and soon expanded to include the sale of films and projectors.[17] Recent research suggests that Méliès was involved in what was perhaps the first fairground film exhibition in France, at the Foire du Mail in Orléans between May 29 and June 17, 1896. Less than two months after he began screening films as part of programs of magic at the Théâtre Robert-Houdin, Méliès partnered with several theatrical colleagues to sponsor this fairground tent show, which featured what was billed as a Cinétographe. The show was cut short when the highly flammable films caught fire and burned down part of the booth.[18]

The Lumières, by contrast, balked at the idea of exploiting their Cinématographe like so many fairground showmen. On October 14, 1895, Louis Lumière wrote his father, Antoine, and told him that the elder Lumière's plan to exhibit the Cinématographe himself to paying audiences pained him and his brother, Auguste; he insisted, "we do not like the prospect of you playing [the] Barnum showing off his magic lantern."[19] Méliès was not averse to such an arrangement and began placing regular advertisements in *L'Industriel forain* in 1896.[20] Like Pathé, Méliès cultivated commercial relationships with fairground film exhibitors. Indeed, many who previewed Méliès's new releases on weekdays at the Théâtre Robert-Houdin and purchased films at the sales office around the corner in the Passage de l'Opéra were fairground exhibitors who screened films in tent shows, often as a complement to various live performances. Méliès relied on fairground shows as a primary market for his films. Trick films such as *Marvellous Suspension and Evolution* (1902) and *The Cabinet Trick of the Davenport Brothers* (1902) were based on well-known fairground illusions and suggest that Méliès was tailoring part of his 1902–1903 output to what he perceived to be the tastes of fairgoers.[21] Moreover, the U.S. market for Méliès's films around this time was comprised not just by vaudeville theaters but also in part by summer amusement parks, where cinema jostled for attention among other fairground amusements.[22]

Voyages in Deep Space

In fairground shows, trips to the moon—taken in various ways—were not at all uncommon. There was even a marionette version of "Le Voyage dans le lune,"[23] one of a number of *féeries* mounted by itinerant puppeteers for audiences of mostly children. Something billed as "Le Voyage dans la lune" was also at the Foire du Mail when Méliès's 1896 film show was there, although what it entailed is not clear.[24] The choice of *A Trip to the Moon* as the English title for Méliès's 1902 film capitalized—whether intentionally or not—on the popularity of other contemporaneous shows and attractions of the same name, including, most importantly, the contemporaneous fairground ride A Trip to the Moon.[25]

Cosmopolitan magazine described Frederic Thompson and Elmer "Skip" Dundy's A Trip to the Moon ride as it was originally presented at the Pan-American Exposition in Buffalo in 1901:

The prospective voyagers take their seats in a darkened auditorium, where the guide expresses to them in pregnant phrases the extraordinary nature of the adventure on which they are embarking. Then, at the back of the stage, in a starlit sky, the aërial ship in which the voyage is to be made is seen descending earthward. It passes out of sight; and the inexperienced suppose that now our scene will change, and that we, remaining in our seats, will be carried in imagination only through the various chapters of the journey. But the order given is, "Leave your seats and follow me!"

Out we troop accordingly, in the glimmering dusk, and pass through a passage and over a gangway to other seats on the deck of the aërial ship itself. Yes, verily, there we sit, while the marvelous vessel waves its wings, and far, far below us, with its electric lights shining, lies the terrestrial city of Buffalo. The broad, bat-like wings wave more powerfully, till at length we seem to leave our earthly moorings and to sail steadily but swiftly through the depths of infinite space. In a few moments, we find ourselves passing through a thunder-cloud, and the lightning flashes round us, and the thunder rolls, the wind howls, and the ship sways in it. But our speed is immense, and anon we have risen above the clouds, and now before us, beneath us, is revealed another planet—actually the moon herself! We descend rapidly, and in a few moments, with a slight jar, we have come to anchor on its surface. The order comes to disembark.[26]

A Trip to the Moon was one of a number of three-dimensional simulations at the Pan-American Exposition that combined elaborate trompe l'oeil backgrounds with lighting and sound effects to create a powerful sense of presence, giving rise to newspaper accounts of "illusions so persuasive that viewers tried to grasp, touch, or enter them, or to interact physically with them in more dramatic ways."[27] These illusory attractions included panoramas and cycloramas such as the Johnstown Flood, depicting the catastrophic 1889 flood destroying much of a western Pennsylvania steel town, and the Battle of Missionary Ridge, which reproduced the final decisive day of this violent 1863 Civil War conflict.[28] All these attractions created what Alison Griffiths describes as an "immersive" sensation, "a more bodily participation in the experience, including allowing the spectator to move freely around the space."[29] As *Cosmopolitan* emphasized, "They are elaborate illusions, ingeniously carried out, so that instead of viewing a performance on a stage, we ourselves are participants in the scene."[30]

In the case of A Trip to the Moon, participation in the attraction involved not just simulated space flight aboard the aerial ship, but also movement through a series of real spaces. One walked from the auditorium across a gangplank to the ship, from the ship across another gangplank to the ersatz lunar surface, past the shop windows of a row of lunar stores and giant sentries to the moon palace—and finally from the palace to the attraction's exit. The immersive experience created by Thompson and Dundy's A Trip to the Moon set it apart from other earlier entertainments of the same name. By contrast, audiences for the Urania Scientific Theatre's 1892 presentation of "A Trip to the Moon" in New York mostly remained in their theater seats as they viewed "an imaginary trip to the moon and back" through lighting and stage effects, magic lantern projections, and a lecture by Garrett P. Serviss that avoided "specifying a means of travel."[31] If the Urania Theatre's journey between the earth and the moon was entirely hypothetical (if ostensibly scientifically accurate), Thompson and Dundy's A Trip to the Moon took fairgoers on a physical journey, complete with jostling, wind in the face, and an alien encounter. Unlike the Urania Theatre's shows at New York's Carnegie Hall, the ride catered not as much to middle- and upper-class audiences as to working-class crowds.

Since both Thompson and Dundy's A Trip to the Moon and Méliès's A Trip to the Moon were informed by H. G. Wells's recent novel The First Men in the Moon, determining to what extent—if any—Méliès might have been directly inspired by the ride is difficult.[32] Apart from serving as a possible inspiration, whether direct or indirect, it is worth pointing out that the film, like the ride, involves a journey to the moon in which passengers begin as passive spectators of a two-dimensional display, but then become more active parts of a three-dimensional experience. In the attraction, the previous description suggests, this occurs when spectators who were comfortably seated in an auditorium were unexpectedly told to leave their seats and step onto the ship. The film includes a comparable early moment where stationary observers who are looking at a two-dimensional representation and listening to a speaker become mobile participants on a journey through three-dimensional space. As Barbenfouillis sketches the planned moon shot on a chalkboard, all of the assembled astronomers are seated—indeed telescopes are magically transformed into stools so that the last to arrive have places to sit. But as soon as the shell's lunar trajectory is drawn on the board, everyone stands up and the boundary separating the spectators from spectacle and speaker is demolished as Barbenfouillis pelts one person in the audience with pieces of paper. Barbenfouillis then steps down among the former spectators and makes physical contact with them for the first time in the form of enthusiastic handshakes as they become participants in the journey to follow, visibly exchanging their heavy robes and tall conical hats for hats, vests, jackets, and overcoats that allow them to move about more freely.[33] After they change clothes, Barbenfouillis waves to the others and leads the travelers out of the room and into the workshops where the capsule is being constructed. Importantly, in this scene, the group actually enters the capsule, moving from foreground to middle ground in order to poke around inside of the shell: they are now fully immersed in a wholly three-dimensional voyage. These deeper staging strategies later give way to the sensational illusion of movement through deep space when the spectator sees the rapidly approaching moon as the capsule presumably hurtles toward its surface.

Circular Panoramas and Moving Sidewalks

Méliès may not have been too familiar with the Pan-American Exposition or with Coney Island, but he was certainly well acquainted with the Universal Exposition held in Paris in 1900. The magicians' magazine *Mahatma* reported that with "Paris being full of visitors," the Exposition gave a major boost to the city's "small theatres."[34] Among these small magic theaters was Méliès's Théâtre Robert-Houdin.[35] There, the magician Carmelli was performing and the film *Cinderella* (1899) was being screened around the time of the Exposition.[36] Cinema had a presence at the Exposition, perhaps most notably through the free screenings of the Lumière Cinématographe that took place several times a day in the Gallery of Machines, where a massive screen was visible from both sides by up to 15,000 people at a time.[37] Unlike Lumière, Pathé, and Gaumont, Méliès did not participate in any of the Exposition's official exhibits,[38] but he did make some nineteen films there in the months from February to May 1900, none of which are known to survive.[39]

The Universal Exposition featured several major "astronomical attractions," as Lynda Nead aptly terms them. Through a giant telescope in the Palace of Optics, visitors saw "views of the moon magnified ten thousand times, so that the observer was brought within fifty to sixty miles of the surface."[40] One could also see a model of the moon as it orbited earth, "accomplishing the phases of its monthly revolution," in the planetarium that was contained within the enormous Celestial Globe not far from the Eiffel Tower.[41] Unlike these attractions, however, Méliès's *A Trip to the Moon* is far more concerned with reaching the moon than looking at it—unlike his earlier *The Astronomer's Dream* (1898) or his later *The Eclipse* (1907). The film also depicts the trip to the moon as a distinctly embodied experience, one that quickly moves from visual observation to the register of physical experience. Thus, *A Trip to the Moon* has more in common with travel rides such as the Maréorama, which simulated a journey through the Mediterranean "on the deck of a steamer worked by a contrivance which causes it to roll and pitch as at sea. Nothing is wanting to complete the deception. There are smoking funnels, steam whistles, etc., while varied scenes of sea and shore pass in review as the spectator steams along the coast."[42] With its mechanical pitch and roll and ersatz vessel flanked by moving backdrops, the Maréorama anticipated the design of Thompson and Dundy's A Trip to the Moon in many ways— although its journey was unequivocally earthbound.

The idea of virtual travel was implicit in Méliès's Universal Exposition actualities, which attempted to simulate cinematically the spectator's physical presence at the fair. In six of the nineteen Méliès films entitled *Paris Exposition, 1900*, the camera was mounted on a moving vehicle to simulate movement through the exposition grounds by boat or by train, creating what Méliès described in a flyer for the series as the "curious effect" of a traveling shot, which permitted spectators to see some of the Exposition's big buildings "parade by."[43] Tom Gunning notes of other similar panoramic views, "Rather than simply reproducing the view, such films seem to recreate the actual penetration of space that traveling involves."[44]

In addition to these "panoramic views," Méliès also made five so-called "circular panoramic views" in which 360-degree panning shots were used to scan the grounds of the fair from various fixed vantage points.[45] Méliès touted these "circular panoramas" as "cinematographic novelties obtained by a new process with a truly gripping effect."[46] Conventional travelogue films, Méliès's advertisement claimed, "can give only a very imperfect idea of the places represented," but these circular panoramas "reproduce in perfect fashion the complete and overall look of each of the most picturesque parts of the Exposition . . . the audience sees the different monuments pass one by one before their eyes, surrounded by crowds, and at the same time can enjoy the view of the streets, the gardens, the bridges across the Seine, etc., exactly as if they had been a centrally-located observer looking all around."[47] Méliès's use of circular panoramas in these films of the Universal Exposition dovetailed with the larger aims of the fair, as Kristen Whissel points out in her discussion of Porter's use of the same technique in the films he took for Edison at the Pan-American Exposition one year later: "Expositions tended to mimic, on a far grander scale, both the panorama's representational ambitions and its effects on spectators: both enclosed the spectator within a world bound by a strictly imposed artificial horizon . . . to intensify the reality effect of—and the spectator's immersion in—a wondrous yet highly artificial world."[48] Although the camera never swivels in *A Trip to the Moon*, the film as a whole creates a panoramic effect as it takes in the various phases of the journey—like the many nineteenth-century "composite panoramas" that surrounded spectators with temporally and spatially distinct visual details rather than immersing them in simulated locations at singular moments in time, emphasizing action and narrative as well as virtual presence.[49]

Méliès also shot three films at the Universal Exposition in which the camera traveled along the moving sidewalk (*trottoir roulant*) and two more films of the moving sidewalk in operation.[50] The moving sidewalk was one of the highlights of the Paris World's Fair; as one journalist explained, the "moving sidewalk . . . connects the two main divisions of the Exposition on the left bank of the river, and has been a great success financially from the first. Instead of sitting down one must stand, and many people prefer to walk, the height and accelerated motion giving to the pedestrian the peculiar sensation of being at least ten feet tall and wearing seven-league boots."[51] In *A Trip to the Moon*, the camera does not move, but the film is nevertheless animated by the dynamism of machine-aided movement. Watching the film, one often has a sense of people sliding by as if transported by a moving sidewalk: the travelers rush past like the well-dressed fairgoers gliding past on the *trottoir roulant* in the Lumière film *Vue prise d'une plate-forme mobile* (1900).

Fairground Amusement

World's Fairs such as the Universal Exposition sought to combine education with entertainment to produce an edifying series of exhibits that together celebrated human achievements. Thus, *Scientific American* praised the Universal Exposition because it "illustrates in the most elaborate manner possible the progress made by man during the last one hundred years in every department of art, science, and industry."[52] As a recent technological invention included in different ways in turn-of-the-century World's Fairs, cinema was similarly associated with edification. Use of the cinematograph at the Pan-American Exposition, for example, was cited as "a source not only of keen pleasure but of educational value."[53] Looking back on the World's Fairs of the previous two years, *Forum* in 1902 stressed the "educational value of World's Fairs" and claimed that Fairs "served . . . the peace and well-being of mankind" and "duty to . . . [one's] neighbor."[54] Although World's Fairs were touted as a means of promoting world peace and fostering international understanding, Robert W. Rydell has demonstrated the extent to which their organization and execution was underwritten by nationalist and imperialist ambitions.[55] Rather than occluding these issues, *A Trip to the Moon* highlights the

Figure 9-2. The Moving Sidewalk, or Mobile Platform, at the Universal Exposition, *Harper's Monthly Magazine*, September 1900.

unfortunate (if comically presented) results of imperialism through the travelers' encounter with the Selenites. Far from peacefully greeting their newly discovered neighbors, the frightened explorers annihilate a number of the creatures before returning to their own planet for a victory parade, an awards ceremony, and a statue honoring the individual (Barbenfouillis) who has just single-handedly obliterated six Selenites.

While *A Trip to the Moon* echoes several attractions from the 1900 and 1901 World's Fairs, the film ultimately aligns itself with the excesses of traveling fairground shows rather than the didactic aspirations of international expositions. The beginning of the film pokes fun at the pretense of the Scientific Congress, and their pomp quickly gives way to illusion (telescopes transforming into stools), quick-sketch (drawing the plan on a chalkboard),[56] and slapstick (throwing paper at a dissenting colleague). Likewise, the next scene, which shows the construction of the capsule, devolves into knockabout comedy as one of the travelers inadvertently tumbles into a pail, causing several workers to stop what they are doing and laugh. The presence of snow on the moon was a serious scientific question in 1902,[57] but Méliès uses a lunar snowfall to drive the travelers underground, where an open umbrella planted in the soil grows into an enormous mushroom (a tableau that is itself a kind of parody of a horticultural exhibit). The explorers in the film do little in the way of observing the moon or gathering samples. Instead, the moon becomes a site for displays of acrobatics (Selenites leaping, tumbling, and contorting themselves), grappling (Barbenfouillis hoisting a Selenite above his head and throwing it to the ground with a move that closely resembles what we see in Méliès wrestling films such as *Fat and Lean Wrestling Match* [1900] and *Side Show Wrestlers* [1908]),[58] and a rapidly edited chase sequence. Though sometimes overlooked in *A Trip to the Moon*, these are each quintessentially Mélièsien moments that derive their appeal less from the technological dexterity of special effects than from the carnivalesque spectacle and humor that would have been entirely familiar to Méliès's target audiences on the French fairgrounds.

Notes

Author's note: An earlier version of this chapter was presented at the Society for Cinema and Media Studies Conference, Philadelphia, March 2008. The careful research of Jeffrey Man yielded a number of additional sources that were extremely useful for expanding and revising it to its present form.

1. Georges Méliès, "Les Debuts d'un film célèbre," *Ce Soir*, Dec. 23, 1937, 8. All translations mine unless otherwise indicated. Other versions of this same story, complete with dialogue, are recounted in Madeleine Malthête-Méliès,

Méliès, l'enchanteur (Paris: Éditions Ramsay, 1985), 268–269; and Jean-Jacques Meusy, *Paris-Palaces, ou les temps des cinémas (1894–1918)*, rev. ed. (Paris: CNRS Éditions, 2002), 105–106.

2. Charles Musser, *Before the Nickelodeon: Edwin S. Porter and the Edison Manufacturing Company* (Berkeley: University of California Press, 1991), 209.

3. Edward Insley, "Paris in 1900 and the Exposition," *Harper's Monthly*, Sept. 1900, 497.

4. In this way, *A Trip to the Moon* could be compared to turn-of-the-century World's Fair–related sound recordings such as "On the Midway" by Issler's Orchestra and "Down the Pike at the St. Louis Exposition," in which running commentary by a guide or fairground barker bridges short segments of music, dialogue, and sound effects. Thank you to Jacob Smith for sharing these recordings with me.

5. See, for example, "The Congresses of the Paris Exposition," *Science*, June 1, 1900, 872–874.

6. Jacques Malthête has found analogs for several sites from the 1900 Paris Exposition in specific tableaux of such Méliès films as *An Impossible Voyage* (1904) and *The Palace of the Arabian Nights* (1905). See Malthête, "Georges Méliès, de la non-fiction à la fiction," *1895*, no. 18 (1995): 76–79.

7. "Musings without Method," *Blackwood Edinburgh Magazine*, July 1900, 110–111.

8. Méliès had earlier made a film (presumably an actuality) of just such a waterborne fairground ride, *Shooting the Chutes* (1898).

9. Georges Sadoul, *Les Pionniers du cinéma (de Méliès à Pathé), 1897–1909*, vol. 2, *Histoire générale du cinéma* (Paris: Éditions Denoël, 1947), 50–52.

10. Charles E. Russell, "The Greatest of World's Fairs," *Munsey's Magazine*, Nov. 1900, 180.

11. On *A Trip to the Moon* as exemplary of the "cinema of attractions," see Tom Gunning, "The Cinema of Attractions: Early Film, Its Spectator, and the Avant-Garde," in *Early Cinema: Space, Frame, Narrative*, ed. Thomas Elsaesser with Adam Barker (London: British Film Institute, 1990), 56–58. See also Gunning, "Lunar Illuminations," in *Film Analysis: A Norton Reader*, ed. Jeffrey Geiger and R. L. Rutsky (New York: Norton, 2005), 74–76.

12. John F. Kasson, *Amusing the Million: Coney Island at the Turn of the Century* (New York: Hill and Wang, 1978), 8.

13. *Le Grand Robert de la langue française: Dictionnaire alphabétique et analogique de la langue française*, 2nd ed. (Paris: Le Robert, 1986), vol. 1, 858.

14. See, for example, Jean de la Vigne, "Mot de la fin," *L'Illusionniste*, Mar. 1903, 122; Van Lamèche, "L'Aquarium ou 'celle-là,'" *L'Illusionniste*, Oct. 1905, 87; and Le Servant de scène, "Chronique théâtrale de la prestidigitation," *L'Illusionniste*, Oct. 1906, 204.

15. *L'Industriel forain*, Aug. 2, 1896, quoted in Jacques Deslandes and Jacques Richard, *Du cinématographe au cinéma, 1896–1906*, vol. 2, *Histoire comparée du cinéma* (Tournai, Belgium: Casterman, 1968), 138. After the demonstration of his Phonoscope projection apparatus, Georges Demenÿ said he got "an avalanche of requests from Barnums and fairgrounds" seeking to exhibit it. Quoted in Laurent Man-

noni, *The Great Art of Light and Shadow: Archaeology of the Cinema*, trans. Richard Crangle (Exeter, U.K.: University of Exeter Press, 2000), 356. See also Deac Rossell, *Living Pictures: The Origins of the Movies* (Albany: SUNY Press, 1998), 51, 90.

16. Richard Abel, *The Ciné Goes to Town: French Cinema, 1896–1914*, rev. ed. (Berkeley: University of California Press, 1998), 10–17.

17. Charles Pathé, *Souvenirs et conseils d'un parvenu* (1926), repr. in *Écrits autobiographiques*, ed. Pierre Lherminier (Paris: L'Harmattan, 2006), 55–57. See also Pathé, *De Pathé Frères à Pathé-Cinéma* (1940), repr. in *Écrits autobiographiques*, 137–151. Compare Léon Gaumont, about whom Vanessa Schwartz notes, "the Musée Grévin dealt with Gaumont . . . rather than Charles Pathé, who was always considered a parvenu and a 'Barnum' of sorts." *Spectacular Realities: Early Mass Culture in Fin-de-Siècle Paris* (Berkeley: University of California Press, 1998), 188, n. 36.

18. Jean-Baptiste Hennion, "Éclairage sur l'année 1896: Éléments chronologiques relatifs à l'introduction du spectacle cinématographique sur les champs de foire français," *1895*, no. 54 (2008): 44–49; *Dictionnaire des cinématographes en France (1896–1897)*, ed. Jacques and Chantal Rittaud-Hutinet with Antoine Morin and Benoît Rittaud (Paris: Editions Honoré Champion, 1999), 345–347. Hennion hypothesizes that the fourteen films reported to have perished in this fire may have been the first films Méliès himself produced in 1896 (47–48).

19. *Letters: Auguste and Louis Lumière*, trans. Pierre Hodgson (London: Faber and Faber, 1995), 27. Compare the text of the original French letter, where the regrettable possibility of Antoine Lumière as "*le barnum*" is more pronounced: *Auguste et Louis Lumière: Correspondances, 1890–1953* (Paris: Cahiers du cinéma, 1994), 47. Instead, Louis and Auguste Lumière proposed a more civilized arrangement whereby operators trained by them would be responsible for the projections and would be paid by concessionaires. They evidently prevailed on their father as this was in fact the system the Lumières soon used to exploit their Cinématographe. On the Lumière's "global strategy," see esp. Jacques Aumont, "Lumière Revisited," trans. Ben Brewster, *Film History* 8, no. 4 (1996): 421–422.

20. *L'Industriel forain*, Aug. 2, 1896, quoted in Malthête-Méliès, 171. Advertisements for Lumière films seem to have appeared in *L'Industriel forain* somewhat belatedly, by contrast, in 1903. *L'Industriel forain*, quoted in André Gaudreault with Jean-Marc Lamotte, "Fragmentation and Segmentation in the Lumière 'Animated Views,' " trans. Timothy Barnard, *Moving Image* 3, no. 1 (2003): 129, n. 8. These advertisements concerned a series of trick films produced by Gaston Velle, a former magician who had recently been hired by the Lumières in an effort, however tardy, to serve the demands of the French fairground market and thus to compete with Méliès and Pathé on their own terms.

21. See my "Fairground Illusions and the Magic of Méliès," in *Travelling Cinema in Europe*, ed. Martin Loiperdinger, *KINtop Schriften* 10 (2008): 34–45. Other Méliès trick films from this period embracing fairground illusion motifs include *Ten Ladies in One Umbrella* (1903) and *Extraordinary Illusions* (1903).

22. Richard Abel, *The Red Rooster Scare: Making Cinema American, 1900–1910* (Berkeley: University of California Press, 1999), 3–6. The U.S. market would

become increasingly important for Méliès after 1903, when, partly in response to the widespread duping of *A Trip to the Moon*, he dispatched his brother, Gaston, to New York to establish a Star-Film sales office and developing laboratory and began producing two negatives of every title with one negative earmarked for export to the United States.

23. Deslandes and Richard, *Du cinématographe*, 87. See also Paul Hammond, *Marvellous Méliès* (London: Gordon Fraser, 1974), 95.

24. Hennion, "Éclairage," 44.

25. See Richard Abel, "*A Trip to the Moon* as An American Phenomenon," this volume, 131–134. A fixture of Luna Park for several years, A Trip to the Moon closed on Coney Island in 1907. Its place was taken by a comparable ride, A Trip to Mars by Aeroplane in 1910. One of the most comprehensive accounts of A Trip to the Moon is Frank H. Winter, "The 'Trip to the Moon' and Other Early Spaceflight Simulation Shows, ca. 1901–1915," part 1, in *History of Rocketry and Astronautics*, AAS History Series, vol. 23, ed. Donald C. Elder and Christophe Rothmund (San Diego, Calif.: American Astronautical Society, 2001), 133–161. For a detailed study of the many versions of A Trip to the Moon in early-twentieth-century traveling carnival shows, see Winter, "The 'Trip to the Moon' and Other Early Spaceflight Simulation Shows, ca. 1901–1915," part 2, in *History of Rocketry and Astronautics*, AAS History Series, vol. 25, ed. Hervé Moulin and Donald C. Elder (San Diego, Calif.: American Astronautical Society, 2003), 3–28.

26. Julian Hawthorne, "Some Novelties at Buffalo Fair," *Cosmopolitan*, Sept. 1901, 490. See also Woody Register, *The Kid of Coney Island: Fred Thompson and the Rise of American Amusements* (New York: Oxford University Press, 2001), 69–73.

27. Michael Leja, *Looking Askance: Skepticism and American Art from Eakins to Duchamp* (Berkeley: University of California Press, 2004), 125.

28. Several "short scenes of specific attractions," including the titles *A Trip to the Moon* (1901) and *Johnstown Flood* (1901) were among Edison's films of the 1901 Pan-American Exposition. Charles Musser, *Before the Nickelodeon: Edwin S. Porter and the Edison Manufacturing Company* (Berkeley: University of California Press, 1991), 176. See also *Edison Films*, July 1901, 3–7.

29. Alison Griffiths, *Shivers Down Your Spine: Cinema, Museums, and the Immersive View* (New York: Columbia University Press, 2008), 2.

30. Hawthorne, "Some Novelties," 491.

31. Xenophon Theodore Barber, "Evenings of Wonders: A History of the Magic Lantern Show in America" (Ph.D. diss., New York University, 1993), 379. See also *Magic: Stage Illusions, Special Effects and Trick Photography*, ed. Albert A. Hopkins (1898, repr., New York: Dover, 1976), 348–353; and Lynda Nead, *The Haunted Gallery: Painting, Photography, Film, c.1900* (New Haven, Conn.: Yale University Press, 2007), 221–224.

32. A Trip to the Moon was often mentioned in accounts of the Pan-American Exposition published in the United States, but neither it nor the Buffalo Exposition itself seem to have garnered nearly the same level of attention in the French popular press. Thierry Lefebvre suggests that Méliès would most likely have been aware of A Trip to the Moon and emphasizes parallels between the ride

and the film. Lefebvre, "*A Trip to the Moon*: A Composite Film," trans. Timothy Barnard, this volume, 51–53. See also Gunning, "Lunar Illuminations," 73–74.

33. Although Barbenfouillis manages to keep the tall, pointed hat atop his head as he bows to his colleagues in the audience, it falls off when he steps up to the speaker's platform, showing the difficulty of moving in this unwieldy ceremonial garb.

34. "Paris Items," *Mahatma*, July 1900, n.p.

35. Hammond notes that Méliès "advertised the activities of the Robert-Houdin in the official guide" to the Universal Exposition. *Marvellous Méliès*, 43.

36. Jean-Jacques Meusy, *Paris-Palaces, ou les temps des cinémas* (1894–1918), rev. ed. (Paris: CNRS Éditions, 2002), 73. Later, Carmelli (Auguste Coëne) ran his own fairground theater, which combined illusions with film screenings that sometimes included Méliès's films. Jacques Garnier, *Forains d'hier et d'aujord'hui: Une siècle d'histoire des forains, des fêtes et de la vie foraine* (Orléans, France: Jacques Garnier, 1968), 288–289.

37. Emmanuelle Toulet, "Cinema at the Universal Exposition, Paris, 1900," trans. Tom Gunning, *Persistence of Vision*, no. 9 (1991): 15–16. On cinema at the 1900 Universal Exposition, see also Meusy, *Paris-Palaces*, 77–98.

38. Toulet, "Cinema at the Universal Exposition," 14. Méliès's former business partner Lucien Reulos, with whom he had marketed a short-lived motion picture apparatus, did participate in the photography exhibits at the Universal Exposition. On this apparatus, see Georges Brunel, *La Photographie et la projection du mouvement* (Paris: Charles Mendel, 1897), 93–99.

39. Jacques Malthête, "Les *Vues spéciales de l'Exposition de 1900* tournées par Georges Méliès," *1895*, no. 36 (2002): 99–100. Each film was 20 meters—or slightly more than one minute—in length.

40. Nead, *Haunted Gallery*, 224.

41. "Some Unique Attractions of the Paris Exposition," *Scientific American*, June 16, 1900, 374. See also Nead, *Haunted Gallery*, 224–226.

42. "The Maréorama at the Paris Exposition," *Scientific American*, Sept. 29, 1900, 198.

43. "Feuille spéciale décrivant les *Vues spéciales de l'Exposition de 1900* editées par Georges Méliès," *1895*, no. 36 (2002): 103–104.

44. Tom Gunning, " 'The Whole World within Reach': Travel Images without Borders," in *Virtual Voyages: Cinema and Travel*, ed. Jeffrey Ruoff (Durham, N.C.: Duke University Press, 2006), 36.

45. In addition, he also made one film that used a semicircular panoramic shot, *Paris Exposition, 1900—From the Trocadero*.

46. "Feuille spéciale," 101–102.

47. "Feuille spéciale," 104–105. The sense of virtual travel which these circular panoramas ostensibly provided is emphasized by the English titles *Panoramic Excursion Round the Champs Elysées* and *Panoramic Circular Tour; "Les Invalides."*

48. Kristen Whissel, *Picturing American Modernity: Traffic, Technology, and the Silent Cinema* (Durham, N.C.: Duke University Press, 2008), 137.

49. See Griffiths, *Shivers Down Your Spine*, 51–56.

50. Lumière, Edison, and Pathé also made films of the moving sidewalk. "Feuille spéciale," 101–106. See also *La Production cinématographique des frères Lumière*, ed. Michelle Aubert and Jean-Claude Seguin (Paris: Bibliothèque du film, 1996), 184–185.

51. Edward Insley, "Paris in 1900 and the Exposition," *Harper's Monthly*, Sept. 1900, 494. See also "Musings without Method," *Blackwood Edinburgh Magazine*, July 1900, 114–115. The escalator, or "moving stairway," an "ingenious piece of American machinery . . . presented now to the public for the first time" at the Universal Exposition was not the subject of as many journalistic accounts as the moving sidewalk. B. D. Woodward, "The Exposition of 1900," *North American Review*, April 1900, 476.

52. "Some Perspectives on the Paris Exposition," *Scientific American*, June 30, 1900, 406.

53. Lillian W. Betts, "The People at the Pan-American," *Outlook*, Sept. 14, 1901, 119.

54. Ordway Partridge, "The Educational Value of World's Fairs," *Forum*, Mar. 1902, 121.

55. Robert W. Rydell, *All the World's a Fair: Visions of Empire at American International Expositions, 1876-1916* (Chicago: University of Chicago Press, 1984). See also Rydell, John E. Findling, and Kimberly D. Pelle, *Fair America: World's Fairs in the United States* (Washington, D.C.: Smithsonian Institution Press, 2000), 45–71.

56. Paolo Cherchi Usai notes the importance of the blackboard in *A Trip to the Moon* in his analysis of another Méliès film that involves a quick-sketch by the filmmaker, "Une autre Méliès retrouvé, analyse de *Le Chevalier mystère* (1899)," *Cinémathèque Méliès*, no. 15 (1989): 15. See also the quick-sketch Méliès performs in *The Astronomer's Dream*.

57. "Is There Snow upon the Moon?" *Harper's Weekly*, Mar. 15, 1902, 339. Professor Pickering of the Harvard College Observatory had hypothesized that there was snow on the moon after observing white areas on the lunar surface that appeared to diminish with exposure to sunlight. There is also snow on the moon in H. G. Wells's novel *The First Men in the Moon*.

58. Both of the latter films explicitly position wrestling contests in the fairgrounds, where they were often staged. See Christiane Py and Cécile Ferenczi, *La Fête foraine d'autrefois: Les années 1900* (Lyon, France: La Manufacture, 1987), 66–94.

Figure 10-1. *A Trip to the Moon*—The Big Dipper.

VICTORIA DUCKETT

The Stars Might Be Smiling

A Feminist Forage into a Famous Film

> Without doubt, too, civilizations may change. It is not in itself inconceivable that ours may, one day, turn away from history, and historians would do well to reflect upon this possibility. If they do not take care, there is danger that badly understood history could involve good history in its disrepute.
>
> —Marc Bloch, *The Historian's Task*

Starting Seriously

A TRIP TO THE MOON IS A peripatetic film. It engages so many art forms, mediums, traditions, and histories, that establishing precisely what we are seeing when we watch the work is difficult. This means that even if sources are identified, arguing that they are the film's determinant texts is difficult. We might begin, most obviously, with the literature available to us.[1] We might then detour into biography or the popular theater[2] or speak, as Lynda Nead does, of *A Trip to the Moon* in terms of the Victorian astronomical imagination. Indeed, as Nead notes in a prescient reading of the image of the rocket landing on the moon, "This spectacular and memorable image can be read as a symbolic

vision of the end of astronomical science based on the transcription of
the observation of the eye and the triumph of a new astronomy based
on the superior gaze and representational capacities of the camera lens."[3]

My difficulty with these various approaches is that they all seem
to move forward into early film, as though Méliès's *A Trip to the Moon*
were really the end point of a necessary advance. What gets lost here
are some very simple facts: the film was as much about the reworking of
established disciplines and discoveries as it was a comedic reflection upon
social change and gendered difference. Méliès might present a clever
lunar landing with a host of new spectacular tricks, but he is comically
clear about who travels, why they travel, and where they actually go.
Much of Méliès's work is therefore less "progressive" than it is humorously regressive and it is actually quite convenient for us to instead focus
on film as a discipline that offers visual proof of scientific discovery or
technological advance. That is, the effort to imagine film in terms of
male adventure or even in terms of Méliès's capacity to personalize an
industrial product is not without purpose because then we never ask
about female intervention in his film, or never ask if he might have
engaged with feminist arguments, or even if we feminists have been too
quick to imagine feminist archaeology in terms of literal absence alone.
Endorsing this view is Lucy Fischer's argument, forwarded in 1979 and
yet to be revised, that with Méliès "The Lady Vanishes" or becomes a
decorative object "to be placed here or there like a throw pillow or a
piece of sculpture."[4] This means that the "artistic tableaux" he presents
are then *really* "artistic tableaux," which illustrate the unfortunate fact
that women have traditionally been imagined as static and contemplative
objects. Méliès thus remains misogynistic, a founding father recuperated
by other founding fathers, someone who illustrates the happy coincidence
between male authorship, popular culture, and avant-garde practice in
early film.

Finding Things Funny

The humor of Méliès's *A Trip to the Moon* is different. The smiles he
provokes from me as I watch women reenact their clearly choreographed
chorus derives not just from my own personal delight in kitsch, but
from the much-gendered comedy that his images set into play. Méliès
not only proactively engaged with feminism, but he did so in a satirical
and witty manner. Indeed, I note how in our focus on the tricks and
magic of his film, we have lost much of his satire and biting commentary.
Hence, even though women do not travel in *A Trip to the Moon*, even
though they do not bumble their way through any number of fantasies

of colonization and control, they nevertheless indicate some fundamental feminist demands. In the first place, the film shows both their public presence and the very labor of their "decorative art" (women are the anonymous chorus girls in sailor suits smiling at us, they are sitting still, balancing their "artistic tableaux"). The film also comically parodies their irrelevance: three secretaries scribble at the Scientific Congress, twelve chorus girls push the rocket that an elderly scientist later negotiates alone, these same girls cheerfully return to sound the shell's departure, and on the moon they either poke their heads inanely through the "Big Dipper" that appears in the sky, pose in their artistic tableaux, or are seated at the foot of the Selenite King. Back on earth they again push the shell, parade with ceremonial guns, and finally join hands to dance in celebration of a trip they never took. This exaggerated female presence, this parade of stockings and smiles and careful, calculated activity reminds us that decorative art was less about private retreat than it was about public agitation.

Occupying quotidian space in spectacular new ways, women engaged in the production of artistic meaning. The satire that they enacted, however, is a little different from the slapstick of the theater. This is the comedy of anachronistic desire, a humoring of the idea that even in the machine age, at a point at which technology was clearly related to the demands of the *femme nouvelle*, women were merrily (and merely) performing for a male audience. As Debora L. Silverman explains in her book *Art Nouveau in Fin de Siècle France: Politics, Psychology, and Style*, the very emphasis on woman as decorative object and decorative artist was a calculated response to the threat of female emancipation in the 1890s. She states, "the craft officials united in forging a specifically cultural route to contain and interiorize women. By celebrating women as queens and artists of the interior, they developed a powerful antidote to the *femme nouvelle*, who threatened to relinquish her role as decorative object and decorative artist."[5] Méliès was not part of this effort to contain the modern woman. When he visually immobilized women within their given shots and ensured their narrative extraneousness, he was not doing this to mark some kind of social and gendered entrapment. Rather, he satirized their gendered immobility, paradoxically making the fixed pose the very one that carried mobile meanings, which I discuss later. In comically undermining the very effort to domesticate and contain the craft movement, he presented women as active, professional figures capable of articulating new forms of engagement in the modern world.

Silverman, noting that technology was closely allied to feminism in late-nineteenth-century France, goes on to explain men's critical reaction to this. Fearing the inversion of sexual roles, authors described fantastic

visions of feminist anarchy and detailed the eradication of sexual difference, projecting a homosocial fear of woman leaving the home to become
a *femme nouvelle* or *amazone*. Silverman states:

> In Robida's vision of the twentieth century, superwomen in male's
> clothing use machines to dominate the earth and skies, dividing their
> time between mechanical wizardry and teaching at the universities.
> More solemn and more apprehensive in tone was an article in
> 1889 by Georges Valbert in the *Revue des deux mondes*, an academic
> counterpart to Robida's lively science fiction. Valbert's "L'Age des
> machines," written one month after the opening of the 1889 exhibi-
> tion, cautioned against two distracting modern forces prefigured in
> the monumental exhibition. One was the levelling depersonalization
> of the new technology, whose standardized and prefabricated iron
> forms threatened individual creativity and autonomy. The other
> was the social effects of this new technology, which would be
> expressed in the elimination of differences between the sexes. . . .
> The model of woman as the embodiment of aesthetic spectacle and
> as the manipulator of a complicated weaponry of seduction would
> be replaced, Valbert feared, by the female-man, rigid, austere, and
> riddled with the appetitive combativeness of professional mobility.[6]

Méliès seems to empty his screen of these women: the cross-dressing
of his sailor girls was an accepted part of theatrical tradition, the embrace
of his two posing women was hardly prompted by same-sex desire, and
women are uniquely absent from the description of technological production (that is, when the men mechanically build the rocket). But there is
something else operating here. There is an excess of display and availability, a saturation of posture and pose, which suggests that women
might actually be parodying the very performances they are setting into
place. Thus, into the otherwise familiar tale of bumbling scientific men
discovering a distant moon, we have a new satirical look at representational traditions. We laugh not because we recognize the women—we
do not—but because they recontextualize the narrative being described.
This is a trip to the moon where aged scientists remain aged scientists
and where youthful female stars disdainfully hurry them on their way.

Case Study: The Moon Man

I now examine the most famous image and scene (well, two scenes) in
A Trip to the Moon. That is, I explore the moment in which the rocket
lands in the eye of the moon and its immediate consequence as a kind

of test case for what it is I am arguing about Méliès's satirical humor and his use of women. I think this scene and the following one is appropriate, not only because it is so familiar to us all, but also because it remains topical today. Still used as a kind of iconographic shorthand in the description of early film (and hence its appearance on the Society for Cinema and Media Studies banner as one of its visually representative "moments"), it is known to specialists and nonspecialists alike. Indeed, I would go so far as to say that where once it might have been the cannon or telescope that represented lunar flight and the comedy of science fiction, with film it has instead become Méliès's moon man. We might begin with Rudolphe Töppfer's comic strips *Monsieur Pencil* (1849) or his *Docteur Festus* (1840)[7] and note that the very first "picture story" not only included space travel but also featured many aspects that made their way into *A Trip to the Moon*: the send-up of the Scientific Institute, huge telescopes, and descriptive wit. There is also similarity in terms of events and props. For example, in *Travels and Adventures of Docteur Festus* the scientists travel as a group, carry an umbrella, and on their descent they fall into the sea with a steam ship at hand; in *Monsieur Pencil*, Mr. Jolibois falls to earth from space and is captured, examined, but then escapes from imprisonment; all these elements overlap with *A Trip to the Moon*.[8] We can further recognize the way in which Töppfer, too, humorously undermines the usefulness of the individually held telescope.[9] We might then move on to the images that we have of the cannon in Jacques Offenbach's operetta *Le Voyage dans la lune* (1875) and note the visual concordance between this, Töppfer's huge exploding telescope, and Méliès's similar cannon launch.[10] More important, we might realize that even if a comedy of fantastical flight is repeating itself in both visual and narrative terms through disparate texts (and discussion could obviously be developed), it is Méliès's moon that has instead become symptomatic of his film and of the humor he was engaging.

And so another path might be chosen. Here, even if we are discarding the telescope as representative object, we are not discarding its associative wit. Méliès's moon is the smiling moon-face of Jules Chéret in his cover for the *Catalogue illustré de l'exposition des arts incohérents* (1886), it is the moon of *La Lune rousse* that preceded this with its comical attacks on bourgeois conformity, and it is, finally, a synthesis of the Incoherents' *La Nouvelle Lune* with its successive mastheads personifying precisely what Méliès depicts in and on the moon: Phoebe on her crescent, the jester looking down on contemporary Paris, the lunatic smile of a man who has escaped reason.[11] Perhaps more obviously, Méliès's moon in *A Trip to the Moon* is the moon in the publicity for his own *Les Farces de la lune ou les mésaventures de Nostradamus* (1891), a moon-face that grins lasciviously down on a Phoebe who rests seductively on her cardboard crescent.[12]

I would like to believe that this humor remains with us today and that we still see the satirical "incoherence" of Méliès's moon in that we fixate on this image rather than the telescope precisely because it offers an intelligent escape from masculine phallocentrism. Although it is never actually introduced as an "incoherent moon," Méliès's moon reflects the comic logic of the "Institut de l'Astronomie Incohérent" and resonates with Méliès's later sketches of the film.[13] In other words, we could interpret this image of the grinning moon as shorthand for the wit and satire of early cinema, meaning as a gesture of critical acknowledgement. Furthermore, the actual silence surrounding Méliès's moon-face could suggest that we have already understood its antagonistic humor, meaning that it might indeed be seen as the cinematic equivalent of placing a smoking pipe in the mouth of the *Mona Lisa*.[14] There would be something very encouraging in this, in the idea that Méliès's voice has actually been lost in the broader terms of his social satire and that there is instead a real need to stress the extent of Méliès's engagement in film (he is "cinema's first *auteur*," a "one-man band," as Tom Gunning has recently explained).[15]

I think, however, that something very different has happened. Méliès's *A Trip to the Moon* has been transfixed within the genre of the trick film and his moon-face has largely come to represent the magic and illusion of film. Gunning's article "The Cinema of Attractions: Early Film, Its Spectator and the Avant-Garde" is largely responsible for this because *A Trip to the Moon* was first described here as "a demonstration of the magical possibilities of the cinema" and early film was conceived in terms of spectacle and exhibition.[16] The fault is obviously not Gunning's alone: he was paradoxically trying to shift attention from narrative to image and to highlight the role of the spectator in the creation of social meaning. Here I will not go to the opposite extreme—I will not ask that we abandon spectacle altogether—but want to suggest that we undertake Gunning's task a little differently. Instead of presuming a visually transparent image and imagining spectatorship in terms of sensorial shock, I view film in terms of visual layers and reflective humor. Indeed, it is only when we mine the historical meaning of a given image that satire can be identified as part of *A Trip to the Moon* and history can actually become relevant. And at this point, when we laugh at what Jean-Louis Comolli (citing Julia Kristeva) calls "*a stratified history*," "a history characterized by discontinuous temporality, which is recursive, dialectical, and not reducible to a single meaning,"[17] we can laugh at the refractive humor of film. It is here, when we see that images also move inward and backward and not just outward and forward, can we move from discussions of men and modernity and assign film some real material agency.

The Lunar Landing

Let us begin, then, with the moment when the rocket lands on a man's eye. This rocket has been fired from a cannon, but it has not actually taken flight, meaning we have not actually seen it fly in the sky. Instead, it is pasted on the moon in some kind of awkward collage, and this is followed by a display of facial distortion. Originally, as Gunning notes in his article "Tracing the Individual Body: Photography, Detectives, and Early Cinema," facial distortion was seen as a way to resist the fixing of the photographic inscription of criminal identity in late-nineteenth-century France. As he explains, facial distortion then entered early film in comedies of criminal capture: in *A Subject for the Rogue's Gallery* (1904) a woman contorts her face but then acknowledges the inevitability of her identification. Caught by a progressively advancing Biograph camera, she weeps.[18] In *A Trip to the Moon*, we have the same momentum—an encroachment on a captured face—but we have a very different comedy. Here the camera does not so much reveal or identify its subject (he is too made up, he lacks a body, there is no narrative involvement), nor does it offer the promise of subsequent revelation. Instead, the contorting face reminds us that we are watching a filmic farce and that for all of our technological know-how, this is still man's fantasy of scientific advancement and of making it to the moon. Hence we might have a superior gaze and greatly increased representational capacities thanks to film, but the material world still escapes us: we reach the moon through a comedy of arrivals and are promised a distorted and incoherent vision of what it might actually be. Even with the eye transformed through new technologies of vision (the camera, film), we are still inventing and "making up" what we can actually see. Again, we can return to Töppfer's *Docteur Festus* because we are like his Astronomer Guignard, marveling over the appearance of a celestial body, which is actually only a trapped man framed in a new circle of vision.[19]

   This argument can be taken a step further. We enter the moon in *A Trip to the Moon* through the head of a man who is performing a comedy of facial distortions. But where does the humor actually lie? Surely it is not the move from reality to make-believe, or from presence to performance, because we are already clearly within the realm of comedy and the fantastic. The grimacing yet smiling moon man signals the fact that comedy can challenge established meanings and representational histories. This is, in other words, the site (like the moon on the banner of *La Nouvelle Lune* or the cover of Chéret's 1886 catalogue) in which the fantastic might very well reign but it reigns with a critical and social purpose. As though to underline this aim, Méliès has his moon man brought—literally—to his senses here, just at the beginning of this fantastic lunar "escape." Indeed, only now that the moon man rolls his tongue, licks his lips, and blinks, does this suggest we have moved from a comedy of arrival to one of sensorial anticipation. Hence, while this face was at first smiling solidly, introducing the humor of the rocket's impossible flight (it appears too suddenly, it is a flat fragment of detail against an otherwise expressive surface), it is now newly mobile. Presenting a comedy of masculine anticipation, it suggests that this surface will not be suddenly cleaned and cleared, identified and named, even in the final moment of photographic intrusion. Better, this man will never weep in recognition of his absurd aims, or be forced into individual accountability, or be asked to remove his makeup. This is the true story, then, of a man who has his head in the clouds.

Joining de Bergerac's Journey

Emphasizing the senses (taste, sight, touch) at the very moment that we enter the moon seems rather paradoxical. Particularly in the instance of sight—where an eye has been effectively blinded through the landing of the rocket—we have man's incapacity to see comically reinforced. While this reveals one of the possible ways in which the absurdity of the Incoherents was brought to film, it also invokes the satire of Cyrano de Bergerac's *Journey to the Moon* (1657).[20] That is, Méliès was bringing to film the sensorial changes described by de Bergerac's text or at least signaling that the moon will become a place in which man is forced to his senses. Hence, just as de Bergerac substitutes the inhalation of the vapor of food for eating on the moon (claiming that this is why kitchen and pastry cooks "eat less than persons of other professions, [but] are still much fatter than they are"[21]), so too does Méliès introduce and dematerialize taste at the very point that we reach the moon. Or, rather, he reverses de Bergerac's vision and makes the scientists leave a vaporous industrial world only to land them on a moon that resembles (and perhaps is) a custard pie. Even more generally, one could argue that Méliès's later focus on physicalized, acrobatic acting (through the contortions of the Selenites, who were "actually" acrobats from the Folies-Bergère) can be paralleled to de Bergerac's contention that the language of the people on the moon (and remember that these were people who walked on all fours) "is expressed by the quivering of the limbs . . . their limbs, accustomed to move about so violently that it does not seem to be a man speaking, but a body shaking."[22] But this jumps ahead: for now, my point is that the smiling moon-face in Méliès's *A Trip to the Moon* was partly modeled on de Bergerac's *Journey to the Moon* and that a watching audience would have been able to decipher and recognize this.

How is this so? Why would de Bergerac's text be relevant or even significant at this particular moment in the film? In the first place, de Bergerac's *Journey to the Moon* had remained very much in the public eye in the late nineteenth century. Proof of this can be related to the fact that the work had recently been published in French (in 1888, 1897, and 1898).[23] It had also recently been translated into English as *A Voyage to the Moon* (1899).[24] Coming on the heels of at least three earlier English translations (one in 1660, another by A. Lovell in 1687, and another by Samuel Derrick in 1754),[25] we have evidence that the late nineteenth century did indeed see a renewed interest in de Bergerac's text. Although the reasons for this are many—people could respond to de Bergerac's fanciful speculations, were similarly engaging the capacity to see oneself as "other," clearly embraced the burlesque,[26] reveled in de Bergerac's joining of the old and the new, and spoke of his "triumphant blend of romance and humor,"[27] it was perhaps the resounding success of Edmond Rostand's 1897 play, *Cyrano de Bergerac*, which ensured his renewed visibility. Played with Ernest Coquelin in the title role to popular acclaim at the Théâtre de la Porte Saint-Martin (he would play the piece for more than 400 performances) and taken the following year to the Garden Theatre, New York (and here played by Richard Mansfield), *Cyrano de Bergerac* was later famously included in the program for Paul Decauville's Phono-Cinéma-Théâtre at the Universal Exposition in Paris in 1900. What this means is that even if an audience was not familiar with de Bergerac's own *Journey to the Moon*, then they were probably at least familiar with his reincarnation as a witty, masked character on the popular stage. Indeed, Emile Cohl's 1899 comic strip, "Une Aventure incroyable" (published in *L'Illustré nationale*), has a play on the moon's physiognomy with a man mistakenly catching his fishing rod on the moon's nose and pulling it to a "de Bergerian" length.[28] Perhaps more specifically, the 1899 English translation of his book has a direct reference to this play explaining on the opening page that Monsieur de Cuigy (the owner of the house where the tale begins) appears as a character in Rostand's play.[29] More concretely, we might recognize the way in which the scene in which Cyrano farcically "returns" from the moon before a startled De Guiche illustrates Rostand's familiarity with de Bergerac's originary text: explaining the seven ways of reaching the moon and humorously invoking all of the fantastic modes of lunar travels de Bergerac described in *Journey to the Moon*. There is travel by the dew's evaporation, by entrapped air, by magnetism, by the tide, by fire, and by the bodily application of grease marrow.[30] There is also overlap in the sense of disorientation at the respective de Bergerac's return to France, or overlap in the smaller detail of floss-silk ("Our Lady's Cotton") being described as "comet hair."[31] More obviously, of course, is the fact that the defining feature of Rostand's de Bergerac is his ungainly nose and capacity to write poetry while de Bergerac describes a moon in which eating becomes a matter of olfactory exchange and goods and services are paid by nobles in verse.[32]

I return, however, to Méliès's moon-face and continue to explain how this might lead us back to de Bergerac's satirical humor. As mentioned earlier, the moon moves his face after the rocket lands, and at this point he comes to his senses by licking his lips and so on. Humorously catching a taste of his own disguise, he seems to promise the realization of the fantastic. Moreover, we then move, like Rostand's more modern hero, into a fantasy in which the moon's mask is not removed. And at this point we might ask if the moon-face is not also playing the same substitutive role as Cyrano does for his friend Christian, describing an attraction for someone who does not otherwise have the language or words to do so, who lacks the capacity to conjure. I do not want to go too far with this parallel because, clearly, Rostand's work is also a departure from de Bergerac's. I think, however, that it is important to ask why this face is witty and humorous; why we do not recoil from its physical excess but instead choose to smile just at the moment that the rocket lands and sticks pointedly out of the moon-face.

The clearest indication that we are now "following" and in a sense replicating the wit and satire of de Bergerac's *Journey to the Moon* is revealed to us, however, in the next shot, when the scientists climb out of the rocket. Turning to look at their surroundings, they see the earth rise moon-like in the sky behind them. This moment is recounted in de Bergerac's conversation with a young adolescent he meets just after his own arrival on the moon. He states (it is the narrator speaking):

> "You see in me . . . a person bewildered by so many miracles that I do not know which one to admire first. To begin with, coming as I do from a world that you here doubtless consider to be a moon, I thought I had landed in another, which the people in my country also call the Moon, and lo and behold, I find myself

in Paradise.". . . [H]e [the adolescent] replied, "what you say is quite true; this earth here is the Moon that you can see from your globe, and this place through which you are walking is Paradise, but it is the Earthly Paradise into which only six people have ever entered: Adam, Eve, Enoch, I (who am the old Elijah), St. John the Evangelist, and you."[33]

Later, as punishment for holding that the moon was his earth and (vice versa), de Bergerac describes how sentence was passed to "declare . . . that this Moon here is not a moon, but a world; and that the world over there is not a world, but a moon."[34]

Satirical Stars

Within this satirical scheme, then, where worlds pluralize and we see ourselves as "other," women appear in the sky. There are the seven smiling stars (all young women) incarnating the form of the Big Dipper as they float above the six restlessly sleeping old men, there is Phoebe in diaphanous robes sitting on her cardboard crescent moon, and there are two women in a formal *tableau vivant* style of embrace, holding aloft a large star. What this means is that while these women are there to be freely looked at and savored as decorative treats, they are also there to be seen differently. Not only do they inhabit the space that has just been vacated by the moon's moon, but they are also a dream that has been realized. Like the scientists, we thus share a vision of bare arms, veils, tights, pointed toes, physical symmetry, and female grace, but we do not "really" see it. And like the scientists we might very well fantasize woman as a decorative and seductive object, but we are nevertheless constantly reminded that these are actually hard-working chorus girls. Indeed, ignoring the way in which each of the young girls has to nod their way into the frame, forcing the painted, circular heart of their respective stars to give way, is difficult. Instead of a slow process of imposition—remember that the male moon-face only gradually appeared within the moon—appearance here is labored and physical. Indeed, what this line of chattering and youthful faces represents is not so much a line of free floating female heads, but a recorded example of a theatrical trick that requires action. We might be watching a trip to the moon, but this is a very earthly and grounded vision of "the star."[35]

The fantasy of the sleeping scientists is, clearly, that these youths are excited over their presence and that they appear precisely because they have arrived. Here we are returned to another, more familiar, fantasy

Figure 10-2. *A Trip to the Moon*—Phoebe, Gemini, and Saturn.

of excited young actresses peeking out onto their theatrical audience before or between curtain calls. In this context, it is little surprising that Phoebe and the *tableaux vivants* models appear after these faces. In other words, it is little surprising that this image of youths desiring to be seen is then followed by the "artistic poses" of the stocking clad women who are "actually" seen. The anonymous circumstance of cinematic spectatorship is thereby comically denied: the moon's fiction is not so much that men have arrived in a distant celestial space but that film unwinds through a play of reciprocated (heterosexual) desire.

Pictorial and Performative Play

There is an alternative way in which male desire is satirized in this tableau. We are on the moon in a clearly fictitious space but the women are nevertheless "real." These are neither the inhabitants of de Bergerac's moon who crawl on all fours, nor are these women the elusive and physically unavailable Roxanne of Rostand's verse. These women are instead physically present and smiling back at us, offering their bodies to be seen. Clearly, Méliès was relying on familiar visual cues here. Most obviously, he returns us to his own *Les Farces de la lune ou les mésaventures de Nostradamus*, a *féerie* produced at his Théâtre Robert-Houdin in 1891. As Jacques Malthête indicates, this included a "tableau" of the goddess Phoebe.[36] Played by Jehanne d'Alcy, the photograph of this scene features the actress clad in a tight corset lying upon a crescent moon, one arm languorously stretched behind her head as the other rests at her side holding a wand with its own crescent on it. Her feet are slightly raised as they rest, crossed, and her eyes are shut. Nostradamus, dressed in a black gown and a pointed hat covered in stars, gestures to her, his back turned toward us.

We have in this figure of the reclining woman, not only a return to Méliès's own theater, but also a return to Lucas Cranach the Elder's *Nymph of the Spring* (1518)[37] (with d'Alcy inverting the direction of the resting nymph).[38] Whereas other visual sources might also be cited (Giorgione's *Sleeping Venus*, c. 1510, or Titian's *Andrias*, 1518, perhaps), the issue is not just that this image provides reference to a famously seductive image of a resting woman, but that her sleep is feigned. Indeed, the importance of Cranach's image is related to the fact that "*Fontis nimpha sacri somnum ne rumpe quiesco*" (I am the nymph of the sacred fountain. Do not disturb my sleep. I am resting.) is inscribed on a picture where sleep is, at best, ambiguous. In the poster publicizing Méliès's performance, Cranach's conjecture has been humored: Nostradamus is inserted into the frame and reaches toward Phoebe, who will no doubt awaken on her crescent moon.

On the live stage, then, this tableau presented the image of a famous *voyant* (Nostradamus) materializing a woman who was visually available. Indeed, not only was d'Alcy obviously and quite literally in Méliès's employ, she was also an actress on the popular stage and so associated in the public imagination with a loose morality. In this way, Cranach's eroticism was very much realized. This same point can be related to the film: Bleuette Bernon, a music-hall performer, appeared on the crescent moon, embodying the same erotic codes of d'Alcy. As Tracy C. Davis explains in her article "The Actress in Victorian Pornography"—and this is a comment that can be related as much to Méliès's film as to his stage practices—there was explicit overlap between the erotic codes in the popular theater and those of late-nineteenth-century pornography. She states:

Theatrical conventions, deeply encoded in the sexual language of society, participated in and reinforced a view of the theatre and

particularly of actresses, for the objects as well as the subjects of
arousal were gendered. The encodings, which almost certainly
were invisible and unintelligible to many spectators, were explicitly
explained in Victorian erotic books, periodicals, and illustrations
that were widely available to men. Thus, while erotica included
images of the theatre and its practitioners, the theatre persistently
contained elements of the erotic, to the consternation (or more
often the delight) of knowing spectators.[39]

Noting how theatrical costume "flagrantly violated the dress codes of
the street and drawing room, flaunting the ankles, calves, legs, thighs,
crotch, and upper torso,"[40] Davis goes on to explain that actual nudity
was not a requirement for sexual titillation. In a comment that, again,
might be read within the context of both d'Alcy and Bernon, she states:
"Simulated nudity (with tights or maillots) was just as powerful [as actual
nudity] and, by Victorian aesthetics, much more beautiful. Scandal arose
by association—posing with a man, posturing indecently (one foot on
a chair, one leg highly elevated, an ankle crossed over a knee, dorsal
views, and contortions) or through an activity (bicycling, climbing, and
arranging the toilette). Thus, momentary deferment of nudity was the
message of the photograph."[41]

When Méliès brought this "simulated nudity" to *A Trip to the Moon*,
he also changed its associative meanings. In this tableau Nostradamus is
replaced by scientists who lie asleep, immobile, beneath the women they
dream and desire. More significantly, Phoebe is seated upright, balancing
on her crescent moon, and seems to be more Manet's *Olympia* (1863) than
Cranach's nymph. That is, she is awake *and* confronting male spectatorial
presence. Moreover, as *phoibos* she is a bright and radiant presence—a
goddess or "star" in the night sky—who is available and visible yet also
distant and untouchable. In a similar way, she appears in a dream but is
at the same time a solid body in the sky; she is a woman who incarnates
the impossible promise of real physical presence. The independence that
Manet suggests (both professional and sexual, his courtesan has a maid and
her hand blocks her genitals) is also part of Méliès's world: Phoebe awakens
the men from their reverie when she casts snow on them. Determining,
therefore, not only how long she will be looked at and dreamed about,
Phoebe also implies that hers is a space that is not to be claimed.

We cannot forget, of course, that Phoebe is joined in this scene of
snowfall by the *tableau vivant* of two women holding aloft a star and by
Saturn leaning angrily out of his planet. These two women are the flip
side to Phoebe's carnality and promise of sexual pleasure. Or, rather, they

offer the satirical promise of innocent worship and thereby hold aloft a six-pointed Marian star as they adopt the clothes, pose, and movement of the Statue of Liberty (the Roman stole, one right arm extended aloft holding a star as a kind of "lunar torch," the left leg moving forward). Within the context of Catholic France at the turn of the twentieth century, these two women would have been readily identifiable (the Statue of Liberty was presented to the United States in 1886). Méliès's doubling of this figure—the fact that he presents two women in a forward-facing embrace—indicates this slippage of identities and terms. We move, then, between Mary and Libertas, between a Catholic Virgin Mother and a Roman goddess demanding liberty and freedom. We also move between church and country, between the singular (Mary) and the many (nameless immigrants), and between two conceptions of "enlightenment." At the same time, we move between two images of the female star on film: she is an innocent woman, a nameless and virginal youth who remains enticingly out of reach, yet she is also a woman who can demand freedom and who might—through film—make visible her challenge to gendered oppression.

In this scene, Saturn is presented as an irascible old man who leans out of his ringed planet and who provides a kind of celestial counterpoint to both the young stars we see before us and earth's (man-made) vaporous industrialization. Saturn is also, clearly, not just a gaseous planet above the vaporous earth: he is also an "earth" that famously has many moons. Again, therefore, we return to de Bergerac's exploration of the earth as a moon and vice versa, only this time there is the witty suggestion that we might partake in a process of endless lunar devolution. Saturn's age also leads us back to de Bergerac and his description of youths ruling over elders on the moon[42] because Saturn's major moon—Titan—mythologically refers to a deity of older gods (the Greek Titans) who were ruled by their youngest member (Kronos). Here the suggestion that Saturn might, in fact, be ruled by his youthful celestial companions or even that Phoebe (as an original Titan) could rule over him as a woman is comically raised.

Caustic Conclusions

It is relevant that it is Phoebe who gestures for the snow to fall and who therefore casts the scientists from her idyll. This is not just a witty inscription of a new celestial hierarchy inaugurated by film ("the star"), but it comically characterizes the limits of French colonial expansion. Indeed, even if audiences were not familiar with de Bergerac using Qué-

bec as his point of earthly departure for the moon,[43] they might have
been familiar with Verne's 1889 novel, *A Family without a Name*, which
was set in Canada in the Patriots Rebellion of 1837. Opening with a
humorous citation from Voltaire's 1757 letter to Mr. de Moncrif, it
characterizes French colonial struggle in the following way: "One pit-
ies that poor human race that slits its throat on our continent about
a few acres of ice in Canada."[44] It was Voltaire's 1758 novel, *Candide*,
which more famously characterized Canada as "a few acres of snow." In
conversation with Candide about France and England as they approach
the English coast, Martin accordingly states, "You know that these two
nations are at war about a few acres of snow somewhere around Canada,
and that they are spending on this beautiful war more than all Canada
is worth."[45] What is interesting about Méliès's citation of Voltaire's dis-
dain is the way it introduces another limit to man's colonial aspirations:
although he might indeed arrive in Canada, woman (and film) will not
be so easily occupied.

When Phoebe gestures for the snow to fall, she not only casts
the scientists from her idyll, she also humorously inverts the famous
Endymion myth. In this way, she challenges both a received story and
its representational history. Hence, rather than have Selene (the Titan
goddess of the moon) ask that a male mortal sleep so that he can remain
sexually available to her, Selene casts the scientists out of her celestial
sphere. Here Phoebe's crescent moon is again relevant, for in many paint-
ings of this myth the crescent moon crowns her face (see, for example,
Nicolas Poussin's *Selene et Endymion*, c. 1630; Sebastiano Ricci's *Endymion
and Selene*, c. 1714; and Jérôme-Martin Langlois's *Diane et Endymion*,
c. 1822). Here, too, de Bergerac again serves Méliès as a comedic foil:
the scientists did not—like his own character who arrives on the moon
only to "find his youth reinvigorated"—become younger or in any way
more attractive to the watching women. They instead arrive as old men
and depart as old men. And as if in final confirmation of their banish-
ment from the celestial sphere, they stumble hurriedly underground.

Shooting Stars

I will stop here, on this image of masculine retreat, because it is just a
brief revision of this famous moment that I wanted to offer. I want to
return, however, to my opening comments about *A Trip to the Moon* being
a peripatetic film and acknowledge that I, too, might have traced different
influences, even into this scene. There is, for example, the comical film of
Percy Honri as a ukulele-playing moon in Mitchell and Kenyon's *Mister*

Moon (1901), which is visually very similar to the smiling moon-face of Méliès's work and which introduces music and sound into discussion as well as another (more "filmic") way of addressing questions of authorship and textual migration.[46] But I wanted to keep my sight on Méliès and on his women, and I wanted to ask if we might see these figures differently. Rather than regarding ourselves as decorative objects—rather than speaking of "dried flowers or fruit"—I wanted to ask whether women could indeed engage in the creation of new aesthetic meanings, particularly through the medium of film. And although I might be criticized for focusing on just two scenes to do this, I also wanted to demonstrate a methodological choice. That is, when I speak of a stratified history, I am not nodding toward an easy interdisciplinarity, but asking that microhistorical studies be used to explode some of the more general historical models we still seem to hold in film studies.

My main difficulty in relation to this method remains tied to the question of source material. How far, in fact, can I look into the image? To what extent might I actually be inventing feminist agency? I don't know. The concept of stratified history certainly gives me leverage, but I am bringing this to a figure who has long been celebrated for his authorial voice, for his authority on film. I am reassured, however, by the fact that Méliès's self-portrait depicts his face breaking through a canvas on which it is written, *"Ad Omnia Leonardo Da Vinci"* ("To everything Leonardo Da Vinci").[47] Unlike the anonymous faces happily breaking through the stars in his Star-Film, Méliès is shown, brushes in hand, looking tired by the strain of his effort. Wit has gone; even his inscription is more a dedication than it is a parodic play on textual interruption. We have here an "actual" still life, a counterpoint to our young female stars, an homage to man's physical and textual entrapment.

Notes

Author's note: I would like to thank Richard Abel, Massimo Locatelli, David Mayer, Elena Mosconi, and Matthew Solomon for their generous suggestions and conversation.

1. Especially H. G. Wells's *The First Men in the Moon* (1901) and Jules Verne's *From the Earth to the Moon* (1865).

2. See Antonio Costa, *La morale del giocattolo: Saggio su Georges Méliès* (Bologna, Italy: CLUEB, 1995), 107, where he joins a discussion of the *féerie* to the Wells and Verne texts.

3. Lynda Nead, *The Haunted Gallery: Painting, Photography, Film, c.1900* (New Haven, Conn.: Yale University Press, 2007), 227.

4. Lucy Fischer, "The Lady Vanishes: Women, Magic, and the Movies," *Film Quarterly* 33, no. 1 (1979): 30–40; citation on p. 32.

5. Debora L. Silverman, *Art Nouveau in Fin-de-Siècle France: Politics, Psychology, and Style* (Berkeley: University of California Press, 1989), 74.

6. Silverman, *Art Nouveau*, 67, 69.

7. See *Rudolphe Töppfer: The Complete Comic Strips*, ed. and trans. David Kunzle (Jackson: University Press of Mississippi, 2007), esp. 351–376.

8. See E. H. Gombrich, *Art and Illusion: A Study in the Psychology of Pictorial Representation* (Oxford, U.K.: Phaidon, 1959), 248. In the context of the comic strip, Gombrich goes on to state that "Töppfer's humorous picture novels, the first which Goethe admired and encouraged him to publish, are the innocent ancestors of today's manufactured dreams."

9. For example, with Töppfer, "twenty-eight salaried observers" perch in trees with their telescopes but observe nothing but the mistakes that their patron sees with his naked eye; with Méliès, these telescopes become chairs during the Congress' meeting. See *Rudolphe Töppfer*, 367.

10. See Antonio Costa, "Georges Méliès alla conquista della luna," online at http://www.iuav.it/Didattica1/pagine-web/facolt--di1/Antonio-Co/clasT---st/03--9-ottobre--Georges-M-li-s.pdf. This is not included in his book (cited above n. 2).

11. See Donald Crafton, *Emile Cohl, Caricature, and Film* (Princeton, N.J.: Princeton University Press, 1990), 272–273.

12. See the poster reproduced in Jacques Malthête, *Méliès, images et illusions* (Paris: Exporégie, 1996), 37.

13. See *Christian Fechner présente Georges Méliès* (DVD, Studio Canal, 2007), "Boniments d'après Georges Méliès dits par André Dussollier," and the sketch reproduced in David Robinson, *Georges Méliès: Father of Film Fantasy* (London: Museum of the Moving Image, 1993), 39. Matthew Solomon has recently suggested to me that these sketches were made in the early 1930s.

14. Remember that Jules Lévy coined the phrase *les arts incohérents* as "an antagonistic foil to the everyday expression *les arts décoratifs*." Crafton, *Emile Cohl*, 30. See also Eugène Bataille, *Mona Lisa with a Pipe*, 1887.

15. Tom Gunning, "Lunar Illuminations," in *Film Analysis: A Norton Reader*, ed. Jeffrey Geiger and R. L. Rutsky (New York: Norton, 2005), 68.

16. Tom Gunning, "The Cinema of Attractions: Early Film, Its Spectator and the Avant-Garde," in *Early Cinema: Space, Frame, Narrative*, ed. Thomas Elsaesser with Adam Barker (London: British Film Institute, 1990), 58. See also the way in which this term has become generally applied: Richard Abel, "The Cinema of Attractions: 1896–1904," *The Ciné Goes to Town: French Cinema, 1896–1914* (Berkeley: University of California Press, 1998), 59–101; partly reprinted in *The Silent Cinema Reader*, ed. Lee Grieveson and Peter Krämer (London: Routledge, 2004), 63–75.

17. Jean-Louis Comolli, "Technique and Ideology: Camera, Perspective, Depth of Field," parts 3 and 4, in *Narrative, Apparatus, Ideology: A Film Theory Reader*, ed. Philip Rosen (New York: Columbia University Press, 1986), 424.

18. Tom Gunning, "Tracing the Individual Body: Photography, Detectives, and Early Cinema," in *Cinema and the Invention of Modern Life*, ed. Leo Charney and Vanessa R. Schwartz (Berkeley: University of California Press, 1995), 27.

19. *Rudolphe Töpffer*, 363.

20. See Costa, *La morale del giocattolo*, 55, where he inserts de Bergerac into a broader cultural panorama. While it is this generality I am critiquing, Costa is a particularly rich source for historical context. He is unique in that he makes mention of de Bergerac.

21. I am citing from the most recent English translation: Cyrano de Bergerac, *Journey to the Moon*, trans. Andrew Brown (London: Hesperus Classics, 2007), 44.

22. De Bergerac, *Journey to the Moon*, 40–41.

23. Cyrano de Bergerac, *Oeuvres comiques: Voyage dans la lune, Histoire des états et empires du soleil, Histoire des oiseaux* (Paris: Librairie de la Bibliothéque nationale, 1885–1889), for the 1888 edition. See also de Bergerac, *Œuvres comiques: Voyage dans la lune, Histoire des états et empires du soleil, Histoire des oiseaux* (Paris: Librairie de la Bibliothèque nationale, 1897); and de Bergerac, *Œuvres comiques: Voyage dans la lune, Histoire des états et empires du soleil, Histoire des oiseaux* (Paris: Librairie de la Bibliothèque nationale, 1898).

24. Cyrano de Bergerac, *The Comical History of the States and Empires of the World of the Moon*, trans. A. Lovell (New York: Doubleday and McClure, 1899).

25. Cyrano de Bergerac, *A Voyage to the Moon, with some account of the solar world: A comical romance done from the French*, trans. Samuel Derrick (London: Vaillant, 1754). The 1660 translation is mentioned in the preface to the 1687 edition.

26. See the preface to de Bergerac, *A Voyage to the Moon*, xxvii, where it is explained that while de Bergerac missed "real genius" it was his "exaggeration, sometimes carried to the burlesque, [which] is the essential trait which makes him what he is."

27. See "Constant Coquelin as the Gascon: Bernhardt Acts Roxanne in Rostand's Play for the First Time," *New York Times*, Dec. 11, 1900, 6.

28. Crafton, *Emile Cohl*, 270. Crafton is here discussing this in terms of Cohl's later film *Clair de lune espagnol* (1909), arguing that Cohl provides his films with his own specific gag motifs (268).

29. De Bergerac, *Comical History*, 9 n. 1.

30. See Edmund Rostand, *Cyrano de Bergerac*, trans. and adapt. Anthony Burgess (New York: Applause, 1985), 112–114. See the description of various modes of travel (de Bergerac is satirizing not only his own travel but also that of religious figures: Enoch, Adam, Eve, Elijah, and St John the Evangelist) in *Journey to the Moon*, 5–7, 15, 19–26. See also how these accounts overlap at times with Töppfer's description of how flight is achieved. *Rudolphe Töpffer*, 246, 263, 367.

31. De Bergerac, *Journey to the Moon*, 30. I do not want to go into this here, but this same "disorientation" is comically played out in Töppfer's work (see *Rudolphe Töpffer*, 255–258). De Bergerac's earthling is also caged and disorientated on the Moon (see *Journey to the Moon*, 34).

32. See, for example, de Bergerac, *Journey to the Moon*, 46: "When an author has composed a piece of poetry, he takes it to the Royal Mint . . . if they

are judged to be of good alloy, they are valued no according to their weight but according to their wit." Note that this nose is mentioned in the 1899 translation. De Bergerac, *Comical History*, xix.

33. De Bergerac, *Journey to the Moon*, 19.

34. De Bergerac, *Journey to the Moon*, 68. Note that we remain with the same six figures—in the sense that there are six men who arrive on de Bergerac's moon just as there are six men who arrive in Méliès's film (and just as there were six men in the French Académie Scientifique. See Maurice Crosland, "Popular Science and the Arts: Challenges to Cultural Authority in France under the Second Empire," *British Journal for the History of Science* 34, no. 3 (2001): 309.

35. John Frazer notes, in a rare acknowledgment of this "labor," "One always sees the presence of the hard-working chorus girls and dancers from Châtelet as they take position for a Méliès tableau." *Artificially Arranged Scenes: The Films of Georges Méliès* (Boston: G. K. Hall, 1979), 14.

36. Malthête, *Méliès, images et illusions*, 36.

37. See Michael Liebmann, "On the Iconography of the Nymph of the Fountain by Lucas Cranach the Elder," *Journal of the Warburg and Courtauld Institutes* 31 (1968): 434, for an explanation of why this image becomes the referential text (there are others of the same subject by Cranach); a reproduction of this painting is in Madeleine Malthête-Méliès and Anne-Marie Quévrain, "Georges Méliès et les arts: Étude sur l'iconographie de ses films et sur les rapports avec les courants artistiques," *Artibus et historiae* 1, no. 1 (1980): 140. The authors relate this pose to Méliès's drawing of "La Grande ourse" and his drawing for "Le Voyage dans la lune," I presume, because they are reproduced on the same page and share the figure of the reclining female.

38. See Malthête-Méliès and Quévrain, "Georges Méliès," 140, where this image is reproduced, and 138, where it is noted, in very general terms, how "The iconographic motif of the woman often makes use of the works of former painters: Cranach and the great Venetians."

39. Tracy C. Davis, "The Actress in Victorian Pornography," *Theatre Journal* 41, no. 3 (1989): 294–295.

40. Davis, "The Actress," 298.

41. Davis, "The Actress," 313.

42. De Bergerac, *Journey to the Moon*, 69–75.

43. De Bergerac, *Journey to the Moon*, 14.

44. Jules Verne, *Leader of the Resistance*, pt. 1, *Family without a Name*, ed. I. O. Evans (Westport, Conn.: Associated Booksellers, 1963), 11. The first sentence of chapter 1 is as follows, and includes an embedded quote: " 'We pity the wretched human race, who for the sake of a few acres of ice are cutting one another's throats' commented the philosophers towards the end of the eighteenth century. The reference was to Canada, for whose possession the French and English were at war."

45. Voltaire, *Candide*, trans. and ed. Daniel Gordon (Boston: Bedford/St. Martin's, 1999), 98. The quote here is: "You know that these two countries have

been at war over a few acres of snow in Canada, and that they are spending more on this lovely war than all of Canada is worth."

46. I would like to thank David Mayer for bringing this film to my attention.

47. See *Self Portrait of the Artist*, n.d., reproduced in Nead, *The Haunted Gallery*, 102. Nead analyzes this image in very different terms.

Figure 11-1. *Le avventure straordinarissime di Saturnino Farandola* (1913).

11

ANTONIO COSTA

Impossible Voyages and Extraordinary Adventures in Early Science Fiction Cinema

From Robida to Méliès and Marcel Fabre

"THE MYTH OF MÉLIÈS SEEMS TO return, once more and for the last time, in early Italian cinema." So Luigi Rognoni, a musicologist and author of a pioneering essay on silent film, concluded his account of Marcel Fabre's film *Le avventure straordinarissime di Saturnino Farandola* (1913),[1] composed on the occasion of a retrospective of Italian silent film held at the 1952 Venice Film Festival.[2] More recently, Kristin Thompson—writing in the Domitor newsletter about the conference, "The Days of Cabiria" (Turin, October 1997)—underscored the importance of the initiative that had allowed her to appreciate the full range of Italian silent film, apart from the usual stereotypes; and she ranked *Saturnino Farandola* first among her numerous "discoveries."[3] Georges Sadoul has already proposed a connection between the illustrations of Albert Robida—the author of the novel on which Fabre's *Saturnino Far-*

This chapter was translated by Elizabeth Alsop.

andola is based—and the impossible voyages of Georges Méliès. This chapter (1) examines the *féerique* aspects of *A Trip to the Moon* as well as other voyages of Méliès, which have more in common with the parodic imagery of Robida than with the visionary literature of Jules Verne and H. G. Wells; and (2) illuminates the continuities between Fabre's film and those of the late Méliès—in particular, *The Conquest of the Pole* (1912).

The Impossible Voyages of Georges Méliès

Thanks to *A Trip to the Moon*, Méliès is often considered one of the founding fathers of science-fiction and "futuristic" cinema, inasmuch as he was inspired by Jules Verne's and H. G. Wells's classic novels of the genre. However, the science-fiction component seems secondary when one considers the fantastic, burlesque quality of the fairy-tale (*féerique*) scenes Méliès first staged at the Théâtre Robert-Houdin, and subsequently filmed in his "cinematographic views." Moreover, we might reasonably assume that Verne's influence may have been mediated through the production of *Le Voyage dans la lune*. From the compelling account of the performance included in Siegfried Kracauer's exemplary study, *Orpheus in Paris: Offenbach and the Paris of His Time*, one begins to appreciate the debt Méliès owed to contemporary theatrical tradition:

> The sensation of the first act was an enormous gun through which the travelers were to be shot to the moon. So enormous was it that it rested on mountains and stretched across valleys, villages, and rivers. The second act showed the landscape of the moon itself. One of its features was a tobacco plant which blossomed in a few seconds. But all these were trifles in comparison with the volcanic eruption in the fourth act.
>
> No sooner are the travelers to the moon sentenced to hard labor in the interior of the volcano then there is a crash of thunder, the earth quakes, lava flows, and flames rise everywhere. One of the travelers takes refuge on an enormous rock. The rock is struck by a ball of fire and flung into space. There is a shower of ashes, then the devastated crest of the volcano is seen; and then the earth, glowing brightly in the distance in the sky, starts growing bigger and bigger until it fills the whole scene.
>
> The purely human plot was by no means overshadowed by the astronomical scale of these events. It was filled with humorous and satirical incidents. Prince Caprice, played by Zulma Bouffar, rouses very earthly feelings in the breast of Princess Fantasia, who, like all the inhabitants of the moon, is incapable of love. The love-affair

between the two proceeds triumphantly in the midst of all the technical wonders. So little, indeed, did the latter predominate that there was actually room for a ballet of snowflakes and a ballet of chimeras.

What gave this pantomime its individuality was the magic of Offenbach's music. Indeed, it held forth a vision of a time when man should no longer be in thrall to technical invention, but should freely use and play with it.[4]

Méliès had already created a distinctive iconography pertaining to the moon and its mythologies in his previous film, *The Astronomer's Dream or the Man in the Moon* (1898), which was in turn derived from one of his theatrical sketches (*Les Farces de la lune ou les mésaventures de Nostradamus*, 1891).[5] In *The Astronomer's Dream*, an astronomer in a long cloak and conical hat finds himself in a fantastical medieval setting. The character is clearly played for laughs, the comedy arising from the moon's mischievous transmutations, which disrupt the astronomer's otherwise ascetic existence. This evil lunar influence is presented as something out of a fable: it seems to hark back to the idea, long present in popular tradition, of a mythical age in which the moon and earth existed side-by-side.[6] On the other hand, it also represents the almost literal realization of the effect the French have dubbed *lunette d'approche*, a phrase used to denote the telescope or similar instruments. In actuality, the mood of the film is more retrograde than forward-looking: the anthropomorphic moon has the features of a playful glutton, and its demonic apparitions are far from horrifying. Méliès's sky is populated by lovely young girls who peer and prance about like actors at a *café-chantant*. In *A Trip to the Moon*, Méliès retains some vestiges of this original lunar iconography—albeit in a substantially more dynamic and developed context—and he will return to it again on other occasions. An often-cited example is *A Moonlight Serenade, or the Miser Punished* (1903), where the moon comes to the aid of the poor Pierrot, and helps him to avenge himself against a greedy, money-grubbing man who does not appreciate his serenades. Particularly worthy of note is the moment in which the lunar disk transforms itself into an eye, which, according to the entry in the American Star-Film catalog, is "the '*Eye of God*' who has seen his wickedness and his avarice and has punished him for his cruelty."[7]

A moon somewhat similar to the one in *The Astronomer's Dream* also appears in *The Dream of an Opium Fiend* (1908), a late and somewhat repetitive film, characterized by a more naturalistic style of acting, and the use of effects that strike one as both more realistic and, in general, less poetic than those of its prototype. Particularly comical are the protagonist's lunar hallucinations, which he experiences in the context of a petty bourgeois sitting room—a far cry from the sumptuous, Oriental opium den in the first scene.

Both the curious combination of elements so widely evident in Méliès's work, and his borrowings from "science-fiction" literature, are responsible for the extraordinary achievements of *A Trip to the Moon*. From the very first scene, one recognizes his talent for intermingling and juxtaposing different iconographic models. On the one hand, we have the scene set in a sort of Gothic cathedral-cum-laboratory, during a rowdy, rather absurd meeting of the Astronomic Club, whose members are all dressed as wizards in long flowing robes and conical hats. On the other hand, we have the futuristic scene in the workshop, where they are assembling the projectile. The first scene unfolds in the indefinite time and space of a fable. But when the astronomers, having exchanged their cloaks for more conventional bourgeois garb, head to the workshop where the projectile is being prepared, the set design changes radically. And the view from the workshop's rooftop terrace onto which the clumsy travelers have crowded to witness the smelting of the "great cannon" reveals an industrial landscape filled with chimneys belching smoke and sulfurous gases. The scene depicting the launch of the projectile strikes us as something halfway between a municipal ceremony, with all its pointless bravado, and a spectacle straight out of the Folies-Bergère. A parade of sailor girls lightens the atmosphere of suspense created by the ominous presence of the cannon, which swallows up the capsule containing the astronomer-astronauts.

We now turn to the most often-cited and discussed scene in the film, the one portraying the projectile's approach to the moon and its impact on the lunar surface. After the order "Fire!" is given on earth, we see the moon appear to come closer until, with a break in continuity, a crude approximation of the lunar round is replaced by a more detailed anthropomorphic rendering—a "face" whose eye is pierced by the projectile, causing some liquid to seep out while the moon grimaces comically. One is dealing here with a fake traveling shot—that is, an apparent forward movement of the camera. As in other Méliès films, the effect was achieved by slowly moving the object being shot toward the camera (which was stationary). Méliès only used effects of this kind to represent the transformation of an object's dimensions as the result of various kinds of magic: in *The Man with the Rubber Head* (1901), we see the alchemist "inflate" his own head to the point of making it explode; in *The Mermaid* (1904), we see a magician whose tricks increase the size of an aquarium so much that it turns into a real ocean. A modern spectator tends to interpret the approach to the moon as a "subjective" point-of-view shot. Some perceive a sort of shift in point of view within this frame, a movement from one subjective vision (the spectators, who identify with the supposed point of view of the astronomers) to another (that of the public who has remained on earth), which is an objective, "omniscient view."[8] John Frazer's comment is even more helpful, as he talks about the "close-up" effect of the moon; "a close-up," he adds, "that is rationalized by special circumstances, similar to G. A. Smith's rationalized iris close-ups in *Grandma's Reading Glass*."[9] In fact, Smith's 1900 film includes various extreme close-ups, which are justified, however, by the grandmother's magnifying glass with which the baby is playing. The most definitive approach seems to be one that acknowledges the film's iconographic sources—for instance, Méliès's aforementioned theatrical sketch, *Les Farces de la lune*, in which he makes use of an identical trick without it being motivated by any voyage through space.[10] Even the astonishing effects—beginning with the "earth light" (as opposed to "moon light") and the eruption of a lunar volcano—are used for the purpose of representing the voyeuristic obsessions of these ad hoc space explorers; that is, they further develop the theme that emerged in *The Astronomer's Dream*. As for the sequence representing the return of the heroes, one could say that the capsule's crash-landing at sea is a pretext for replicating the underwater scenes that Méliès had long succeeded in realizing with his ingenious tricks. And the scenes of celebration, for their part, accentuate the cartoon-like quality of the astronauts with their medals of the Order of the Moon (reproductions-in-miniature of the anthropomorphized lunar face pinned to the vain savants' collars) and the monument to science that returns to the image of the scientist-as-alchemist in a long cloak and conical hat, arrogantly resting his foot on the face of a moon that resembles the one in *Les Farces de la lune*.

As for the theme of the fantastic voyage—which very often is a voyage through space—Méliès dedicated many other films to the topic, films occasionally marked by a creative zeal even greater than that in *A Trip to the Moon*. This is certainly the case with *An Impossible Voyage* (1904), which offers the variant of a voyage to the sun and which takes its title (and nothing else) from a play by Verne and Adolphe d'Ennery—a "fantastic play" in three acts, performed for the first time on November 25, 1882, at the Théâtre de la Porte Saint-Martin.[11] *An Impossible Voyage* never achieves the results of *A Trip to the Moon*. The more complex arrangement of spaces, the more spectacular nature of the scientific assembly ("The Institute of Incoherent Geography"), the greater realism of "The Machine-Shop," with its set full of perfectly synchronized moving gears—all this, and the film's undeniable technical advances, still is not enough to mitigate against the lingering impression of mannerism and redundancy. The approach to the sun (which appears to be a replica substantially less convincing than the one used for the moon), is portrayed in an even more overtly comic key, but with far more predictable results. On balance, the terrestrial scenes depicting the various, disastrous movements of the travelers on earth—the "movement" gag at the station, a train crossing a bridge before a suggestive alpine backdrop, the scene of Crazyloff swooping down on a beach at the Inn of the Righi and crashing through a wall—are more innovative and interesting than the scenes in space. Still, one cannot forget the shot of an interstellar train crossing the galaxy, and the film achieves a highly lyrical, almost Chagall-like quality—and above all, the frozen bodies of the explorers who, in order to protect themselves from the extreme heat of the sun, take refuge in a giant ice box. Even the crash-landing at sea and subsequent underwater scenes allow for some effective iterations of the theme (the octopus and the apotheosis of aquatic divinity).

It may be no coincidence that the "rediscovery" of Méliès occurred at the height of the Surrealist movement, when people were also discovering Cyrano de Bergerac's voyages to the sun and moon.[12] If the library of Doctor Faustroll (one of Alfred Jarry's inventions, less famous but no less significant than Ubu Roi) included the work of Cyrano de Bergerac,[13] any ideal collection of films devoted to "pataphysical" science would have to include Méliès's "science-fiction" voyages. And out of "pataphysics" and carnivalesque humor grew another of Méliès's extremely successful variations on the celestial theme, *The Eclipse* (1907). The iconography is the same, although the execution is somewhat less refined than in *An Impossible Voyage*. The schoolroom astronomy lesson, the allotment of telescopes, the assigned posts from which to view the spectacle—all seem designed to invest the astronomical passion of these wizards-in-training with voyeuristic significance. The sun's eclipse by the "full moon" takes the form of a slow, comical ballet, full of flirtatious winks and sexual allusions. And the subsequent aerial visions (in which the sense of "traveling" is obtained by moving the backgrounds) have a similarly ballet-like rhythm, with the regular apparition of beautiful—if somewhat uncelestial—women. The film ends with the students' telescopes trained on the rear end of an astronomer who, having leaned too far over the balcony, has fallen facedown into a wooden barrel, his legs flailing.

Near the premature end of his filmmaking career, Méliès returned to the theme of the voyage with *The Conquest of the Pole*, which was produced by Pathé, Star-Film having by this time lost its independence. The film, completed on the eve of the successful exploration of the North Pole, confirms that Mélièsien fantasy was more inspired by theatrical machinery (the abominable snowman) than futuristic iconography—

even though, in this case, there is no missing Doctor Maboul's curious invention, the "aerobus," which bears an uncanny resemblance to the "aeromobiles" invented by illustrator Jean-Marc Côté at the end of the nineteenth century (and publicized, more recently, by Isaac Asimov).[14] In actuality, Maboul's "aerobus" is the result of a singular bricolage—science fiction produced from a combination of extraordinary and familiar, everyday, elements. Méliès's inventions are strikingly similar to Côté's: both share a passion for marine backgrounds: the zoomorphic appearance of a fuselage with a bird's head (which seems to recall the fantastic carriage-horse in *The Merry Frolics of Satan* [1906]), the silhouette of a common omnibus, and a toy in vogue at the time.

The exposition of the various phases of the enterprise follows the same order as in his other travel films: a scientific congress characterized by bizarre and extreme behavior; the selection and preparation of the aircraft; the departure, and journey through the stars; the arrival, and misadventures in a mysterious realm; and finally, the fortuitous return and rejoicing.

Some variants, however, are worth noting: above all, a dispute with some suffragettes who want to participate in the expedition, and the misguided efforts of their female president, who, attempting to follow the

Figure 11-2. *The Conquest of the Pole* (1912) .

company in a small propeller plane, runs straight into the steeple of a bell tower. Equally charming are the car-related gags involving admirers who use various means of transport to accompany the expedition and a "surprise hit" from the scorpion constellation, which creates some serious difficulties for the aerobus. Even if discerning signs of a search for a more fluid, more refined syntax in the combination of dynamic elements in the frame (one thinks, for instance, of the galaxy-crossing sequence) were possible, the language of the film seems decidedly primitive, considering the rapid evolution of cinematographic language. As Sadoul has written—with a felicitous analogy to visual art—the film is "a masterpiece that has the perfection of a Giotto. But it is a Giotto completed during the time of Michelangelo and Raphael."[15]

The Extraordinary Adventures of Saturnino Farandola

When *The Conquest of the Pole* debuted, references to Verne were as frequent as they were ambiguous. We now turn to two of them. The Pathé-Frères weekly bulletin announced, "There isn't one of [Méliès's] works that hasn't enjoyed the success, the vogue, and the popularity of a Jules Verne novel."[16] And for its part, the weekly *Le Cinéma* declared the film "a masterpiece from the Jules Verne of the film camera."[17] In reality, Méliès's late film seems to be a parody of the iconography and mythology of Verne's *Extraordinary Voyages*, more than a reprisal of it. And if anything, it has more in common with the satiric "*actualités reconstituées*," which were one of the trademark features of Star-Film; I am thinking, for instance, of *An Adventurous Automobile Trip* (1905). In fact, by this point, trips to the North and South Poles were news items, not just the subject of literary speculation: the American Robert E. Peary had reached the North Pole on April 6, 1909, and Roald Amundsen had reached the South Pole on December 14, 1911.[18] Moreover, as we have already seen, this film makes specific reference to the emerging feminist movement, which is portrayed in a comic, even grotesque, key.

     In light of these considerations, the reference to Robida's illustrations—made in due course by Sadoul—would seem to warrant further examination. Particularly deserving of attention is *Saturnin Farandoul*, which, adapted into a film by Fabre, would constitute an important episode in the "survival" of Méliès's style in early cinema.

     The novel *Saturnin Farandoul* was published in installments between 1879 and 1880.[19] The result is an extremely odd adventure book, halfway between an homage to Verne's novels and a parody of them (because it introduces a satire of Verne's vision of the ideology of industrial progress and colonial expansion). It came equipped with an extremely thick apparatus of illustrations, which Fabre drew on extensively in his film adaptation—particularly, their use of cartoonish exaggeration and casual disregard for standards of naturalism or verisimilitude. The significance— and, perhaps, the limitations—of Ambrosio's production (which proved to be a notable success),[20] can be seen more clearly if one looks directly at the work from which it originated and at its author, Albert Robida.[21]

Albert Robida (1848–1926), an illustrator and writer, collaborated with the *Journal amusant*, *Paris comique*, and *La Vie Parisienne*, and founded *La Caricature*. He was the author and illustrator of various works in addition to *Saturnin Farandoul*, including *Le Voyage de M. Du Mollet* (1883) and *Le Vingtième Siècle, roman d'un Parisienne d'après-demain* (1883). Moreover, he was one of the intellectuals who often enlivened the cabaret evenings at the Chat Noir, famous for its productions of shadow plays. Founded by Rodolphe Salis in 1881, the Chat Noir took its name from Edgar Allan Poe's eponymous story. Various other artists also collaborated with the Chat Noir, among them Caran d'Ache, the author of *L'Epopée*, a true blockbuster of the shadow theater. Another celebrated work, *La Tentation de Saint Antoine*, was produced in 1887 by Henri Rivière from a text by Gustave Flaubert.[22] For the Chat Noir, Robida produced, in collaboration with Rivière, *La Nuit des temps* (1889), which has rightly come to be considered a precursor of science-fiction cinema: it depicts the destruction of Paris by aerial warfare.[23] Robida had already explored the theme of aerial warfare in 1879 in his *Saturnin Farandoul* when he described and drew the aerial battle between Phileas Fogg and Farandoul. In *La Nuit des temps*, the only original script performed at the Chat Noir (the others being based on literary sources), Robida had his characters drink a magical potion that first transported them to a prehistoric era before projecting them into the twentieth century—lending his work the science-fiction quality of Verne's novels.[24]

But Robida did not imagine only the destruction of Paris; he also participated in its reconstruction. I allude to his role as director and set designer of Vieux Paris, created for the 1900 Universal Exposition. Images of Vieux Paris survive in various photographs taken on the occasion of the exposition. Visitors viewed the reconstruction of medieval Paris from a steamboat on the Seine, so creating convincing traveling shots was easy for filmmakers like Méliès, who made three such views as part of his *Paris Exposition, 1900* series, recorded as numbers 251–253 in the Star-Film catalogs. There is also Paul Morand's curious recollection of the exposition's inaugural ceremony, in which Loubet is described as someone who "crossed old Paris, the masterpiece of that great artist and great poet, Robida." He was remembered as "the author of *Le Vingtième Siècle* who foresaw theater in three languages, transatlantic flight, the

talking newspaper, television, black members of parliament, female law-
yers, man-made islands, and the fall of Russia." And, Morand adds, "the
first magistrate of France admires the precision with which the Pont au
Change has been reconstructed, the little old workshops on the rue de
Rempart, the ancient Louvre, the Villes Etuves, the Grand Châtelet, the
Pré-aux-Clercs."[25] There is also a delightful guide, illustrated by Robida,
in which the work on Vieux Paris—rebuilt and restored to allow visitors
to the exposition a half-historical, half-fantastical journey—is meticulously attributed to architects and landscapers, the workers responsible
for the river and the platform, for electric light and sanitary services. To
everything is appended the name Albert Robida, *"Maître de l'Œuvre."*[26]

This genial writer-illustrator of the Chat Noir constitutes a sort of
union, or "hyphen," between Méliès and Fabre's film. The undeniable
connection goes beyond the obvious iconographic parallels and can be
seen in the similarly derisive spirit with which both depict the ideology
of progress. Sadoul, as we have already hinted, refers to Robida in his
discussion of Méliès's *An Impossible Voyage*; he writes, "One thinks above
all of the sketch books of Robida, to which Méliès has some kinship,
sketch books that seem to have inspired him more than once."[27]

Bruno Traversetti has noted that in 1879, when Robida published
Saturnin Farandoul, Jules Verne was fifty-one and had published "little more than a third of the novels that would together constitute his
Extraordinary Voyages."[28] And here's what he had to say about *Saturnin
Farandoul*: "The work, which is animated by a playful, ingenious, innovative superabundance and a happy, paradoxical spirit, appeals to the
enormous popularity that Verne's novels have enjoyed in recent years,
with its gentle derision of positivist sentiment."[29] As Traversetti demonstrates through a series of telling quotations, the fascination of *Saturnin
Farandoul* derives from a dense series of intertextual allusions—allusions
to the universe of Verne, which would have been familiar to the readers
of Robida's text. In short, Verne's *Extraordinary Voyages* constitute the
source that lent credibility to the fantastic world being represented and
at the same time is itself both the object of never-ending expansion and
the parodic undoing of that universe. Following in Traversetti's footsteps,
I provide some of these excerpts, along with a few of my own additions.

The first is taken from the fourth chapter of the first part, which
is dedicated to Farandoul's underwater love affair with the beautiful
Mysora, in which Robida brings together the divers of Captain Nemo's
Nautilus and a troop of monkeys—that is, the "milk brothers" with whom
Farandoul had been raised: "The man who appeared so providentially
in the cave was none other than the celebrated Captain Nemo, known

to all readers of Jules Verne, that is to say, to the entire universe, so we need not draw his picture."[30]

The second excerpt comes from the tenth chapter of the second part, which recounts the aerial battle fought by Farandoul and Fogg using chloroform bombs (with the image of thirty balloons hit by chloroform, drifting aimlessly away from the battlefield; and of the balloon-admiral, Fogg, who continues to resist despite being riddled with bullets). But here is what happens after Farandoul's victory: "Everyone boarded the first steamship for Europe. A sacred duty called Farandoul to Paris. He wanted personally to deliver to Mr. Jules Verne all the details of the glorious but deplorable end of Sir Phileas Fogg."[31]

Finally, during the search for the King of Siam's White Elephant, Farandoul and his men meet "an attractive man who had the look of a Russian official with a big mustache and a long beard." They enjoy a modest meal of bear meat with him. Only at this point do we come to learn that his name is Michel Strogoff, that he was the first civilized person Farandoul and his men had met, and that he was welcomed as an old friend.[32]

A last, irresistible, example appears in the fourth chapter of the fifth section, in which Farandoul arrives at the North Pole and discovers Captain Hatteras living there: "Another of Verne's heroes! At the North Pole, so far from the rest of the world, Farandoul again encounters one of these deadly men! He leaves to discover the Pole, overcoming a thousand dangers, and succeeds in discovering this mysterious island . . . and fatality! The North Pole is inhabited. And by whom? By a hero of Jules Verne, by Captain Hatteras!"[33]

But the most compelling interpretation of Robida's intertextual universe may be Antonio Faeti's:

It is a frenetic epic, which leads the reader into an entire library, in which the protagonist must navigate through the seas of allusion to nearly all the travel literature of his time, touching all the myths, desecrating all the symbols, construing the most far-fetched plots, which continuously weave in and out of different literary territories, with only the briefest of warnings, and extracting from them characters, stereotypes, situations. Naturally, Verne is one of the most common targets: his captain Nemo resurfaces in the pages of Robida but, blinded by his impenetrable pride, he allies himself with Saturnin and a pack of giant apes to fight the Malaysian pirates. Phileas Fogg, who here is the general of the Southern troops in the war of secession, falls asleep with his army, struck

by a chloroform bomb. Ettore Servadac travels on horseback to a
flying minaret, while Michel Strogoff traverses Manchuria on the
back of a white elephant.[34]

Faeti sees *Saturnin Farandoul* as "a smiling, anti-Darwinian polemic"
and writes about the "regressive course of Farandoul's anti-evolutionary
march." In fact, the novel begins with Farandoul, raised by a community
of apes who despair not only that the small half-human is unable to grow
a tail—notwithstanding the interventions of a venerable old ape, who performs countless treatments on him—but also because he fails to develop
the grace and ability of his "milk brothers." It ends with the return of
Farandoul to the island of the monkeys, his childhood home, "founding
a republic in which all his numerous friends and followers agree to share
equal rights and responsibilities with a village of monkeys."[35] Faeti notes,
"Only the German scientists asked to be repatriated, so as to make the
scientific congress of Berlin aware of their Polar mission."[36]

We have spoken of the literary sources, but in this context we must
also speak of iconographic sources because Robida's book is illustrated.
And Fabre was directly inspired by Robida's iconography, which in turn
is nothing other than an ironic-hyperbolic reworking of the illustrations
that appeared in the Hetzel editions of Verne's *Extraordinary Voyages*.
More than by Robida's illustrations, Fabre was inspired by the unre-
strained imagery of the fantastic cinema of Méliès and his emulators,
offering us in some sense one of the most curious and charming examples
of fantasy-adventure film in a sort of uninterrupted visual delirium.

After this somewhat lengthy but necessary preamble, let us linger
for a bit on the film *Saturnino Farandola* and its creator, Marcel Fabre, a
figure deserving of more in-depth studies than have been done to date.
I will limit myself to highlighting a few essential facts.[37]

An actor of Spanish provenance (his real name was Marcel Fernán-
dez Peréz), Fabre came to cinema from the circus, and established himself
in the comic sketches Pathé and Éclair produced. Hired by Ambrosio of
Turin in 1911, he created, in competition with Cretinetti, the character of
Robinet that made him famous all over the world (in some films, Robinet is flanked by Robinette, played by Nilde Baracchi). In 1913 he also
directed some comedies in the Fricot series that, along with *Saturnino
Farandola* and *Amor Pedestre* (1914), are usually considered to be among
his best work. He subsequently emigrated to the United States where he
pursued various activities: he tried to revive interest in the character of
Robinet, he worked for various production companies (Pasha, Sanford,
Arrow), and he even directed some Westerns with Pete Morrison. After

losing a leg in a work-related accident, he dedicated himself to the job of scriptwriter for Universal. He died in 1929, universally forgotten.[38]

When Fabre was making *Saturnino Farandola*, Méliès had recently abandoned filmmaking. The underwater scenes and the aerial battle with the sky full of propeller planes recall various scenes in Méliès, even if the Mélièsien aspects seem magnified and made to serve the development of the plot. Of course, the reference to Méliès is obligatory. Yet on its own it would be a minor thing and of little value were it not for the film's emerging connections to this literary (and iconographic) source material on which—as we've already seen—Méliès himself drew. To this, one must add that translating all the narrative material in this overflowing novel—let alone the whole system of intertextual allusions contained within Robida's prose—into a single film (or even a series of four episodes with a combined length of 3,660 meters) would be impossible.[39] And this is not considering the fact that the copy available today is only 1,612 meters long. This "abridged" version, although it retains almost all of the episodes described in Vittorio Martinelli's synopsis,[40] most likely eliminates the lulls that some have complained about (more than "bizarre," the film is described as "interminable" on the index card Martinelli and Aldo Bernardini devoted to Fabre).[41] It also allows viewers to fully appreciate the whirlwind of innovations in a film in which literally everything happens.

In the first part, we witness the terrible shipwreck in which Saturnin's parents lose their lives. Before succumbing, the two manage to save the baby by placing it in a floating cradle that, pushed by the currents, reaches the island of the monkeys. Raised by Great Apes, Saturnin soon discovers his "difference." Despite the cures the wizard administers, his situation does not improve. On leaving the island, he is welcomed onto the ship *La Bella Leocadia* commanded by Captain Lombrico, who "civilizes" him and teaches him to speak. Having succeeded Lombrico as commander of the ship, he meets the beautiful diver Mysora during his marine explorations; unfortunately, a whale swallows her. Professor Croknuff, who directs the Melbourne aquarium, acquires the whale, which gets stranded on the beach, and brings it to his aquarium, where the cetacean regurgitates the beautiful diver. Aware that Mysora is a prisoner of Professor Croknuff, Farandoul declares war on the scientist, calling on the army of the monkeys for help. The war ends with the destruction of the detested Croknuff's aquarium and the liberation of Mysora.

The second episode, *Alla ricera dell'elefantino bianco*, actually corresponds to events recounted in the fourth part of the novel. Farandoul (played by Fabre), in an elegant captain's uniform that makes him look a bit like Corto Maltese *avant la lettre*, makes his way through a fabulous Oriental realm in search of the white elephant that has abducted the King of Siam's head of police. Included in this part are several visually stunning special effects and curious episodes such as the beautiful Mysora leading the Siamese riders in their military drills or the one in which a cruel villain carries out sadistic acts on his prisoners in a way that recalls Méliès's *The Terrible Turkish Executioner* (1903) in its use of dummies. Then there's the scene in which the beautiful Mysora distributes opium cigarettes to the soldiers of the guard so she can tie them to each other by their pigtails; this allows Farandoul to launch a daring escape with his men, who have been held captive in wooden boxes. The major concerns of the second episode are cinematography (the suggestive backlighting of which resembles the effects of shadow plays), set design, and bizarre scenarios, noted more for their accumulation of strange details than any real advancement of the plot. The third episode, entitled *La regina dei Makalolos* in Martinelli's filmography, shows us Farandoul liberating the two queens of Makalolos.

The last episode proceeds from a title that informs us that the state of South Milligan is considering a plan to move Niagara Falls "within its own borders." From here, a conflict erupts between Farandoul, who commands the troops of North Milligan, and Phileas Fogg, who has sided with the Southerners. They are allied with the Indians, who are only a little less far-fetched than the ones who had appeared in Giulio Antamoro's *Pinocchio* (1911), produced by Cinès a few years previously. More improbable still are the troops of North Milligan, who march as if they are in a circus parade, under the gaze of Farandoul. Among the soldiers in fur hats is also a squad of divers (whose presence is incomprehensible unless one knows that in the novel the first part of this strange war of secession takes place in the deep sea). The war sequences demonstrate the effects of the chloroform bombs and the "war machine," a sort of gigantic vacuum that sucks up the besieging forces. Particularly striking are the battle scenes among the clouds. This sequence—which owes much to Robida's visionary iconography, as well as to the flight sequence toward the Pole in Méliès's *The Conquest of the Pole*—seems to us today to be poised between the universe of Méliès and that of the great Karel Zeman, whose film *The Fabulous World of Jules Verne* (1958)—which was inspired by, among other things, Verne's novel *Facing the Flag* (1897)— seems not entirely unaware of Fabre's film.

If we compare Fabre's film, first screened in December 1913 (even though the censor's approval came in the early days of 1914), with the aforementioned *The Conquest of the Pole* of 1912, we see that the differences lie primarily in the richness of the design solutions, in the variety of spaces used, and the genius of the sets. But from the point of view of language, we see many of the same challenges already evident in Méliès's cinema: the difficulty of integrating those elements produced by artificial means, such as the reconstructed sets, with more naturalistic ones. In the scenes on the island of the monkeys, the coexistence of "fake" and real monkeys produces a strange effect. Rather than "integration"—which lies at the heart of the principle of "functional equivalents" that became the guiding logic of classical narrative style according to David Bordwell, Janet Staiger, and Kristin Thompson's well-known formulation[42]—one can instead discuss the effect of combining scenographic effects (costumes, makeup, and so forth) and natural ones. Actors clumsily disguised as monkeys share the frame with a number of smaller, real monkeys, according to the logic of accumulating attractions that, however unsuccessful in terms of narrative integration, in our eyes, gives these images a certain antiquated air. One might think of the model of the circus, where the acrobatic performances of clowns and jugglers exist alongside those of more or less exotic animals. If herein lie the "linguistic" limits of Fabre's film, here too also lie the sources of its fascination. As in Méliès, the logic of *Saturnin Farandoul* is still more "marvelous" than it is "fantastic."[43] And this is the source of its old-fashioned appeal—one last homage to the style of Méliès, soon to be rendered obsolete by developments in technology and cinematic language.

Notes

1. Produced by Ambrosio, and known in the United States as *The Extraordinary Adventures of Saturnino Farandola*, the film was adapted and directed by Marcel Fabre (with uncredited help from Luigi Maggi) from the celebrated novel by Albert Robida with a mile-long title, *Voyages très extraordinaires de Saturnin Farandoul dans les 5 ou 6 parties du monde et dans tous les pays connus et même inconnus de M. Jules Verne* (Paris: Librairie illustrée; M. Dreyfous, 1879–1880). Author's note: I was able to study this edition on microfilm at the Bibliothèque nationale in Paris.

2. Luigi Rognoni, "Cinema muto italiano a Venezia," *Bianco e nero*, no. 7–8 (1952): 99. See also Rognoni, *Cinema muto: Dalle origini al 1930* (Rome: Bianco e Nero, 1952).

3. Kristin Thompson, "Conference: I giorni di Cabiria, La grande stagione del cinema muto torinese, Turin, October 1997," *Domitor Bulletin* 12, no. 1 (Jan. 1998): 12.

4. Siegfried Kracauer, *Orpheus in Paris: Offenbach and the Paris of His Time*, trans. Gwenda David and Eric Mosbacher (New York: Knopf, 1938), 335–336.

5. See Jacques Malthête and Laurent Mannoni, *L'Œuvre de Georges Méliès* (Paris: Cinémathèque Française, Éditions de la Martinière, 2008), 72–73.

6. This myth inspired a story by Italo Calvino, who reimagined popular stories and legends as science fiction in *Cosmicomics*. See Italo Calvino, *Cosmicomiche vecchie e nuove* (Milan: Garzanti, 1984), especially "La distanza della luna," 103–115.

7. *Complete Catalogue of Genuine and Original "Star" Films (Moving Pictures) Manufactured by Geo. Méliès of Paris* (New York: Geo. Méliès, 1905), 39.

8. See Anne Marie Quévrain," A la redécouverte de Méliès," *Cahiers de la Cinémathèque*, no. 35–36 (1982): 163; and Richard Abel, *The Ciné Goes to Town: French Cinema, 1896–1914* (Berkeley: University of California Press, 1994), 72.

9. John Frazer, *Artificially Arranged Scenes: The Films of Georges Méliès* (Boston: G. K. Hall, 1979), 96.

10. As Jacques Deslandes observed, "the trajectory of the shell approaching the moon in the 1902 film, which will seem so astonishingly cinematic to many historians, is already wholly inscribed in the series of magic sketches staged in 1891." *Le Boulevard du cinéma à l'époque de Georges Méliès* (Paris: Éditions du Cerf, 1963), 41.

11. See Jules Verne and Adolphe d'Ennery, *Voyage à travers l'impossible* (Paris: Pauvert, 1981); on the relationship between the film and Verne and d'Ennery's play, see Malthête, *Essai de reconstitution du catalogue français de la Star-Film suivi d'une analyse catalographique des films de Georges Méliès recensés en France* (Bois d'Arcy, France: Centre national de la cinématographie, 1981), 207.

12. Cyrano de Bergerac, *L'autre monde; ou, les états et empires de la lune et du soleil* (Paris: Cercle du livre de France, 1940).

13. See Luciano Erba, introduction, Cyrano de Bergerac, *L'altro mondo: Storia fantastica di un viaggio sulla luna* (Rome: Theoria, 1982), 11.

14. Isaac Asimov, *Futuredays: A Nineteenth-Century Vision of the Year 2000* (London: Virgin, 1986); illustrations by Jean-Marc Côté.

15. Georges Sadoul, *Le Cinéma devient un art (1909–1920)*, pt. 1, *L'avant-guerre*, vol. 3, *Histoire générale du cinéma* (Paris: Denoël, 1951), 136.

16. *Bulletin hebdomadaire Pathé-Frères*, no. 12 (1912), quoted in Malthête and Mannoni, *L'Œuvre de Georges Méliès*, 284.

17. *Le Cinéma*, no. 9 (Apr. 26, 1912), quoted in Malthête and Mannoni, *L'Œuvre de Georges Méliès*, 284.

18. Malthête and Mannoni, *L'Œuvre de Georges Méliès*, 284.

19. Robida, *Voyages très extraordinaires de Saturnin Farandoul.*

20. See Vittorio Martinelli and Aldo Bernardini, *Il cinema muto italiano 1914*, pt. 1 (Turin, Italy: Nuova ERI, 1993), 52–54.

21. Fundamental to an understanding of Robida's work and personality is Philip Brun's book, *Albert Robida (1948–1926): Sa vie, son œuvre suivie d'une bibliographie complète de ses écrits et dessins* (Paris: Editions Promodis, 1984).

22. See Jac Remise, Pascal Remise, and Régis van de Walle, *Magie lumineuse: Du théâtre d'ombres à la lanterne magique* (Paris: Balland, 1979), 302–311.

23. See Jean-Pierre Bouyxou, with Roland Lethem, *La Science-fiction au cinéma* (Paris: Union générale d'éditions, 1971), 31.

24. See *Le Chat Noir*, ed. Mariel Oberthür and Thierry Groensteen (Paris: Réunion de musées nationaux, 1992), 49. Worth noting is that by 1863 Jules Verne had already written (if not yet obtained Hetzel as a publisher for) a novel titled *Paris au XXe siècle*, recently published by Hachette (Paris, 1994), in an edition by Piero Gondolo Della Riva; on the date of composition of the novel, see pp. 16–17. Editor's note: In English translation as *Paris in the Twentieth Century*, trans. Richard Howard (New York: Random House, 1996).

25. Paul Morand, "Il palazzo delle illusioni o l'esposizione universale," in *La Belle Epoque* (Rome: Gherardo Casini, 1987), 388–389.

26. *Le Vieux Paris: Guide historique, pittoresque et anecdotique Exposition universelle de 1900* (Paris: Ménard et Chaufour, 1900).

27. Georges Sadoul, *Les Pionniers du cinéma (De Méliès à Pathé), 1897–1909*, vol. 2, *Histoire générale du cinéma* (Paris: Éditions Denoël, 1947), 292.

28. Bruno Traversetti, *Introduzione a Verne* (Rome: Laterza, 1995), 3.

29. Traversetti, *Introduzione a Verne*, 3–4.

30. Robida, *Voyages très extraordinaires de Saturnin Farandoul*, 53.

31. Robida, *Voyages très extraordinaires de Saturnin Farandoul*, 320.

32. Robida, *Voyages très extraordinaires de Saturnin Farandoul*, 629ff.

33. Robida, *Voyages très extraordinaires de Saturnin Farandoul*, 706.

34. Antonio Faeti, *Guardare le figure* (Turin, Italy: Einaudi, 1972), 171–172.

35. Faeti, *Guardare le figure*, 172.

36. Robida, *Voyages très extraordinaires de Saturnin Farandoul*, 800.

37. See Paolo Cherchi Usai and Livio Jacob, *I comici del muto italiano* (Pordenone, Italy: Le Giornate del cinema muto, 1985); and Antonio Costa, "Marcel Fabre," in *Dizionario dei registi del cinema mondiale*, ed. Gian Piero Brunetta, vol. 1 (Turin, Italy: Einaudi, 2005), 599–600.

38. Aldo Bernardini and Vittorio Martinelli, "Robinet," in *I comici del muto italiano*, 116–123.

39. Fabre's film was originally presented as a serial in four episodes titled, respectively, *L'isola delle scimmie*, *Alla ricerca dell'elefante bianco*, *La regina di Makalolos*, and *Farandola contro Phileas Fogg*.

40. Martinelli and Bernardini, *Il cinema muto italiano 1914*, 52.

41. Bernardini and Martinelli, "Robinet," 116.

42. David Bordwell, Janet Staiger, and Kristin Thompson, *The Classical Hollywood Cinema: Film Style and Mode of Production to 1960* (London: Routledge and Kegan Paul, 1985).

43. On the distinction between the "marvelous" and the "fantastic" see Gérard Lenne, *Le Cinéma "fantastique" et ses mythologies* (Paris: Éditions du Cerf, 1970). "[T]he domain of the marvelous contains the germ of what will become the 'fantastic' " (93).

12

Viva Paci

No One-Way Ticket to the Moon

Time is never time at all
You can never ever leave without leaving a piece of youth
And our lives are forever changed
We will never be the same

—Smashing Pumpkins, "Tonight, Tonight"

Monsieur Méliès et moi faisons à peu près le même métier, nous enchantons la matière vulgaire.

—Apollinaire

W HEN, ON DECEMBER 16, 1929, at the Grande Salle Pleyel in Paris, the Gala Méliès[1] got underway—the result of a strange collaboration among Studio 28 (the ciné-club that gave birth to Parisian cinephilia) and its director Jean Mauclaire; a smattering of headlines in conservative papers (*Le Figaro* and *L'Ami du peuple*); and Maurice Noverre, an old-world aesthete so enamored of Méliès he dedicated several issues of his review, *Le Nouvel Art cinématographique*,[2] to him—it was such, one imagines, that the public conceived *a new regard for certain old things.* . . . First reflection.

This chapter was translated by Elizabeth Alsop.

When, on November 15, 1979, at the Whitney Museum of American Art, Tom Gunning shared his thoughts on some forms of noncommercial cinema, "An Unseen Energy Swallows Space: The Space in Early Film and Its Relation to American Avant-Garde Film," an idea somewhere at the nexus of history, theory, and cinephilia took shape. As Gunning explained, "the impetus for the comparison comes partly from avant-garde filmmakers themselves, from artists such as Ken Jacobs, Ernie Gehr, Hollis Frampton, and others who have directly included elements from early films in their own work. Likewise, it was undoubtedly my encounter with films by these and other avant-garde filmmakers that allowed me to see early films with a fresh eye."[3] This comment gives rise to a second reflection: *early days and experiments have things in common. . . .*

When, on May 15, 2008, the extravagant cultural association known as the Sprocket Society presented an evening of Méliès at the Northwest Film Forum in Seattle,[4] *A Trip to the Moon* was accompanied by a soaring, explosive score—one that was discordant, and truly modern: Pink Floyd's "Set the Controls for the Heart of the Sun" (1968).[5] Third reflection: *Méliès's imagery naturally inspires the transgression of cinematic limits. . . .*

These three dates correspond to events that would go on to have varying impacts on the history of cinema,[6] but they where chosen—at the beginning of this chapter—as symptoms of a more widespread phenomenon. They help to distinguish some of the fundamental continuities between Méliès's work (and *A Trip to the Moon*, in particular) and that of others; meaningful intersections, and fruitful interactions, between the nineteenth and twenty-first centuries.

Images that span epochs; searches for new ways of representing cinematic space and time that look back to the origins of cinema (origins much indebted to Méliès) to reenergize the moving image; fascinating achievements resulting from the synthesis of sound and image. These are the three avenues this chapter pursues: anachronism, experimentation, and music. In our analysis, Méliès and *A Trip to the Moon* will find themselves in orbit around the musical comedy, experimental cinema, video art, and music videos.[7]

"Il faut suivre son temps" / "Non, moi je suis mon inspiration"[8]: The intermediality at work in Méliès's time. . . .

À leur projection, le public pourrait s'apercevoir que, si les bandes de Georges Méliès étaient en avance sur leur époque, nos films modernes sont, pour la plupart, très en retard sur la nôtre.

—Maurice Maigrance, *L'Ami du peuple*, July 14, 1929

As this book continually reminds us, *A Trip to the Moon* was—even in its own time—a film that made use of many sources and insinuated itself into still more, part of a continuous, productive exchange of images and ideas. From the recurring trope of the "voyage through space" to the musical spectacle, popular culture strongly influenced the world of the film, which was one of Méliès's longest (it runs for more than twelve minutes, whereas the median length of his work from the same year is around three minutes).

This was certainly the case with popular literature of the time featuring lunar voyages. It was also the case with other typically *fin-de-siècle* phenomena: from the postcards portraying various stages of the moon's waning (often, an anthropomorphic moon),[9] to the amusement parks that—in the nineteenth century—used variations on the theme of "a trip to the moon" as the basis for some of their most popular attractions.[10]

Even if Méliès was working in a popular vein and with well-worn ideas,[11] he did not shy away from experimentation: separating his work for the general public from his experimental work is nearly impossible. In this sense, Méliès could be compared, as he already has been, to Norman McLaren or Charlie Chaplin: all three of them solitary, autonomous innovators, capable of applying their talents to everything.[12]

And if Méliès drew on the mass-produced products of his day and age, it was he who really created them:[13] one thinks, for instance, of Segundo de Chomón's productions for Pathé, such as *Excursion dans la lune* (1908), *Les Lunatiques* (1908), and *Voyage à la planète Jupiter* (1909);[14] and even of some series of illustrations and comics, which were flourishing in the United States thanks to the colossal success of films by Méliès and his imitators. A prime example is a strip from Winsor McCay's *Little Nemo in Slumberland* (published December 3, 1905, in the Sunday pages of the *New York Herald*),[15] in which little Nemo (an obviously Vernian name, the web of cross-references thickens!) journeys to the moon-face after an interstellar voyage on his bed.

We are talking here about work that borrows not only its images from Méliès (the anthropomorphic moon, for instance), but also its shot composition, choreography, and rhythmic movements. Yet we are still far from the idea of "adaptation," in the sense that these images of lunar travel are themselves "traveling" images, which lend themselves to citation, to being turned into clichés, nearly to the point of plagiarism—something that came as an upsetting surprise to Méliès and that dealt a tough blow to Star-Film.[16] In this sense, because of the film's commercial good fortune and tendency to lend itself to "derivative products" (to use the parlance of our times), *A Trip to the Moon* emerged at the turn of the twentieth century with the same currency and ability to circulate as many of the "fetish" objects in today's mass culture.

In *A Trip to the Moon*, one can easily discern the film's debt to the contemporary music-hall tradition. In this one film, Méliès—who was a great illusionist even before he was a filmmaker, a creator of theatrical *féeries*, of tricks and machinery for the stage, and even something of a choreographer—displays his full range of theatrical technique. Thus, the Selenites are acrobats from the Folies-Bergère, the *soubrettes* playing the stars are ballerinas from the Théâtre du Châtelet, and the astronomers (whose leader is played by Méliès himself) come from the Théâtre de Cluny and other famous music halls. (For instance, Bleuette Bernon, a music-hall singer, can be seen languidly reclining on a crescent moon).[17]

This intermediality, the migratory potential so inherent in the imagery of *A Trip to the Moon*, naturally launches us into the orbit of musical comedy, experimental cinema, video art, and music videos, all alluded to earlier. In *A Trip to the Moon*, a paradigmatic example of the "cinema of attractions" (the film was made in 1902),[18] images, elements, and motifs operate and circulate independently as fully autonomous attractions. Sometimes originating as attractions in Luna Park, or one of the music halls, such material ends by finding its way into that most "attractive" of genres—the musical comedy—by way of the Mélièsien extravaganza. The Mélièsien extravaganza: a style whose influence can be seen in the work of more recent artists, from Florenz Ziegfeld to Busby Berkeley, and from Jean-Christophe Averty to Ernie Gehr. We will also encounter Méliès's work, and *A Trip to the Moon* in particular, as direct intertexts for a diverse range of works belonging to different traditions (such as that of Al Razutis, Jonathan Dayton, and Valerie Faris), and as a "citation," here and there.

"*Vous êtes anachronique*"[19]:
Méliès at work in our intermediatic times

> And no one called us to the land
> And no one knows the where's or why's.
> Something stirs and something tries
> Starts to climb toward the light.
>
> —Pink Floyd, "Echoes"

By now it is a critical commonplace to emphasize how much early cinema—its way of organizing the cinematic spectacle, its way of being presented to the public—should be seen as a vehicle for displaying "attractions": both because the film's scenes, or tableaux, were relatively independent of each other and because the films (which were only as long as they needed to be) were part of evening-long programs of other films or scenic attractions. After this point, one is still dealing with similar material, but with the gradual lengthening of the film there is a corresponding inclination toward narrative continuity between scenes. The phrase "cinema of attractions" is usually used to designate a period in cinema that lasted until about 1908. This cinematic mode did not disappear at the end of this period, and over time it has remained undeniably present in certain types of film spectacle. To this end, Tom Gunning has sensibly proposed identifying the various moments in film history in which the attraction intermingles with narration in film—sometimes to the point of overwhelming it. After the early period and long after *A Trip to the Moon*, Gunning suggests that in many genres, the interaction between narration and attraction continues to regulate the flow of films. Musicals, burlesques, horror movies, science fiction, and special-effects films[20] are—apart from the early Mélièsien examples—the main cinematic sites in which audiovisual elements show themselves to be autonomous: spectacular sequences, moments that almost totally suspend narrative progress, examples of real technical bravura that boldly call attention to themselves.

Without delving into the surprising and complex correspondences between the theoretical and historical category of the "cinema of attractions" and the rules of musical comedy (as I have done elsewhere),[21] I would like to focus on the relationship between Méliès's work and the musical by highlighting some of the similarities between Méliès, Ziegfeld, and Berkeley. And we can start with the impressions of one of experimental cinema's founding fathers, Stan Brakhage—and these are truly "impressions" given the historical unreliability of the entire text of which this is a part. Additionally, over the course of this chapter, we will see that everything is related and witness the formation of a network of elective affinities among these individuals and the movements they embody. Here Brakhage addresses Méliès's relationship with the bodies in his films and, particularly, with the bodies of his stars—his women:

> He imagined her multiplicity in the sense that she could be turned into anything—as a variety of being rather than a number of images of being . . . a transformation in quality rather than quantity—himself, The Magician, controlling the various charms of this femme fatale. He limited her in his imagination to the tradition of stage magic: she was always thus, the "helper" of The Magician: and otherwise, he drew upon the whole mythic history of woman, from oracle of Delphi to mermaid, from goddess to witch. In her divine aspects he had the courage to give her power over men—to loose demons against them . . . to turn men into beasts, etc.: but she was always

putty in the hands of The Magician—or almost always—and could
be made to jump through hoops like circus dogs, vanish in a puff of
smoke at The Magician's slightest annoyance: she could be made-up
out of anything . . . a dress-maker's dummy . . . the hoop she'd
jump through . . . thin air itself. But whatever George's control
over her, she was a magnificent imagining—greater than if she were
just George's creation—inasmuch as she had a divine aspect which
George adored and was certainly, in all her aspects, essentially an
original: and, as such, we will call her "George's Love."[22]

Brakhage—long before questions of "gender"—sensitive to this imagery,
describes Méliès as both a creator of female metamorphoses and a captive
of them, his gaze bewitched by them. Seen in this light, Méliès emerges
as the Ziegfeld of the cinematic screen, a demiurge of female imagery
that multiplies magically. In Brakhage's reading, Méliès (1861–1938),
technically an older brother to Ziegfeld (1869–1932), reincarnates the
popular culture of the spectacle (based on magnificence and glitter, on
strange and breathtaking creations) traditionally associated with Ziegfeld.
This culture is fully incarnated in the grand spectacle of the *variétés*
and particularly in the revue à la Ziegfeld. Cinema has frequently paid
homage to the impresario Florenz Ziegfeld—the most important producer of Broadway musicals[23]—most notably in the MGM musical trilogy
comprised of *The Great Ziegfeld* (Robert Z. Leonard, 1936), *Ziegfeld Girl*
(Robert Z. Leonard, 1941, musical numbers directed by Busby Berkeley),
and *Ziegfeld Follies* (Vincente Minnelli, 1946).[24]

"Son destin était exemplaire, c'est l'exemple même du génie écrasé par le fric et par l'opinion publique ricanant, était victime des sondages. . . . "[25]

The first in this series, *The Great Ziegfeld*, a three-hour biopic, particularly exemplifies the marvelous story of the Ziegfeld protagonist, his march
toward glory, his difficulties, his decline, and the world of the spectacle
to which he belonged: a description that will strike spectators familiar
with Méliès's history as a variation on a theme, namely the adventures
of the Magician of Montreuil.

     This affinity between Méliès and Ziegfeld, which is principally
biographical, would be of little interest were it not for the fact that
here, the web of interconnections—which represents the backdrop to
this chapter—becomes even more tangled. One could easily maintain that
Berkeley, the great choreographer and director, is Ziegfeld's cinematic
alter ego.[26] In his mise-en-scène, the woman is almost infinitely multi-
plied in a series of freestanding frames that lack any temporal, spatial,

or narrative contiguity with the rest of the film. The resulting imagery reminds us not only of Méliès, but even more, of Brakhage's *reading* of Méliès. To return to the earlier excerpt, Brakhage's vision of Méliès seems to be mediated by the Berkeley who reimagined Ziegfeld on screen.[27] The fantasy that proliferates[28] in every frame, the indifference to spatial and temporal continuity, the playful and vaguely salacious transformation of the stars (that is, the women) within the shot:[29] all this is undeniably characteristic of Méliès's cinema, and it will persist and even become— along with the vertical high angle shot into theatrical space—one of the hallmarks of Berkeley's musical comedies during the 1930s.

Let us take *Ziegfeld Girl* as an example. The dance and musical numbers contained within the diegesis of the film are a selection from the revues that the character Ziegfeld is preparing at the New Amsterdam Theater. And here, the issue that famously dogged Méliès can already be raised: the fact that such films can be seen as filmed theatre—literally, production numbers shot from a fixed, frontal vantage point. Yet the very fact of their being executed for the camera—and, in the process, enhanced by it, through editing and special effects—differentiates them from theatrical performances, both in Méliès and in Berkeley. Editing in the film brings together and allows us to compare the *clou* of the various spectacles. Berkeley's touch is obvious from the setting itself: namely,

Figure 12-1. *Ziegfeld Girl* (1941) .

those immense stairs up which the Berkeley girls parade. As "juxtaposed attractions" (*attractions juxtaposées*)[30]—that is, attractions within the attractions—the girls are glittering apparitions in enchanting costumes (another signature touch); editing ensures that they are offered to us one after another in long individual shots. One shot after another in a concatenated sequence, like a catalog: one girl after another, one costume after another, one vision "occulting" another, the spectacle plays out on a surface that is no longer a real, three-dimensional space in which we could locate ourselves, but rather, against a backdrop—a *plan-tableau*[31]—whose edges coincide with those of the frame, and in which a diegetic "offscreen" does not exist, just as it did not exist in Méliès's films, not even in the relatively developed narrative of *A Trip to the Moon*. Offscreen space, in Berkeley as in Méliès, is the offscreen as a space of work, a space in which to rearrange sets and change costumes, a space that does not elicit the spectators' gaze. The images within each shot, each of them an attraction, are radically centripetal.

Bridging between *A Trip to the Moon* and *Ziegfeld Girl* can occur in many ways: in Méliès's film, his *vedettes* (literally, the stars) were ballerinas from the Théâtre du Châtelet troupe. The "stars" of Ziegfeld (the character) and Berkeley (the creator) are also ballerinas: and in *Ziegfeld Girl*, the relationship between ballerina and star becomes literal, especially in the theatrical trailer for the film in which the ballerinas' faces are framed in star-shaped iris shots—then, in a magic mirrors, then, in musical notes arrayed in a five-sided star shape. Such figures seem to have sprung directly from Méliès's visual imaginary.

As in the Star-Film catalogs, allusions to other films in MGM's Ziegfeld cycle recur frequently in this film, creating the comforting sensation of déjà vu. For instance, the final portion of the revue performed in *Ziegfeld Girl* is lifted directly from the 1936 film and is made up of a series of *plans-tableau*, visually linked in such a way that the spectator has the impression of having assisted in compiling a highlight reel of Ziegfeld revues, each one a vital part of the genre's heritage. The intended effect is to maximize the public's pleasure: their viewing pleasure, which is in turn augmented by their delight at recognizing an old familiar number. It is a strategy similar to the one used to compile an anthology.[32] One thinks back to the comment made earlier—the fact that Méliès relied on an iconography that at times preceded him. Thus Méliès's spectator, too, could experience the extraordinary pleasure of seeing something at once astonishing and well-known.

One apparition after another, in a whirlpool of accumulated imagery that culminates in a wide shot featuring a superabundance of elements in the frame: in this film—as in so many of the others Berkeley choreographed—the final wide shot gives the impression of an "apotheosis shot," complete with a falling curtain to conclude the *féerie*. Obviously, terms like "final apotheosis" and "*féerie*" recall Méliès. Méliès possibly inherited the solution of the final apotheosis from the theatrical spectacle, from variety shows featuring magic, *tableaux vivants*, ballet, and *féeries* in revue form. It is in his trick films, above all, that he makes most abundant and delirious use of it. This type of finale—which fell into disuse once narration began to regulate editing—resurfaced in the 1930s, especially in films Berkeley choreographed.

Noël Burch demonstrated that the *féeries* and trick films of early French cinema (films constructed, to use his terminology, according to a "primitive mode of representation") were predicated upon an accumulation of elements and could only end with this sort of final excessive display or apotheosis,[33] that is, a euphoric gloss. The *plans-tableau* of the ending, which serve to reunite many of the elements that attracted the spectator's attention during the film, are actually indebted to the principles of the revue, the sort of music-hall spectacle in which all of a cabaret's main attractions would be re-presented—that is, re-viewed. And the musical comedies Berkeley choreographed resolve their paratactic structure in much the same way—with a final apotheosis, in which all the accumulated attractions are made to circulate one last time. For this reason, then, the penultimate shot of *A Trip to the Moon*—a sort of "revue" that re-presents all the salient images—shows us all the astronomers, accompanied by the corps of star ballerinas, in a layered composition, a comical chaos of movement that ends with the distribution of the medals: flashy accessories that—once conferred on the astronauts—evoke the face of the anthropomorphic moon one final time. Medals, in fact, far too big to actually be hung around the neck, but which serve to restore to the center of the frame the image that had undoubtedly left its imprint in the minds of the spectators.

"Aujourd'hui le cinéma a près d'un siècle et ses enfants, ses petits enfants, la télévision, le clip, la vidéo ont des désires de rêves multipliés. Ouvrons donc ensemble le livre d'images de Georges Méliès par où toute la magie toujours recommence. C'est très instructifs: dans toutes les nouvelles images il y a toujours le regard de Méliès."[34]

Following this theme of the "revue," we can tease out another thread from this tangle of cross-references, another of the many routes leading in and out of Méliès's work. Jean-Christophe Averty, a great innovator of

French television, has often boasted of his Mélièsien heritage;[35] in fact, he dedicated *Le Magicien de Montreuil-sous-bois* to Méliès. It is essentially a televised revue (presented as part of the series *Le Théâtre de la jeunesse*) inspired by the events of Méliès's career. Realistic scenes, performed in period costume (for instance, an extremely plausible Jean-Marc Thibault in the role of Méliès) alternate with ballets and visionary dance numbers that, while taking images and shot compositions from Méliès's films as their point of departure, soon devolve into pure kinetic delirium in which even the elements of the setting are mobilized.[36] The television screen is used as a surface without depth; the choreography is staged so that all the elements are centripetally arranged, ideal for frontal viewing. Thus the screen becomes a flat surface on which to design—the way Méliès used the format of sheet music to organize the components of his spectacle. Gazing at Averty's work, and at the ballerinas' legs (white legs, the bodies obscured by black bodysuits worn against a black background) flashing a bit of lace in the midst of this kaleidoscope of motion, one automatically thinks of Berkeley. At such moments, the kinship between them seems closer than ever.

When Averty mixes moving images of the ballerinas' legs à la Berkeley with Mélièsien settings, this complex of cross-references fully reveals itself. And it seems clear to us that Berkeley's rather strange 1930s settings may actually represent a reworking of Méliès. The primary components of both Méliès's and Berkeley's productions—bodies, costumes, designs, panels, lighting, and effects—were made of the same material with the same substance and were meant to be shot from the same flattened, frontal perspective. The flat surface (*à plat*) becomes a scene (*tableau*), which in turn becomes a wondrous spectacle. And it is all this that Averty takes up in his work, not only in *Le Magicien de Montreuil-sous-bois*, but also in *Ubu Roi* (1965) and *Le Songe d'une nuit d'été* (1969).

Averty, like Méliès, remained indifferent to the changing taste of spectators: he had one timeless style, which he used to pursue an alternative path to creating moving images, a path that today we place under the sign of the "cinema of attractions."

When considering Averty as one of the original creators of video art, it is worth noting, "A shift has occurred from the production of marvel tied to the imaginary, towards an intensification of the manipulation of perception. . . . Spectacle is also, and often above all, one of technical performance."[37] It is also important to acknowledge that the gap separating Méliès's early cinematic imaginary and Averty's still-nascent television aesthetic is minimal,[38] and attributable purely to evolutions in media technology. Technical bravura was always one of the hallmarks of the "cinema of attractions." One is struck by the remarkable consistency among the many images that exploit the possibilities of the surface—the quality of flatness (*à plat*), and the potential for transformations and apparitions therein. After Méliès, in a certain sense, visual transformations of the surface all seem to hark back to the Magician of Montreuil. From the light-and-shadow silhouette of the skyscraper located on the eponymous *42nd Street* (Lloyd Bacon, 1933, with choreography by Berkeley), to the spaceships and enchanted plants in the music video produced by Jonathan Dayton and Valerie Faris for Oasis's song "All Around the World," one finds throughout the culture of the moving image, figurative elements that can trace their roots directly back to this aspect of Méliès's style.[39]

This allusion to a song with a Vernian theme ("All Around the World") and to a music video with Mélièsien imagery—more than *A Trip to the Moon*, the video is indebted to his *The Eruption of Mount Pelee* (1902) for its small paper models and collage—represents another major strand in the web of references linking Méliès to popular culture.

The synching of a musical excerpt with images was doubtless a common feature of early cinema, something that occurred at the moment of the film's projection. Therefore, there is no reason Méliès should be considered a priori a founding father of the music video, more than any of the other creators of his day. And yet a number of music videos seem to bear the stamp of Méliès's paternity.

Having mapped some of the many connections—episodic, perhaps, but also symptomatic—between Méliès and the revue, the musical comedy on film, the invention of *auteur* television, and the early days of music videos, we are now in the position to acknowledge both the strong intermediality of Méliès's work (and its most marked iconographic qualities, such as those present in *A Trip to the Moon*), and its relative timelessness—thanks to the ongoing efforts of artists to "metabolize" it in their own work, and thus, transform and revitalize it. At the same time, the many elements to which we have connected Méliès's work converge naturally in a form that is neither as radically contemporary nor as far removed from the cinema as it initially seems: the music video.[40]

The most obvious example is the music video produced by Dayton and Faris for "Tonight, Tonight" (Smashing Pumpkins, 1996). To begin with, the iconography featured on the cover of the album, *Mellon Collie and the Infinite Sadness*, reveals its evident affinity for Méliès's universe, in general, and *A Trip to the Moon*, in particular. The music video is a direct quotation from *A Trip to the Moon*, one that begins with the shuttle's departure for the moon; the particulars of the narrative are progressively modified, but also draw on other Méliès films. For instance, instead of a projectile shot toward the moon from a Vernian cannon, as in *A Trip to the Moon*, it features a "multitasking" vehicle such as the one in *An Impossible Voyage* (1904). In Dayton and Faris's work, the retro influences often hark back to the origins of cinema and to a cinematic era in which the principle governing continuity among images was pure motion, and thus, rhythm: the moment, in short, when cinema was closest to music.[41] Similarly, the video for the song "Otherside" (Red Hot Chili Peppers, 2000) partially recalls the visual universe and story of *The Cabinet of Dr. Caligari* (Robert Wiene, 1919) and makes explicit the visual affinity between early cinema like Méliès's and the use of settings straight out of German Expressionism, which refers back more or less directly to Méliès.

Let us also consider a scene in *Moulin Rouge!* (Baz Luhrmann, 2001): "Dance across the Sky," a duet performed by the two protagonists and sung to the tune of "Your Song" (Elton John, 1969). If the set design already evokes Méliès's painted backdrops, more than the stylized though still naturalistic Paris of Renoir in *French Cancan* (1955), one of the alternative versions of this number[42] refers to Méliès and the moon in *A Trip to the Moon*, as well as to the ladylike stars not only in *The Eclipse* (1907), but also in *A Nightmare* (1896), *The Astronomer's Dream or the Man in the Moon* (1898), and *An Impossible Voyage* in decidedly explicit fashion.

Shifting 180 degrees, from pop-rock to contemporary Japanese songwriting—without recourse to the logic of "recycling" so diffuse in popular culture—and standing, as it were, on the brink of postmodernism, we once again discover the influential force of Méliès and his astral imagery in two experimental films Teiji Ito scored: *The Very Eye of Night* (Maya Deren, 1958) and *Moonplay* (Marie Menken, 1962).

Figure 12-2. Outtake, *Moulin Rouge!* (2001).

We have already discussed how logical it seems to us to speak of Méliès as an experimental filmmaker in the same mode as McLaren (or Chaplin, following McLaren's own suggestion), and we have already addressed his kinship with the avant-gardes of the first half of the twentieth century. In conclusion, then, establishing one final connection between Méliès and the experimental cinema of the second half of the twentieth century—specifically, to a handful of films structured around a musical extract (sophisticated relations, in a sense, of the music video genre)—will be easy. Maya Deren's films seem to anticipate McLaren's *Pas de deux* (1968), filtered through Méliès's celestial and astrological images—above all, those that surface in the final two parts of *The Eclipse*: "The Wandering Stars" and "An Unexpected Bath." In *The Very Eye of Night*, female stars, zodiac signs, and ballerina constellations shoot across a black background, the images captured in a diagonal high angle shot. The superimpositions and the monochromatic backdrop, speckled with stars, distances this from Deren's other dance films—*A Study in Choreography for Camera* (1945) or *Meditation on Violence* (1948).[43] Here the bodies become true accessories, props prime for dismemberment, depending on

Figure 12-3. *Rabbit's Moon* (1950).

the shot, as was often the case in early cinema and trick films. In this piece of Deren's, the flatness of the images renders the figures in her long, static shots similar to those of Méliès. In Marien Menken's film, *Moonplay*—which Teiji Ito also scored—a few shots of the moon captured by a telescope undergo some visual transformations.

Before leaving the subject of 1950s experimental filmmaking, we must also consider Kenneth Anger's lunar dream in *Rabbit's Moon* (1950),[44] in which Méliès moon imagery—in particular, from *A Nightmare, The Astronomer's Dream, The Magic Lantern* (1903), and *A Moonlight Serenade, or the Miser Punished* (1904)—finds a direct echo. The spectator is confronted with the image of a romantic struggle between Pierrot and Colombine,[45] with the interventions of Harlequin and the magical appearance of some white rabbits that emerge from a fortune-teller's hat, with a full moon that metamorphoses and vanishes only to reappear, and with a magic lantern that records everything, allowing the dream to be projected from the very beginning. Anger, experimenting with samples of romantic imagery, glorifies some of the images to which Méliès himself often returned, and in his sense, romanticizes both the imaginary of precinema and, at the same time, the cinematic apparatus itself.

"This then is an elegy for Méliès. Once, having created films terrestrial, aerial and igneous. . . ."[46]

Let us conclude this chapter—a sort of brief *catalogue raisonné* testifying to the permanence and continuing relevance of Méliès's work—with a few observations on two experimental films by Al Razutis, from the series *Visual Essays: Origins of Film* (1973–1982). Both of them, *Melies [sic] Catalogue* (1973) and *Sequels in Transfigured Time* (1974), are poetic, rather melancholy montages—but like Méliès's films, they are also playful. Seemingly unrelated to the works just discussed[47] (in which the relationship between sound and image played a central role), these films, further examples of the migration of Méliès's forms and figures, really deserve in-depth analysis and a chapter of their own—and above all, a long overdue rediscovery.

Long after the era of "visionary films" (to borrow P. Adams Sitney's expression), and in an age of digital circulation in which images lack authorial protection (we ourselves have made extensive use of YouTube to track the present-day circulation of images from *A Trip to the Moon*), Razutis's "found footage films"—"art" and "artisanal" films, films that noticeably play with the notion of the "unique copy"[48]—are, in fact, rarely seen. The rediscovery of this series of films, made up of montages of early cinema, would be auspicious: also because (as we underscored at the start with the quote from Tom Gunning) these films, along with some of Razutis's contemporaries, specifically advocated for the rediscovery and the renewed circulation of early cinema, and of Méliès and *A Trip to the Moon* to begin with. (For *A Trip to the Moon*, see above all *Sequels in Transfigured Time*.) The rediscovery of early cinema proposed by *Tom Tom The Piper's Son* (Ken Jacobs, 1969), *Eureka* (Ernie Gehr, 1974), or the first of the *Visual Essays: Origins of Film*, preceded even the wave of renewed interest that followed the famous Brighton congress in 1978.[49] Following Sitney's formulation,[50] "structuralist" films—like those of Ernie Gehr,[51] Ken Jacobs, Hollis Frampton, and Al Razutis—specifically called for serious tributes to early cinema[52] to reflect, deconstruct, and reconstruct the status of "origins."

In *Melies* [*sic*] *Catalogue* and *Sequels in Transfigured Time*, excerpts from Méliès's body of work follow one after another, thus celebrating the utterly "attraction"-based suppression of a narrative based on characters' actions: instead, we encounter fleeting fugitive apparitions, objects transformed through "reframings" (*recadrages*) so as to assume a new, unsettling aspect, at once familiar and foreign, and superimpositions and inversions of tints (often positive/negative) performed by Razutis.[53]

The title of the first of these, *Melies* [*sic*] *Catalogue*, already points us toward an important aspect of Méliès's work: it functions like a catalog. That is, throughout Méliès's work,[54] as in the Star-Film catalogs, one finds various fragments that parallel each other and remain relatively unchanging, delineating a series of motifs and patterns: in fact, there is little stylistic difference between *A Nightmare* and *The Conquest of the Pole* (1912). In Razutis's "found footage," one finds these recurring motifs, for instance: reframings to alter scale, long shots with a crowd of agitated people in the center of the frame, close-ups of heads or masks—from that of the moon, to that of *The Four Troublesome Heads* (1898), to that of the giant in *The Conquest of the Pole*. One hears:

> Hommage a
> Georges Melies
> (1961–1938)
> Directeur du Theatre Robert Houdin
> Auteur, Acteur, Decorateur,
> Auteur en Scene
> Cinematographiques Mordernes
> Createur du Spectacle
> Cinematographique[55]

Melies [*sic*] *Catalogue* includes fragments corroded by wear, burnt strips of celluloid that aspire to be recognized (and thus remembered) as Méliès's images—and because Méliès himself burned them, Razutis's aesthetic choice seems that much more touching today. The superimposition of these images—the one, Méliès's, and the other, the burnt black perforated end of the celluloid—suggests we read them as the apocalypse of film.

The impression of fragility and fear of obsolescence that always haunt early films are staged here with the Mélièsien fragments threatening to disappear with every cut. The eye of the moon pierced by the projectile and the breaking up of agitated bodies are only the distant echo of a work one dreams of reconstructing. (And remember, too, that Razutis made the film in 1973, that is, before the preservation and mass distribution of Méliès's work made it more easily accessible.)

The era in which these homages came into being was not yet one of philological perfection (we have already spoken of the pre-Brighton era), and it witnessed certain comical mix-ups, readily understandable to us today, and a reminder of one of the factors contributing to Méliès's ruin. Earlier, we recalled how Méliès had truly inaugurated a new mode, and how Pathé (and Segundo de Chomón) made underhanded use of it. Here, Razutis intercuts Chomón's images with those of Méliès. Thus the constellations, the zodiac, the ascent to the starry vault, the antics and acrobatics of the leaping gods, à la Méliès, which Razutis shows alongside Méliès's images are taken from *Voyage à la planète Jupiter*. And the same thing occurs both in *Melies* [*sic*] *Catalogue* and in *Sequels in Transfigured Time*. In the latter, Razutis renders Méliès's images almost unrecognizable by inserting countless obstacles between what we see on screen and our own recollection of Méliès—inverting positive and negative (or right and left), superimposing two or more stills at once, and using "freeze frames." The result is a sense of excitement whenever we *do* succeed in "understanding" the image, as we waver continually between alienation and attraction.

The first part of *Sequels in Transfigured Time* revisits the lunar imagery of *A Trip to the Moon*. The cartoons—superimposed along the image's bottom margin—evoke the sort of sensations that images like this tend to elicit:

> as if under a macroscope
> all hieroglyph & metaglyph
> emulsion formed, light borne
> kinetographs

Kinetographs: says Razutis. This written allusion appears in a sort of "cave painting" that the spectator's avid and attentive gaze—eager for signs of

Méliès—discovers to be a depiction of the lunar travelers, contending with the flora and fauna of the moon cave (an image created with the "tricks" enumerated above). *Kinetographs:* cinematic graphemes, originary signs of the cinema, according to the cinephilic neologism that appears on the images from *A Trip to the Moon* in *Sequels in Transfigured Time.*

We feel the need to affirm at the end of this journey that the freedom we have allowed ourselves in this chapter—to move between work that is by nature commercial and popular (such as musical comedy, television programs, and music videos) and that which is defined by the author's craftsmanship and experimentation—was, if perilous, hopefully also compelling. The common thread in these heterogeneous works, which belong to diverse eras, traditions, and media, leads back to Méliès and in particular to *A Trip to the Moon*—the apex of his success and the beginning of his cultural drift, a "drift" marked by the unchecked circulation of his images. For us today, so far from Star-Film's concerns about distribution, this circulation is a heuristic instrument that can be used to measure a film's impact. Méliès's work in particular—even in its own time—served as a bridge between mass-produced, popular work, and work crafted by an auteur. For us today, it is no longer just a bridge, but a full-blown spatial corridor in which one can move backward and forward, from one decade to another: *no one-way ticket to the moon.* . . .

Having presented this vast network of modes and motifs, and having transcended the conventional limits separating one institution from another, we have ultimately considered *A Trip to the Moon* as a seminal—not to mention intermedial—artifact. We have proposed—proposed, yes, but the images have helped us to substantiate our hypothesis—that its reception by experimental filmmakers, creators of music videos, and cutting-edge artists, encouraged them to use Méliès's film as a springboard for making new work. *A Trip to the Moon*—constructed as an index of entertaining, concatenated images, of familiar fragments from an era with its own culture of images and rhythms, as a true cave of wonders, a *wunderkammer*, of colors and pure movement—is, in our reading, a genuine cradle of a culture.

It pleases us, then, to conclude with the words of Georges Franju who at the end of his moving film *Le Grand Méliès* (1953)[56] in his notes for a "waltz" through the last century, honors the memory of Méliès:

> And this is the end of the story that I started to tell a little while ago. But the little waltz is still here. And I think perhaps you understand now why without Georges Méliès this movie and many others could never have been made.

Notes

Author's note: The research for this text was part of a postdoctoral project research (FQRSC, 2008/2010) at McGill University's Department of Art History and Communication Studies: "Entre attractions et musée: cinéma, exposition et nouvelles technologies." Many thanks to Al Razutis for having generously allowed the screening of several of his films, presented in brief in this chapter, and to Ernie Gehr for his availability and some bibliographic suggestions.

1. At the Gala Méliès, in addition to the program on Méliès, there was also a screening of Cecil B. De Mille's *The Cheat* (1915), with Sessue Hayakawa—a reference point for the elegant French "First Wave." See Richard Abel, *French Cinema: The First Wave, 1915–1929* (Princeton, N.J.: Princeton University Press, 1984); and *Fotogenia: La bellezza del cinema*, ed. Guglielmo Pescatore (Bologna, Italy: CLUEB, 1992).

2. For a detailed analysis of the rediscovery of Méliès at the end of the 1920s, see Roland Cosandey, "L'Inescamotable escamoteur, ou Méliès en ses figures," in *Georges Méliès, l'illusionniste fin de siècle?* ed. Jacques Malthête and Michel Marie (Paris: Presses de la Sorbonne Nouvelle, 1997), 45–96; and Roland Cosandey, "Georges Méliès as *L'Inescamotable Escamoteur*: A Study in Recognition," in *Lo schermo incantato: Georges Méliès (1861–1938) / A Trip to the Movies: Georges Méliès, Filmmaker and Magician (1861–1938)*, ed. Paolo Cherchi Usai (Rochester, N.Y.: International Museum of Photography at George Eastman House; Pordenone: Edizioni Biblioteca dell'Immagine, Le Giornate del Cinema Muto, 1991), 57–111. See also Christophe Gauthier, "Le Cinéma des nations: invention des écoles nationales et patriotisme cinématographique (années 1910–années 1930)," *Revue d'histoire moderne et contemporaine* 4, no. 51 (2004): 58–77. On the relationship between the Gala Méliès and the historical avant-gardes, see Antonio Costa, *Il cinema e le arti visive* (Turin, Italy: Einaudi, 2002).

3. Tom Gunning, "An Unseen Energy Swallows Space: The Space in Early Film and Its Relation to American Avant-Garde Film," in *Film before Griffith*, ed. John L. Fell (Berkeley: University of California Press, 1983), 356.

4. "The Sprocket Society . . . seeks to cultivate the love of the mechanical cinema, its arts and sciences, and to encourage film preservation by bringing film and its history to the public through screenings, educational activities, and our own archival efforts." See www.sprocketsociety.org/events/melies/Georges_Melies-Impossible_Voyager_2008.pdf.

5. A quick search on YouTube uncovers some rather strange pairings of Méliès titles (particularly *A Trip to the Moon*) and contemporary music. See especially "A Trip to the Moon vs. Pink Floyd" (www.youtube.com/watch?v=_1ACaTnUZ70) to the tune of "Echoes" (1971); or the montage by British underground singer Doron Deutsch who alternates live images of his band, filmed on a cell phone, with tinted fragments of *A Trip to the Moon*: www.youtube.com/watch?v=vfwvnS3QPUU&eurl.

6. The first, an important event in terms of valorizing the concept of "cinematic patrimony" (a relatively new concept in 1929) at the Gala Méliès,

and at the same time, consecrating the relationship among popular, retro, and avant-garde work that would span the twentieth century. The second, contributed by Gunning: a little taste of the shift in film historiography post-Brighton, which today informs our way of looking at early cinema (as it does the majority of authors in this collection). The third, a program of screenings accompanied by soaring music: the umpteenth example of the tendency in recent times to appropriate images from early cinema in order to reinscribe them in the performative context of a "happening."

7. At this point, we should acknowledge some of the more or less well-known works of contemporary visual art that will not be part of this chapter: Red Grooms and Rudy Burckhardt, *Shoot [in] the Moon* (1992, 16 mm); Paul Glabicki, *Five Improvisations* (1979, classic animation, 35 mm); William Kentridge, *Fragments for Georges Méliès* (2003, video for installation, in particular see the fragment, *Journey to the Moon*).

8. Remarks taken from dialogue in *Le Magicien de Montreuil-sous-bois* (Jean-Christophe Averty, 1964), available in the web archives, "Inamédiapro."

9. See Johanne Sloan, "Modern Moon Rising: Imagining Aerospace in Early Picture Postcards," in *Strange Spaces: Explorations into Mediated Obscurity*, ed. André Jansson and Amanda Lagerkvist (Surrey, U.K.: Ashgate, 2009), 279–296.

10. See Thierry Lefebvre, "*A Trip to the Moon*: A Composite Film," trans. Timothy Barnard, this volume, 49–63; and John F. Kasson, *Amusing the Million: Coney Island at the Turn of the Century* (New York: Hill and Wang, 1978). Even today are found rides directly inspired by Verne and Méliès, including Voyage Cosmique, which debuted in the spring of 1995 at Disneyland Paris. To advertise the ride, clips from *A Trip to the Moon* were shown alongside shots of Luna Park on the television news show broadcast by France 3 on May 26, 1995 (available in the web archives, "Inamédiapro").

11. See Richard Abel, *The Ciné Goes to Town: French Cinema, 1896–1914* (Berkeley: University of California Press, 1994), 70–73.

12. See Norman McLaren, "Hommage à George Méliès," *Asifa* [Montréal], no. 15 (April 1987): 3–4; translated in pamphlet included in DVD box set *Georges Méliès: First Wizard of Cinema (1896–1913)* (Flicker Alley, 2008). See also Gilles Delavaud, "Méliès et Chaplin, du cinéma d'attractions au film-attraction," in *Georges Méliès, l'illusionniste fin de siècle?* 357–379.

13. But one must also bear in mind that Méliès himself draws on décors, costumes, movements, and gags, thus weaving a web of recurring, and reassuring, iconographies. As for the "trip through space," the anthropomorphic moon, and the galactic choreography, one finds many relevant titles in the Star-Film catalogs, among them, *A Nightmare* (1896), *The Astronomer's Dream or the Man in the Moon* (1898), *Alcofrisbas, The Master Magician* (1903), *A Moonlight Serenade, or the Miser Punished* (1904), *An Impossible Voyage* (1904), *The Merry Frolics of Satan* (1906), and *The Eclipse* (1907), to which one could add *Les Farces de la lune ou mésaventures de Nostradamus* performed at the Théâtre Robert-Houdin in 1891.

14. At the end of this chapter we will see in the discussion of Al Razutis that the Méliès/Chomón misunderstanding persisted for several decades.

15. The reproductions of the McCay panels can be found in a published version of the collection: Winsor McCay, *Little Nemo in Slumberland: So Many Splendid Sundays!* (New York: Sunday Press Books, 2005).

16. "[T]he first positives . . . forwarded to U.S.A. . . . were copied, (countertyped), and sold in large number, by Edison and Lubin of Philadelphia, perhaps also by some others, for the number of copies sold in America was enormous relatively [*sic*] to the number printed in my laboratory." Méliès, "Reply to Questionary [*sic*]," this volume, 233.

17. Méliès, "Reply to Questionary [*sic*]," this volume, 234.

18. The paradigm of the "cinema of attractions" would influence film scholarship after André Gaudreault and Tom Gunning's seminal article, "Le Cinéma des premiers temps: Un défi à l'histoire du cinéma" (1985), in *Histoire du cinéma: Nouvelles approches*, ed. Jacques Aumont, Gaudreault, and Michel Marie (Paris: Publications de la Sorbonne, 1989), 49–63. A contemporary study that includes an English translation of this article and revisits this group's terms is *The Cinema of Attractions Reloaded*, ed. Wanda Strauven (Amsterdam, Netherlands: Amsterdam University Press, 2006). For an extended exploration of the concept of "attraction," its usefulness to film theory and the art of the spectacle, and its ongoing relevance to film history, even contemporary history, see Viva Paci, "De l'attraction au cinéma" (Ph.D. diss., Université de Montréal, 2007).

19. Remarks taken from dialogue in *Le Magicien de Montreuil-sous-bois*.

20. Tom Gunning, "Attractions, truquages et photogénie: l'explosion du présent dans les films à truc français produits entre 1896 et 1907," in *Les Vingt premières années du cinéma français*, ed. Jean A. Gili, Michèle Lagny, Michel Marie, and Vincent Pinel (Paris: Presses de la Sorbonne Nouvelle; AFRHC, 1995), 183.

21. Work dealt with in my doctoral thesis, "De l'attraction au cinéma."

22. Stan Brakhage, *The Brakhage Lectures: Georges Méliès, David Wark Griffith, Carl Theodore Dreyer, Sergei Eisenstein* (Chicago: Good Lion/School of the Art Institute, 1972). Transcripts of lectures given as part of a course at the School of the Art Institute of Chicago during the fall and early winter of 1970–1971 are available at http://www.ubu.com/historical/brakhage/brakhage_lectures_revised.pdf, Web Collection Ubuclassics, 2004, p. 11.

23. In addition to the infamous *Show Boat, Whoopee!* and *Rio Rita* (which would be adapted into films), Ziegfeld's most influential productions were the *Follies*. He staged more than twenty versions of them in 1907—the first at the Jardins de Paris theater on Broadway (*Follies of 1907*) to the last *Ziegfeld Follies* staged in 1931. Others would follow but were financed by other producers.

24. See Gerald Mast, *Can't Help Singin': The American Musical on Stage and Screen* (New York: Overlook, 1987). On the reasons for the decline in the theatrical spectacle à la Ziegfeld see Gerald Bordman, *American Musical Theatre. A Chronicle* (New York: Oxford University Press, 1978). The plot of a Warner film during the golden era of musical comedy recounting the clash between the culture of the grand revue and the ascent of sound film can function as a summary and epilogue of the stories of all the "Ziegfelds" on Broadway, thwarted above all by the U.S. 1929 financial crisis as well as by improvements in production, by the pomp of Hollywood's major players, and by the additional attraction offered by the standardization of sound film.

25. Jean-Christophe Averty to Bernard Pivot, in "Ouvrez les guillemets," May 21, 1973, RTF/ORTF (available in the web archives, "Inamédiapro"), is one of his clear vindications of Georges Méliès's legacy.

26. On Busby Berkeley, see Martin Rubin, *Showstoppers: Busby Berkeley and the Tradition of Spectacle* (New York: Columbia University Press, 1993).

27. As for the affinity between the avant-garde and the popular (a subject with which this chapter began by remembering the 1929 Gala Méliès) and, in particular, the affinity between the world of U.S. experimental film and the imaginary of Busby Berkeley, it is worth remembering that as part of a retrospective at New York's Anthology Film Archives in 2005 (see the DVD case for *Unseen Cinema: Early American Avant-Garde Film 1893–1941*, which includes the program) experimental films were paired with animation, with "views" from early cinema, and with choreographed sequences from Berkeley. This choice of programming—by Bruce Posner and David Shepard—seems to us to have finally rescued Berkeley from the purgatory of "kitsch" or "camp" in which "gender studies" seems to have stranded him. On "kitsch" and "camp," see Susan Sontag, "Notes on Camp" (1964), *Against Interpretation and Other Essays* (New York: Picabo, 1966).

28. Some of Benayoun's ideas about Berkeley could be reread with Méliès in mind, and his comments would retain their relevance: see Robert Benayoun, "Berkeley le centupleur," *Positif*, no. 74 (1966): 29–41.

29. The chorus of the song by celebrated lyricists Warren and Dubin, "Dames," in Ray Enright's film of the same name, *Dames* (1934), with choreography by Berkeley, is worth noting: "Go see a show for? Tell the truth, you go to see these beautiful dames. . . . Who cares if there's a plot or not, when they've got a lot of dames."

30. The expression *"attraction juxtaposé"* is from Livio Belloï, "Reconfigurations: La question du plan emblématique," in *La Firme Pathé Frères, 1896–1914*, ed. Michel Marie and Laurent Le Forestier (Paris, AFRHC, 2004), 179–192.

31. This expression, *plan-tableau*, is included in Pascal Bonitzer, *Peinture et cinéma: Décadrages* (Paris: Cahiers du cinéma/Éditions de l'étoile, 1987); it attempts to collapse the distinction between film and painting. According to Bonitzer, one finds an "unstable mixing between the high (painting) and the low (cinema), between movement (the shot) and stillness (the *tableau*)" (30). The *plan-tableau* is fairly independent from the continuity of the montage and may actually suspend the flow of narration. Méliès, for his part, uses the expression *"tableau"* to denote two levels of fragmentation in his films, as André Gaudreault reminds us in *Cinéma et attraction: Pour une nouvelle histoire du cinématographe* (Paris: CNRS Éditions, 2008), 219. For Méliès, in his writings and in the descriptions in the Star-Film catalogs, *"tableaux"* sometimes indicate those fragments of film associated with one décor (which include more shots), and at other times, lesser elements. Gaudreault reminds us that from the point of view of marketing, the more tableaux there are, the more they are emphasized in the publicity for the films in the catalog: for instance, *A Trip to the Moon* boasts thirty tableaux in the catalog, but only involves seventeen changes in décor.

32. Actually, one of the most suitable forms for presenting Berkeley's work is the anthology: in the Warner box set *The Busby Berkeley Collection* (2006), which includes *42nd Street*, *Gold Diggers of 1933*, *Footlight Parade*, *Dames*, *Gold Diggers*

of 1935, an entire disc (*The Busby Berkeley Disc*) is dedicated to a compilation of Berkeley's best pieces, shown one after another.

33. Noël Burch, *Life to Those Shadows*, trans. and ed. Ben Brewster (Berkeley: University of California Press, 1990); see esp. 186–201.

34. Frédéric Mitterrand, as a *bonimenteur* who performs directly facing the television camera, is the common thread running through the short films that comprise *Méliès 88*. The film was commissioned by the channel La Sept, produced by TF1 and INA in 1988, and directed by Bénédicte Lesage and Christian Janicot. This tribute to Méliès comprises nine short films, all dealing with subjects Méliès never addressed. The directors advocate the importance of 1980s experimental work in video, television, and animation done in the 1980s. All proclaim themselves to be direct disciples of Méliès, that great master of special effects and imaginative solutions. The works include: *The Duel*, Zbig Rybczynski; *La Providence de Notre-Dame des flots*, Gérard Krawczyk; *Le Topologue*, Marc Caro; *Gulliver*, Jean-Pierre Mocky; *Bénie soit elle par qui le scandale arrive*, Aline Issermann; *Les Sept péchés capitaux*, Philippe Gautier; *Rêve d'artiste ou le cauchemar de Méliès*, Pierre Etaix; and *Le Rêve de Radjah*, Jean-Louis Bertucelli (available in the web archives "Inamédiapro").

35. On Averty see Anne-Marie Duguet, *Jean-Christophe Averty* (Paris: Dis Voir, 1991), and Gilles Delavaud, *L'Art de la télévision: Histoire et esthétique de la dramatique télévisé (1950–1965)* (Paris: INA/de Boeck, 2005).

36. Like the giant clock inspired by the props in Méliès's *The Clockmaker's Dream* (1904). In Averty's film, numbers transform themselves into musical bars, which reveal themselves to be the arms of ballerinas, locked in sinuous, collective movements.

37. This interpretation of the early days of video art and of Averty's creations is proposed by Duguet in *Jean-Christophe Averty*. See also Christine Ross, *Images de surface: L'Art vidéo reconsidéré* (Montreal: Editions Artextes, 1996).

38. Another French television program not only *about* Méliès, but which also borrows his style, imagery, and experimental energy is the aforementioned *Méliès 88*. In particular, Pierre Etaix's short film, *Rêve d'artiste ou le cauchemar de Méliès*—full of Mélièsien images, including a sad career finale and a rudimentary use of 3D to create a model of the Montreuil studio (we *are* in 1988 . . .)—underscores the affinity between early cinema and digital animation. Each of the contributions in *Méliès 88* displays some technical dexterity: from video images to digital animation.

39. One could ostensibly continue the trajectory from Méliès, to Berkeley, to Averty, all the way to McLaren. And here, one thinks not only of the McLaren of *Pas de deux* (1968), but also the McLaren of *Neighbours* (1952), in which "stop motion"–descendant of the Mélièsien "substitution splice"—recalls another aspect of Méliès's style. McLaren, among other things, dedicates various contributions to Méliès; see Norman McLaren, "Hommage à George Méliès."

40. Without being able to provide a more in-depth analysis of music videos and to trace their continuities with film, we will limit ourselves to naming three artists who, straddling both forms, help to make our case: Michel Gondry—the

great descendent of Méliès and Averty—Jonathan Dayton, and Valerie Faris. As for the genre's older roots, we will just mention Gaumont's phonoscènes and later Warner's Vitaphone. See Martin Barnier, *En route vers le parlant* (Brussels, Belgium: Editions du Céfal, 2002); and Édouard Arnoldy, *Pour une histoire culturelle du cinéma (Au-devant de "scènes filmées," de "films chantants et parlants" et de comédies musicales)* (Liège, Belgium: Editions du Céfal, 2004).

41. One could follow numerous paths here, and we will suggest one—that dealing with questions of "pure cinema," abstraction (versus narration), and rhythm (versus realist *découpage*). See *Cahiers du mois*, no. 16/17 (1925), especially the pieces by Georges Charensol, Henri Chomette, René Clair, and Germaine Dulac.

42. It recalls the version labeled "Unseen Footage of Abandoned Edits" on the second disc of the *Moulin Rouge!* 2-DVD set (Twentieth-Century Fox, 2001).

43. See also Lucy Fischer, "The Eye for Magic: Maya and Méliès," in *Maya Deren and the American Avant-Garde*, ed. Bill Nichols (Berkeley: University of California Press, 2001), 185–204.

44. At least three versions of *Rabbit's Moon* exist (multiple versions as in early cinema)—from 1950, 1971, and 1979, with two different soundtracks and with different coloring. The 1950 version was edited with some songs by the Flamingos, The Dells, The Capris, Mary Wells, and The El Dorados; and the 1979 version, with "It Came in the Night," by the group A Raincoat (1976).

45. See also Lucy Fischer, "*Rabbit's Moon*: The Pierrot Figure in Theater, Painting, and Film," *Millenium Film Journal*, nos. 10–11 (Winter 1981–82): 123–139.

46. A line Al Razutis recites in the third and final part of his film *Sequels in Transfigured Time* (1974).

47. We must remember that we have identified certain similarities between the avant-garde work of Maya Deren, Marie Menken, and Kenneth Anger and that of Razutis, both in terms of their rhythms and their ambitions. Let us also remember that Berkeley's musical comedies discussed in this chapter have been recycled and recirculated today precisely because of the atmosphere of the 1960s and 1970s that was so receptive to experimentation. See the series *Unseen Cinema*.

48. *Melies [sic] Catalogue*, in particular, with its images that consume themselves right before our eyes.

49. The reference, of course, is to the FIAF Congress in Brighton, where more than 600 films made between 1900 and 1906 were presented, uncovering new areas of exploration.

50. P. Adams Sitney, "Structural Film," *Visionary Film: The American Avant-Garde, 1943–1978* (Oxford, U.K.: Oxford University Press, 1979), 369–397.

51. Ernie Gehr in particular continues this daunting work on early cinema in both his films and his videos; see *Essex Street Market* (2004) and *Workers Leaving the Factory (after Lumière)* (2004). For Méliès, see *The Astronomer's Dream* (2004). For *Eureka* (1974), see J. Hoberman, "Metro Picture: J. Hoberman on Ernie Gehr," *Artforum* 43, no. 6 (Feb. 2005): 41.

52. André Habib suggests two approaches to recycling imagery in experimental film. One is that of the "structuralists" such as Razutis; one thinks of his

Lumière's Train Arriving at Station (1953), along with the above-mentioned Méliès variations—or perhaps Ken Jacobs's *Tom Tom The Piper's Son.* The other is that of the "melancholic-rag picker," such as Bill Morrison's *Film of Her* (1997) and *Decasia* (2002), Peter Delpeut's *Lyrical Nitrate* (1991), or even Gustav Deutsch's *Film Ist 1–6* (1998) and *Film Ist 7–12* (2002). See André Habib, "Des fragments de premiers temps à l'esthétique de la ruine," in *Networks of Entertainment: Early Film Distribution 1895–1915,* ed. Frank Kessler and Nanna Verhoeff (Eastleigh, U.K.: John Libbey, 2007), 320–326. See also Bart Testa, *Back and Forth: Early Cinema and the Avant-Garde* (Ontario, Canada: Art Gallery of Ontario, 1992), and Gunning, "An Unseen Energy Swallows Space."

53. Here, we have deliberately evoked the definition of *cinéma pur* proposed by the editors of *Cahiers du mois* no. 16/17 (1925): 85 ("complete suppression of script, apparition and transformation of objects lit and seen from a new angle that makes them unrecognizable, chemical crystallization, ultra-rapid movement [creating] unknown visions—inconceivable apart from the union of the lens and the moving strip of film").

54. Pathé, on the other hand, produced the films of 1911 and 1912 without substantial changes.

55. Recited by the final cartoon in *Melies* [*sic*] *Catalogue.* The punctuation, capitalization, and use of accents should be attributed to Razutis.

56. Franju would dedicate another brief film to Méliès: *Méliès père et fils* (1977), installment 136 of the television series *Chroniques de France.* His *Le Grand Méliès* was produced by Fred Orain, who at the time assisted in the transition from auteur cinema to television that was still ripe for invention and anticonformism. *Le Grand Méliès,* which premiered on April 3, 1953, at the Marignan cinema, would have been welcomed by Madame Méliès, Jehanne d'Alcy, as a flop, "*une botte de navet.*"

Appendix

A September 1902 film catalog supplement from the Warwick Trading Company, the authorized distributor for Star-Film at this time, contains one of the most extensive pieces of contemporary publicity for *Trip to the Moon* (listed here without the indefinite article)—a numbered list of its "scenes" (tableaux) and a narrative synopsis.[1] This catalog description is followed by a transcription of a 1930 document written in English in Méliès's own hand, responding to nine questions about *A Trip to the Moon* put to him in a letter from Jean Acme LeRoy; his somewhat idiosyncratic English spelling, punctuation, and usage, are retained without alteration.[2] This document is followed by two articles authored by Méliès. While neither refers specifically to *A Trip to the Moon*, both shed light on Méliès's filmmaking practice. The first essay, "The Marvelous in the Cinema," originally published in 1912, was Méliès's intervention in a debate that took place in the pages of *L'Écho du cinéma* in the wake of a contest that challenged readers to submit storylines for "impossible films" that could be realized cinematically.[3] Méliès unsurprisingly affirms impossible subjects, but also advocates a pluralism of genres and approaches. This inclusiveness is consistent with *A Trip to the Moon*, which embraces variety and combines several of the modes discussed by Méliès. The second essay, "The Importance of the Script," was originally published in 1932, but has heretofore been available only in a French translation of a Spanish translation of Méliès's article.[4] Despite not having made a commercial film for close to two decades, Méliès inserts himself into discussions of the current cinema, explaining that scripts are less important for films of certain genres—particularly for the fantasy films that made his reputation years earlier.

Notes

1. *Warwick Film Blue Book Supplement*, no. 2 (September 1902), 1–6. The synopsis is reprinted nearly word-for-word in the catalog description for Lubin's unauthorized reproduction, "A Trip to Mars," *Complete Catalogue of Lubin's Films*, January 1903, 7–9.

2. Cote 22, box 2, fonds Georges Méliès, Bibliothèque du film, Paris. A copy can be found in the Georges Méliès subject file, Film Department, Museum of Modern Art, New York. While the questions could not be located, one can infer them from Méliès's answers. Méliès's replies, run together as a continuous text, were published in French translation as "*Le Voyage dans la lune*" in Georges Sadoul, *Lumière et Méliès*, ed. Bernard Eisenschitz (Paris: Lherminier, 1985), 231–232. Compare Madeleine Malthête-Méliès, *Méliès, l'enchanteur* (Paris: Éditions Ramsay, 1995), 267–268, where only Méliès's answers to questions 1, 5, 6, and 9 are translated, along with LeRoy's ostensible questions, and Méliès's reply is dated 1933.

3. Géo. [*sic*] Méliès, "Le Merveilleux au cinéma," 2 parts, *L'Écho du cinéma*, no. 6 (May 24, 1912): 1–2; no. 7 (May 31, 1912): 2. See also Marina Dahlquist, *The Invisible Seen in French Cinema before 1917* (Stockholm: Aura förlag, 2001), 228–229. The winning entry is described in "Les Films impossibles," *L'Écho du cinéma*, no. 4 (May 10, 1912): 2.

4. Georges Méliès, "L'Importance du scénario," *Cinéa et ciné pour tous réunis*, n. s., no. 24 (April 1932): 23, 25. Compare Méliès, "Importance du scénario," in Sadoul, *Lumière et Méliès*, 219, esp. fn.

A FANTASTICAL . . .

TRIP TO THE MOON.

An Extraordinary Cinematographic Series in 30 Pictures.

SCENES, DECORATIONS, MACHINERY & ACCESSORIES

by G. MELIES.

No. 4399. Total Length, 800 feet.
Price, Plain – – – – – £32 0 0 net.
"   Coloured – – – – – £64 0 0 net.
Duration of Exhibit, 16 minutes.

Supplied to the Trade on and after
September 10th, 1902.

SCENES.

----

1. The Scientific Congress at the Astronomic Club.

2. Planning the Trip. Appointing the Explorers and Servants. Farewell.

3. The Workshops: Constructing the Projectile.

4. The Founderies. The Chimney-stacks. The casting of the Monster Gun.

5. The Astronomers enter the Shell.

6. Loading the Gun.

7. The Monster Gun. March Past of the Gunners. Fire!!! Saluting the Flag.

8. The Flight through Space. Approaching the Moon.

9. Landed Right into the Eye!!!

10. Flight of the Shell into the Moon. Appearance of the Earth from the Moon.

11. The Plain of Craters. Volcanic Eruption.

12. The Dream (the Bolies, the Great Bear, Phœbus, the Twin Stars Saturn).

13. The Snow Storm.

14. 40 Degrees below Zero. Descending a Lunar Crater.

15. In the Interior of the Moon. The Giant Mushroom Grotto.

16. Encounter with the Selenites. Homeric Flight.

17. Prisoners!!

18. The Kingdom of the Moon. The Selenite Army.

19. The Flight.

20. Wild Pursuit.

21. The Astronomers find the Shell again. Departure from the Moon.

22. Vertical Drop into Space.

23. Splashing into the Open Sea.

24. At the Bottom of the Ocean.

25. The Rescue. Return to Port.

26. Great Fete. Triumphal March Past.

27. Crowning and Decorating the Heroes of the Trip.

28. Procession of Marines and the Fire Brigade.

29. Inauguration of the Commemorative Statue by the Mayor and Council.

30. Public Rejoicings.

SYNOPSIS

The astronomers are assembled in a large hall embellished with instruments. The President and members of the Committee enter. Everybody takes his seat. Entrance of seven men-servants carrying the telescopes of the astronomers. The President takes his chair, and explains to the members his plan of a trip to the moon. His scheme is approved of by many, while one member violently opposes same. The President after some argument throws his papers and books at his head; the protesting party finally being thrown out of the club room amidst general disorder.

Upon order being restored, the trip proposed by the President is voted by acclamation, but at the moment of leaving nobody has the courage to accompany him. The furious President declares he will go by himself. At this stage five learned men make up their minds to go with him; their colleagues break out in applause, the men-servants bring travelling suits, and the six astronomers exchange their gala robes for appropriate dress for the trip.

President Barbenfouillis selects to accompany him five colleagues Nostradamus, Alcofrisbas, Omega, Micromegas and Parafaragaramus to pay a visit to the construction workshops of the projectile destined to carry them to the moon. They enter the interior of the workshops, where smiths, mechanics, weighers, carpenters, upholsterers, etc., are working hard at the completion of the machine. Micromegas accidentally falls into a tub of nitric acid. After the termination of the inspection, a workman descends from the top of the roof and informs the astronomers that if they would ascend to the roof they would witness a splendid spectacle: the casting of the gun. The astronomers hasten to a ladder and climb on to the roof, where they finally arrive. Against the horizon the chimneys are seen belching forth volumes of smoke. Suddenly a flag is hoisted by order of the President. At the signal a mass of molten steel is directed from each furnace into the mould for the gun. The mould pours forth flames and vapor. This causes much rejoicing among the enthusiastic astronomers.

On the top of the roofs of the town pompous preparations have been made; the shell is in position ready to receive the travellers. These arrive, respond to the acclamations of the crowd, and enter the shell. Marines close the breech through which they have passed.

A number of gunners are now pushing the shell up an incline into the mouth of the gun (of which only the back part is visible.)

In the next scene the cannon is fully visible in the distance. It is loaded, the breech is closed; everyone is anxiously waiting for the signal which starts the shell on its voyage. Arrival of Marine artillery, commanded by an officer. The officer gives the signal; the gunner occupies his post, and, at the word of command, the gun is fired. The crowd flocks together from all parts and gazes at the shell as it disappears into space.

In the midst of the clouds the moon is visible at a distance. The shell coming closer every minute, the moon magnifies rapidly until finally it attains colossal dimensions. It gradually assumes the shape of a living, grotesque face smiling sanctimoniously.

Suddenly the shell arrives with the rapidity of lightning, and pierces the eye of the moon. The face at once makes horrible grimaces, whilst enormous tears flow from the wound.

The picture changes, and shows the immense lunar plains with their seas, ampitheatres [sic] and craters. The shell comes down with a crash. The astronomers get out, and are delighted at the landscape which is new to them, whilst against the horizon the earth is rising slowly into space, illuminating the picture with a fantastic light.

The astronomers inspecting the strange country see craters everywhere. One of them suggests descending a crater into the interior, but just as they are about to carry out their intention, an eruption takes place, the unfortunate men being violently thrown in all directions.

The astronomers show signs of fatigue after the rough trip which they have just had. They stretch themselves out on the ground and go to sleep. In their dreams they see passing in space, comets, meteors, &c.—seven gigantic stars, representing the great bear, appear slowly, and out of the stars come faces of women who seem annoyed at the presence of these intruders in the moon. Then the stars disappear in space and are replaced by a lovely vision of Phœbus on the crescent, of Saturn in his globe surrounded by a ring, and of charming young girls holding up a star. They all discuss the arrival of the terrestrials in the moon and decide to punish them in an exemplary manner.

By order of Phœbus, snow is falling in from all quarters, covering the ground with its white coat; the astronomers are comically agitated under the covers with which they have wrapped themselves in order to sleep.

The cold becomes terrible. The unfortunate voyagers wake up half frozen, and decide without hesitation and in spite of the danger, to descend into the interior of a great crater, in which they disappear one by one, whilst the snowstorm is still raging.

The astronomers arrive in the interior of a most curious grotto, filled with enormous mushrooms of every kind. One of them opens his umbrella in order to compare its size with a mushroom, but the umbrella suddenly takes root and transforming itself into a mushroom starts growing gradually, attaining gigantic proportions.

The astronomers suddenly notice strange beings coming out from underneath the mushrooms and approaching them, while making singular contortions. These are the Selenites or inhabitants of the moon. These fantastical beings rush on an astronomer, who defends himself, and with a stroke of his umbrella he knocks a Selenite down, who bursts into a thousand pieces. A second suffers the same fate, but the Selenites are arriving in numbers. The terrified astronomers, to save themselves, take flight, with the Selenites in pursuit.

Succumbing to numbers, the astronomers are captured, bound and taken to the palace of the king of the Selenites.

On a splendid throne, surrounded by living stars, the Selenite King is seated. He commands that the inhabitants of the earth, who have dared penetrate into his State, be fetched, and suggests to sacrifice them before the united Selenite army. The astronomers are making superhuman efforts to free themselves of their impediments. President Barbenfouillis makes a dash for the King of the Selenites, and, lifting him like a feather, throws him violently on the ground. The unfortunate king bursts like a bomb-shell. The astronomers run away in the midst of the general disorder. The Selenite army is pursuing them.

The astronomers run at full speed, turning round each time they are pressed too closely, and reducing the fragile beings to dust, who continue to chase, but, single handed, are not capable of attack, as all their force lies in their number.

The still increasing number of Selenites obliges the astronomers to take desperately to flight again, and they pass through fantastical, picturesque landscapes, still pursued by the Selenites, amongst whom they institute a regular massacre.

At last the astronomers have found their shell, and quickly shut themselves in the interior; thanks to the advance, they have succeeded in gaining over their adversaries. Only one, the President, has been left behind. He arrives, closely pressed by two Selenites. He causes the first to burst by striking him with his hands, and kicking the other violently with his feet, he despatches him into space, where he also bursts, then he rushes to the rope which hangs from the point of the shell balanced on the edge of the moon, and letting himself slide down the rope, he gives it an impetus which causes the shell to precipitate itself into space. A Selenite who at this moment clings to the shell in order to hold it back is being drawn with it, and hanging on to the projectile, accompanies it in its drop.

The shell falls with sickening rapidity. Barbenfouillis clinging to the rope underneath tries to enter the projectile, whilst the unfortunate Selenite, half mad, clings desperately to the shell to save himself from falling off.

The Sea appears. The waves break into foam, the shell is attaining a white heat by the friction with the air in its maddening drop and dashes right into the sea, causing enormous columns of water to gush up. The sea closes over the shell again, and a thick vapour is rising, caused by the scorching hot metal dropping into the water.

We continue following the course of the shell into the depths of the ocean, where amongst the debris of ships, marine plants, the medusae, corals, and fishes of all kinds, the projectile reaches land at last. Enormous bubbles of air escape from the bottom of the sea and reach the surface. The shell balances, and, thanks to the hermetically sealed air in its interior, is rising slowly to the surface under the bewilderment of the fishes.

The shell is being picked up by a mail steamer, which, taking it in tow, returning to port. The Selinite [sic] is still seen clinging to the shell.

In the market place of the town the authorities are assembled, the crowd awaiting the appearance of the astronomers. The procession arrives; the municipal band advances, followed by marines drawing the decorated shell. Finally the astronomers arrive, amidst a general ovation.

The Mayor congratulates the astronomers on their happy return. Crowning them, he confers upon them the Order of the Moon.

The march past of the fire brigade and marines takes place. On the square appears the commemorative statue of the trip, representing President Barbenfouillis vanquishing the moon, with this device: "Labor Omnia Vincit."

The marines, the astronomers, the crowd, the Mayor and councillors join in chorus dancing round the statue to the President.

Reply to Questionary

GEORGES MÉLIÈS, 1930

1—The idea of "Trip to the Moon" came to me from the book of Jules Verne, entitled: "From the earth to the moon and round the moon." In this work the human people could not attain the moon, turned round it, and came back to earth, having, in fact, missed their trip. I then imagined, in using the process of Jules Verne, (gun and shell) to attain the moon, in order to be able to compose a number of original and amusing fairy pictures outside and inside the moon, and to show some monsters, inhabitants of the moon in adding one or two artistical effects (women representing stars, comets, etc.) (snow effect, bottom of the sea, etc)

2—Trip to the moon was begun in May 1902

3—The negative was finished in August 1902

4—The first prints were sold in France the same month—August 1902

5—I dont [sic] know exactly when they were sold in U.S.A. (Probably one or two months after.) As soon as the first positives were forwarded to U.S.A., probably through commission agents, they were copied, (countertyped) and sold in large number, by Edison and Lubin of Philadelphia, perhaps also by some others, for the number of copies sold in America was enormous relatively [sic] to the number printed in my laboratory.

6 The cost was about 10.000 francs, sum relatively high for the time, caused specially by the mechanical sceneries and principally the cost of the cardboard and canvas costumes made for the Selenites, or moon inhabitants, knees, heads, feet, all these articles being made specially and consequently expensive. I made myself the models, sculpted in terra cota [sic], and the plaster moulding; and

the costumes were made by a special masks manufacturer, accustomed to mould cardboard.

7–The subject was not copyrighted in U.S.A. It is why it was such [sic] copied everywhere, and it is also the reason why I open an office in N.Y. in order to have my following films copyrighted, and an agent (my brother) in U.S.A for preventing, as much as possible, the piratery [sic].

8–No dates, the film having not been copyrighted.

When I made "Trip to the Moon" there was [sic] not yet "Stars" amongst the artists, their name was [sic] never known nor written on bills or advertisements. The film was named Starfilm—and the name Mélies [sic], itself, did not appear on the screen, though I performed the principal characters. The people employed in Trip to the Moon was entirely acrobats, girls and singers coming from music halls, the theatrical actors having not yet accepted to play in cinema films, as they considered the motion picture as much below the theatre. They came only later, when they knew that music hall people gained more money in performing films than themselves in playing in theatres for about 300 francs a month, and such was generally the case for most of them.

In the cinema, they could gain more than the [sic] double. 2 years after my office was, every night, full of theatrical people coming for [sic] asking to be engaged.

I remember that in "Trip to the Moon," the Moon (the woman in a crescent,) was Bleuette Bernon, music hall singer, the Stars were ballet girls, from théâtre du Châtelet—and the men (principal ones) Victor André, of Cluny théâtre, Delpierre, Farjaux—Kelm—Brunnet, music-hall singers, and myself—the Sélenites were acrobats from Folies Bergère.

I think to have replied about all what you want to know, will give more details if wanted by you.

GM

The Marvelous in the Cinema

GEORGES MÉLIÈS, 1912

I've read the articles the *L'Écho du cinéma* has devoted to "impossible films," articles that interested a lot me since as you know a specialty of mine has been the creation, in cinematography, of the most extravagant impossibilities; or at all events it's a specialty that's been imposed upon me by my clients themselves because to begin with I, like everyone else, did a bit of everything. I've been one of the founders, not of the *Cinématographe* as a device, but of the cinematographic industry; I am even the first to have done theater of all kinds in the cinema: comedy, drama, buffoonery, war scenes, fairy plays, tricks, and so on, at a time when people restricted themselves to taking *the arrival of a train in a station*, or a *public square* with its milling crowd and its vehicles, or a *collapsing wall*. What's more, I'm very happy that the idea I had of making the cinema serve, not for the servile reproduction of nature, but for the spectacular expression of artistic and imaginative conceptions of all kinds has in actual fact created the true cinematographic industry. In effect, it's *cinematographic theater* that's been the cause of the formidable success of the cinematograph, which without it would remain a barely known laboratory tool.

Today, cinematography has been divided into an infinite number of branches and this is by no means over; each day brings us new inventions, thanks to the fantastic development this industry has undergone and to the considerable number of minds that animated photography puts to work.

This article was translated by Paul Hammond.

I'm certainly very happy and very proud of a result that, I say in all modesty, I hadn't predicted at all at the outset.

If I've reminded you of these facts it's because of the strangeness, as I see it, of the controversies and polemics that are raised about this marvelous tool, the unprecedented success of which is precisely linked to the variety of its applications.

Why do some people rail against comedy? Others against buffoonery or clowning? Still others against drama that is serious, historical, mythological, artistic, long, short? Why do certain people only accept the cinema as a tool for *reportage*? Why do others go on the warpath against fantastic, trick, amazing views? Why? But I'm not going to stop. Let it be understood once and for all, then, that there's enough for every taste. That the public consists of *Mr. Everyman*, men of science, honest bourgeois, happy people and sad, sensitive people and scoffers, women, children, street Arabs, and so on; and that, as a consequence, the infinite variety of the cinematograph is its main factor of success. What one person finds magnificent, another finds stupid, and vice versa, according to one's temperament or one's inclinations, according to one's level of education, according to one's artistic tastes or lack of elevation.

Let those who want comedy shoot comedy; let those who want seriousness or tricks shoot one or the other; let those who want long views shoot them long; let those who make short performances shoot them short. But what's the meaning of this polemic against long views? Only the *interest of the subject* and the *takings it may bring in* for the exhibitor ought to be taken into account by the producer because his own interest is involved. If buffoonery lends itself to the rapid, condensed, bewildering, crazy acting style of the cinematograph, it is obvious that the expression of an eminently artistic or literary way of thinking calls for a measured, calm, studied acting style, a perfect pantomime capable, in a word, of interesting people whose minds are cultured and who know how to recognize art wherever it's found (even in burlesque and caricature). It follows that to be restricted to around twenty meters in an interesting view obliges the artistes to *compress*, as the technical term has it, to such a point that their acting becomes epileptic and the action incomprehensible. I consider this way of doing things butchery and a genuine act of sabotage.

Why, let everyone have their freedom! And let Messieurs the exhibitors choose, each according to his clientele and the length of his show, the films that suit them among the countless novelties that appear. The producer will himself manage to recognize *the genre people like* and the one *that sells*; but don't forget, too, that bit by bit one shapes the education of the public, and that taste has jolly well changed since the *farces* of the early days. One wants beauty today, and to what is it owed if not to *artistic films* that have made the public more demanding. They are generally long, though, but together are more interesting and stirring than a series of short views in which the same "tall stories" are endlessly repeated in all shapes and sizes, works by unknowns without personality and without originality. That is where we're at, however; this war against the important film seeks to impose quality and not quantity. One sees lots of *titles* on the program, however foolish or nondescript the views. What an error! What a mistake! Believe me, my dear readers, apart from its scientific, educational, and edifying applications, in which it will become *all-powerful*, I'm certain the cinema *will only remain in public favor through art in all its forms*.

Make drama, comedy, novels, fairy plays, outrageous fantasy, impossible voyages, crude farce—make what you will, but in each genre let the *artistic note*, the *research*, the *care taken in the execution and in the acting* be apparent to the eyes of all.

If you make a *composed film*, a theatrical composition for the cinema, in a word, whatever your genre, *be someone*. For you the cinema is only a tool, nothing else, an intermediary between *you the filmmaker* and the public, don't forget: it is a work one judges, and at all costs avoid the banal film; the one that *has no guts* and displays the incompetence of its creator.

I'm speaking only of cinematographic theater, of course; the rest, the so-called open-air view, which is highly interesting, indispensable, even, to a program, is a matter for our excellent reporters and cinematographic correspondents, who also work wonders right now in their genre.

I've managed to get a long way away from my subject because I've been so often dreadfully upset on hearing the cinema judged by people who do not know the first thing about it that a certain sadness has been my lot.

You can't please 'em all, as the saying goes; hence the need for variety in cinema programs. Myself, I've often been saddened by the judgments of certain snobs who, even though large and small alike saw but an amusing spectacle in my compositions, would exclaim: "My God, how stupid such things are!" (You can see I'm not bragging.)

Had it been necessary for these unfortunates, generally incapable of any job of work, to realize what a genre like mine costs in terms of thought, work, difficulty, trial and error, and money, they would certainly have been of the opinion of the majority.

What these snobs lacked was the artistic faculty that enables the artist to disregard his personal tastes, to unquestioningly accept a subject chosen by a filmmaker, and to merely examine, without bias, *the artistic effort contained in its execution.* Good heavens! Who is not aware that fairy themes are "stupid"? Doesn't the same apply to all mythological fictions? To all tales, all fantastic subjects? And yet how many masterpieces—in painting, in music, as well as literature—have produced by embroidering on these supposedly *stupid* themes by people who are themselves hardly aware of their intellectual inferiority?

They ought to understand that the *creation of the impossible* is not within everybody's reach, and that in the arts this creation is most difficult.

You see just how inferior actual theater is to cinema in the production of the fantastic with the aid of old, out-of-date tricks, and despite the collaboration of hundreds of skilled individuals, engineers, scene shifters, authors, actors, directors, producers, chief mechanics, and so on.

Has the theater ever created the admirable fantasies, the perfect illusions, the marvelous diableries and journeys through imaginary worlds that the cinematograph has? Of course not, because today the theater has recourse to cinema to offer the public gaze what its material resources are incapable of creating.

I stop there and I go back to *impossible films*. I think I'm qualified to speak to you of them, right? Well! I've had to give up on one film, which really was impossible. And yet, 100,000 francs in cash was offered me, and the person insisted for five months! (He was an extremely wealthy Russian client.) The deal was tempting, I thought long and hard about it; to my shame, I preferred to let it go rather than to make something that was not quite right. I have been forced to admit that from time to time the word *impossible* exists in French, I who am credited with having proved beyond doubt that *anything is possible* in cinematography!

This film was the *exact* reproduction of the Flood! But as my means did not enable me to make the rain fall for forty days and to inundate the highest mountains on the globe in situ, as I remained perplexed by the animals to be shut up two-by-two in the ark, including the mammoths, elephants, rhinoceroses and other mastodonts (not to mention the animals from way back: the diplodocus, ichthysaurus, pterodactyl, megalotherion, and so on), as I considered that the infinitely small, lice, fleas, bugs and other parasites would be invisible in the cinema, I have had to admit defeat, although just this once! Here, I was sure to be unequal to the subject; I was sure not to make art, but to diminish the scenario instead of embellishing it; I preferred to pull out. But I recognize that some have sought to attempt, moreover without success, works beyond human strength. It is better, in my opinion, to refrain from this. The person who composes a cinematographic subject involving fantasy must be an artist enamored of his art, never flinching before any task or any problem, working without respite and seeking to make the skeleton of the scenario disappear beneath the delicate arabesques he envelops it in, just as a painter makes the canvas of the picture disappear beneath the artistic strokes of his palette. It is always to this that I apply myself; this has been and still is my passion and my joy. The creators of films made in a "slapdash" way know nothing of these artistic joys, and the pleasure the beautiful realization of his ideas gives the artist. But it is fair to say that this is all one to them: every profession comprises conscientious workers and saboteurs.

Let me briefly sum up this overlong article: in my view production is too rapid and too numerous in cinema. Quality is better (here as elsewhere) than quantity. It is essential that scenes be well thought-out and well executed. It is, *above all, essential to the splendid future in store for cinematography* that the cinematographic view always presents, and in every genre, *eminently artistic qualities*. The nondescript view used as so-called *padding* should not have a place in any program.

If misused, it is these sorts of views that drive away the public, a public won over today by a splendid invention.

The Importance of the Script

GEORGES MÉLIÈS, 1932

An important personality in the cinema world having recently expressed, in *Comœdia*, this opinion: that, in a film, the script had only *slight importance*, or at the very least a *relative importance*, two well-known "scriptwriters" have been to ask me mine on this subject. In so doing they have done me great honor, because since 1914 I have scarcely dabbled in cinema at all, or at all events I have ceased producing, and it may be that today my own ideas are considered reactionary by the young. One is always rather "old hat" for the young; the only consolation of he who is getting on is that the men of the current generation will be "old hat" in their turn for the next one. Finally, because I'm asked my opinion, let's get on with it, with no thought for "what will people say?" The fact of the matter, I believe, is that the script *may*, in effect, *have no importance* in certain films, but that on the contrary it has a prime, even major, importance in many others.

We must try not to subject cinema, as is advocated today, to a single formula, when this art offers infinite possibilities. By seeking to impose on everybody the same method, the same technique, the same rhythm, as is said today, we oblige filmmakers to cast all their works in the same mold, and we suppress in them the originality that is, for all that, the key factor when it comes to keeping the curiosity of the public alive. In all likelihood, it is to a *lack of originality* that film's current stagnation, of which I've heard many people complain, is due. I continually hear

---

This article was translated by Paul Hammond.

people say: I went one day to the cinema, and there was nothing interesting playing. Always the same stories: the husband, the wife, the lover, telephones, automobiles, luxurious drawing rooms, dance halls, jazz bands, and so forth, then, naturally, to end: the eternal, lingering kiss that has started a fashion, to the point that young people today do not hesitate to "take a leaf out of someone's book" and to indulge in this charming exercise in public, on the bus, or in the métro. Now, from where does this lack of originality come if not from the monotony of the script in the first place, and from methods, ever the same (dissolves and close-ups), used now in an invariable way? It has to be admitted that those famous American scripts whose silliness and vacuity one takes pleasure, at every moment, in recognizing, have gradually invaded the European screen, and it is on this vacuity I believe that the lack of interest of the themes depicted hinges, despite all the talent displayed by the actors.

The actor indeed counts for something—his importance is indisputable—but he cannot make a good work from a bad script, no more than the artiste in the theater can make a "success," whatever his courage or his talent may be, of a work whose very subject is worthless. So in my opinion the following conclusion must be reached, namely that aside from documentaries it is necessary that for everything which is a novel, drama, or comedy, that for every work, in short, in which there is a study of characters and psychology, the script be ingenious and interesting in itself. This by no means prevents producers from cramming it with all the episodic events they take to be necessary for embroidering the film and delighting the eye of the spectator.

In the name of the beauty of the film, they can even make use of all the magnificent resources of modern lighting, as well as all those that shooting from the most varied "angles" (thanks to the perfecting of cameras) affords them. But all this is mise-en-scène, in other words "the sauce"; but that is no reason to neglect the "fish," which is, in fact, the main thing.*

I was saying at the beginning of this brief article that there were nevertheless certain films about which I am totally in agreement with the personality I refer to earlier. And here I feel particularly comfortable about giving my opinion because it is a question of films of fantasy and imagination, the artistic, demonic, fairy, or fantastic films I made a specialty of while practicing all the other genres.

In these sorts of films, the importance lies in the ingenuity and unexpected nature of the tricks, in the picturesqueness of the sets, in the

---

*Translator's note: Méliès is alluding to the saying "*la sauce vaut mieux que le poisson*," meaning the minor detail has more weight than the main one.

artistic positioning of the dramatis personae, and in the invention of the star-turn and the finale. Contrary to the way things are usually done, my procedure for constructing these sorts of works consisted of inventing the details before the whole thing, a *whole* that is nothing other than "the script." One can say that the script is in this case only the thread intended to link "effects" without much of a relationship to each other, just as the compère of a revue is there to connect together scenes that are extremely incongruous. I grant that the script has no more than a secondary importance in this kind of composition.

For twenty years I made fantasy films of all sorts, and my chief preoccupation was for each film to find original tricks, a sensational main effect, and a grand finale. After which, I used to try and find which era would be most suitable in terms of costuming my characters (often the costumes were required by the tricks, even), and once all this was well established, I got down, last of all, to designing the sets to frame the action in accord with the chosen period and costumes. As for the script, the "fable," the "tale" in itself, I worked this out at the very end, and I can therefore state that done thusly the script was without any importance because my only aim was to use it as an "excuse for mise-en-scène," for tricks or for tableaux with a pleasing effect.

I was appealing to the spectator's eye, trying to charm or intrigue him (hence the script was unimportant); but it is different when the filmmaker appeals to his mind, to his intelligence, because then mise-en-scène, however fine, is no longer sufficient. I trust no one will tear out my eyes for having spoken this frankly; I'm not in the habit of concealing what I think. I reckon, moreover, that what I've just said can offend nobody; all opinions are free, each person can work in accordance with his personal taste, and the main thing is, first of all, to please the public of the day.

Contributors

Richard Abel is the Robert Altman Collegiate Professor of Film Studies in the Department of Screen Arts and Cultures at the University of Michigan. Most recently he edited the award-winning *Encyclopedia of Early Cinema* (Routledge, 2005), published *Americanizing the Movies and 'Movie-Mad' Audiences, 1910–1914* (California, 2006), and coedited *Early Cinema and the "National"* (John Libbey, 2008). Currently he is completing research for *Menus for Movie Land: Newspapers and the Movies, 1911–1915*.

Elizabeth Alsop is a doctoral candidate in Comparative Literature at the City University of New York Graduate Center. Her research interests include modernism, narrative theory, and film studies. She currently teaches literature at Queens College, and Italian and film at Hunter College.

Timothy Barnard is a translator, publisher, and film historian living in Montreal. His research focuses on early cinema, French cinema, Latin American cinema, and the films of Jean-Marie Straub and Danièle Huillet. He is coeditor of *South American Cinema: A Critical Filmography, 1914–1995* (Texas, 1999) and is currently translating Jean-Luc Godard's *Introduction to a True History of Cinema and Television*.

Paolo Cherchi Usai is director of the Haghefilm Foundation in Amsterdam, Netherlands, a nonprofit agency for the support of research and scholarly studies in film preservation and curatorship. Cofounder of the L. Jeffrey Selznick School of Film Preservation at George Eastman House in Rochester, New York, and of the Pordenone Silent Film Festival, he is author of the experimental feature film *Passio* (2007), adapted from *The Death of Cinema* (British Film Institute, 2001).

His latest book is *Film Curatorship: Archives, Museums, and the Digital Marketplace*, coauthored with David Francis, Alexander Horwath, and Michael Loebenstein (Synema—Gesellschaft für Film und Medien/ Österreichisches Filmmuseum, 2008).

Ian Christie is a film historian, curator, and broadcaster. He has written and edited books on Powell and Pressburger, Russian cinema, Scorsese and Gilliam; worked on many exhibitions, including *Spellbound: Art and Film* (Hayward Gallery, 2006) and *Modernism: Designing a New World* (Victoria and Albert Museum, 2006); and coproduced the 1994 BBC television series on early cinema *The Last Machine: Early Cinema and the Birth of the Modern World*, as well as writing the accompanying book. A fellow of the British Academy and former Slade Professor of Fine Art at Cambridge University, he is currently professor of film and media history at Birkbeck College, director of the London Screen Study Centre, and vice-president of Europa Cinemas.

Antonio Costa is full professor of film history at the Università Iuav, Venice. He is a member of the board of directors of Storia del cinema italiano at the Centro Sperimentale di Cinematografia, Rome, and has collaborated with many journals, including *Cinema & Cinema*, *Fotogenia*, *Bianco e Nero*, *Hors Cadre*, *Iris*, *Duel*, *CiNéMAS*, *Secuencias*, and *Archivos de la Filmoteca*. He is the author of *La morale del giocattolo: Saggio su Georges Méliès* (1980; CLUEB, 1989), *La meccanica del visibile: Il cinema delle origini in Europa* (Casa Usher, 1983), *Saper vedere il cinema* (Bompiani, 1985), *Cinema e pittura* (Loescher, 1991), *Immagine di un'immagine* (Torino 1993). He also edited the Italian versions of *Hitchcock* by Chabrol and Rohmer (1986), of *L'Organisation de l'espace dans le Faust de Murnau* by Rohmer (2002), and of *The Art of the Moving Picture* by Vachel Lindsay (2008). His most recent books are *Il cinema e le arti visive* (Einaudi, 2002), *I leoni di Schneider: Percorsi intertestuali nel cinema ritrovato* (Bulzoni, 2002), *Marco Bellocchio: I pugni in tasca* (Lindau, 2005), and *Ingmar Bergman* (Marsilio, 2009).

Victoria Duckett is a fellow in the School of Culture and Communication at the University of Melbourne and teaches early film history in the School of Media and Performing Arts at the Università Cattolica, Milan. She received her Ph.D. from UCLA. In 2006, she curated the Sarah Bernhardt programs at Il Cinema Ritrovato (Bologna, Italy) and is currently completing a book entitled *"A Little Too Much is Enough For Me": Sarah Bernhardt and Silent Film*.

André Gaudreault is a full professor in the Département d'histoire de l'art et d'études cinématographiques at the Université de Montréal, where he leads the research group GRAFICS (Groupe de recherche sur l'avènement et la formation des institutions cinématographique et scénique). His books include *Du littéraire au filmique: Système du récit* (rev. ed., Armand Colin, 1999), *Le Récit cinématographique* (Nathan, 1991), with François Jost, *Pathé 1900: Fragments d'une filmographie analytique du cinéma des premiers temps* (Sorbonne Nouvelle, 1993), *Au pays des ennemis du cinéma* (Nota Bene, 1996), with Germain Lacasse and Jean-Pierre Sirois-Trahan, *Cinema delle origini: O della "cinematografia-attrazione"* (Il Castoro, 2004), *Cinéma et attraction: Pour une nouvelle histoire du cinématographe* (CNRS, 2008), *American Cinema, 1890–1909: Themes and Variations* (Rutgers, 2009), *From Plato to Lumière: Narration and Monstration in Literature and Cinema* (Toronto, 2009), and *Film and Attraction: From Kinematography to Cinema* (Illinois, 2011). He is also director of the scholarly journal *CiNéMAS*.

Tom Gunning is the Edwin A. and Betty L. Bergman Distinguished Service Professor in the Department of Art History and the Committee on Cinema and Media at the University of Chicago. He is the author of *D. W. Griffith and the Origins of American Narrative Film: The Early Years at Biograph* (Illinois, 1991) and *The Films of Fritz Lang: Allegories of Vision and Modernity* (British Film Institute, 2000), as well as more than 100 articles on early cinema, film history and theory, avant-garde film, film genre, and cinema and modernism.

Paul Hammond's first book was *Marvellous Méliès* (Gordon Fraser, 1974). Since then he has written on Surrealism and cinema; postcard eroticism; puns (with Patrick Hughes); filmgoing and bibliomania (with Ian Breakwell); and the "Constellations" of Miró and Breton. His most recent book, coauthored with Spanish film historian Román Gubern, is *Luis Buñuel: Los años rojos*; those years being the 1930s. As a translator from French, he has translated Borde and Chaumeton's classic study of film noir and Leiris's lyrical analysis of bullfighting.

Frank Kessler is professor of film and television history at Utrecht University. He is a cofounder and coeditor of *KINtop: Jahrbuch zur Erforschung des frühen Films* and has published numerous articles in the field of early cinema, in particular on early nonfiction films, on the genre of the *féerie*, and on acting. From 2003 to 2007 he was the president of DOMITOR, the international association dedicated to the study of early cinema. He coedited *Networks of Entertainment: Early Film Distribution, 1895–1915* (John Libbey, 2007).

Thierry Lefebvre is maître de conférences in information science and communication at the Université Paris-Diderot. He is the author of several books, including *La Chair et le celluloid: Le cinéma chirurgical du Docteur Doyen* (Jean Doyen, 2004) and *La Bataille des radios libres, 1977–1981* (Nouveau Monde, 2008). He also co-edited two books about Étienne-Jules Marey, *Sur les pas de Marey: Science(s) et cinéma* (L'Harmattan/ SÉMIA, 2004), with Jacques Malthête and Laurent Mannoni, and *EJ Marey: Actes du colloque du centenaire* (Arcadia, 2006), with Dominique de Font-Réaulx and Mannoni.

Viva Paci is professor of film theory in the École des médias at the Université du Québec à Montréal. She received her Ph.D. from the Université de Montréal, with a dissertation entitled "De l'attraction au cinéma." She is a member of the Centre de recherche sur l'intermédialité (CRI) and of GRAFICS. Paci is the author of *Il Cinema di Chris Marker* (Hybris, 2005) and of *L'Imprimerie du regard: Chris Marker et la technique*, with André Habib (L'Harmattan, 2008), as well as of articles in *Cinema & Cie*, *CiNéMAS*, *Intermédialités*, *Sociétés et représentations*, *Comunicazioni sociali*, and *Médiamorphoses*.

Murray Pomerance is professor in the Department of Sociology at Ryerson University, and the author, editor, or coeditor of numerous volumes including *The Horse Who Drank the Sky: Film Experience Beyond Narrative and Theory* (Rutgers, 2008), *A Family Affair: Cinema Calls Home* (Wallflower, 2008), *City that Never Sleeps: New York and the Filmic Imagination* (Rutgers, 2007), *Cinema and Modernity* (Rutgers, 2006), *American Cinema of the 1950s: Themes and Variations* (Rutgers, 2005), *Where the Boys Are: Cinemas of Masculinity and Youth* (Wayne State, 2005), *BAD: Infamy, Darkness, Evil and Slime on Screen* (SUNY Press, 2004), *Enfant Terrible! Jerry Lewis in American Film* (NYU Press, 2002), and *Ladies and Gentlemen, Boys and Girls: Gender in Film at the End of the Twentieth Century* (SUNY Press, 2001). He is editor of the "Horizons of Cinema" series at SUNY Press and the "Techniques of the Moving Image" series at Rutgers University Press, and coeditor, with Lester D. Friedman and Adrienne L. McLean, respectively, of the "Screen Decades" and "Star Decades" series at Rutgers.

Matthew Solomon is associate professor of Cinema Studies at the College of Staten Island, City University of New York. He is the author of

Disappearing Tricks: Silent Film, Houdini, and the New Magic of the Twentieth Century (Illinois, 2010). His work on early cinema has also been published in *Theatre Journal, Nineteenth Century Theatre and Film, Cinema & Cie, KINtop Schriften*, and a number of other anthologies.

Index